MANAGEMENT AND BUSINESS IN
BRITAIN AND FRANCE

MANAGEMENT AND BUSINESS IN BRITAIN AND FRANCE

The Age of the Corporate Economy

Edited by

YOUSSEF CASSIS
FRANCOIS CROUZET
TERRY GOURVISH

CLARENDON PRESS · OXFORD
1995

Oxford University Press, Walton Street, Oxford OX2 6DP
Oxford New York
Athens Auckland Bangkok Bombay
Calcutta Cape Town Dar es Salaam Delhi
Florence Hong Kong Istanbul Karachi
Kuala Lumpur Madras Madrid Melbourne
Mexico City Nairobi Paris Singapore
Taipei Tokyo Toronto
and associated companies in
Berlin Ibadan

Oxford is a trade mark of Oxford University Press

Published in the United States
by Oxford University Press Inc., New York

British Library Cataloguing in Publication Data
Data available

Library of Congress Cataloging in Publication Data
Management and business in Britain and France: the age of the
corporate economy, 1850–1990 / edited by Youssef Cassis, François
Crouzet and Terry Gourvish.
Revised papers originally presented at a conference held at the
London School of Economics on 17–19 September 1992.
Includes bibliographical references and index.
1. Industrial management—Great Britain—History—Congresses.
2. Industrial management—France—History—Congresses.
3. Executives—Training of—Great Britain—History—Congresses.
4. Executives—Training of—France—History—Congresses.
5. Consolidation and merger of corporations—Great Britian—History—
Congresses. 6. Consolidation and merger of corporations—France—
History—Congresses. I. Cassis, Youssef. II. Crouzet, François,
1922- . III. Gourvish, T. R. (Terence Richard)
HD70.G7M275 1995   95-17981
338.0941—dc20
ISBN 0–19–828940–5

1 3 5 7 9 10 8 6 4 2

Typeset by Best-set Typesetter Ltd., Hong Kong
Printed in Great Britain
on acid-free paper by
Biddles Ltd., Guildford & King's Lynn

Preface

THIS volume owed its origin to the editors' belief that it was timely to encourage comparative work among scholars in Britain and France. To that end preliminary plans were drawn up in 1991. Then a meeting, supported by the Maison des sciences de l'homme and the Economic and Social Research Council, was held at the Université de Paris IV Sorbonne in February 1992. It was attended by Professors Louis Bergeron, François Caron, François Crouzet, Patrick Fridenson, and Maurice Lévy-Leboyer, for France, and Dr Youssef Cassis, Dr Terry Gourvish, and Mrs Sonia Copeland, for the UK. The group drew up a provisional programme under the theme 'Management in the Age of the Corporate Economy, 1850–1990'. Three elements were isolated for special attention: the family firm, a controversial but surviving feature in both countries; education and training, at the centre of the debate in both countries on economic performance; and mergers and survivals, a central issue in business organization. The conference was duly organized by the Business History Unit at the London School of Economics on 17–19 September 1992. After substantial revisions to the twelve papers presented at the conference, the volume was assembled in the course of 1993–4. While it was agreed that the different state of business history in the two countries often hindered a truly comparative approach it was hoped that this volume of case-studies would encourage future work in the field. A second conference, to be held in France in October 1995, will address the theme 'Les Stratégies de commercialisation et de marketing'.

The editors would like to thank the many people who helped them in their endeavours. They are particularly grateful to Etsuo Abe, Theo Barker, Dominique Barjot, François Caron, Roy Church, Leslie Hannah, Akira Kudo, Maurice Lévy-Leboyer, Reiko Okayama, Geoffrey Owen, Yves Lequin, Steven Tolliday, and the others who attended the conference and enhanced the quality of the debate. Maurice Aymard kindly encouraged the project at the start, as did Pierre de Longuemar of the Banque Paribas. Sonia Copeland, the Unit's administrative assistant, organized the conference with her customary charm and efficiency. The retyping and translation of manuscripts was carried out promptly and with good humour by Veronica Comyn, Janice Harrison, Ann Hartman, Katie Short, and Alex Wardle. The editors would also like to express their gratitude to the funding organizations which generously supported the conference, namely the Fondation Crédit Lyonnais, the

Institut d'histoire de l'industrie, the Baring Foundation, and the Nuffield
Foundation.

Y.C.
F.C.
T.G.

London and Paris
September 1994

Contents

List of Figures

List of Tables

List of Contributors

ERIC BUSSIÈRE, *agrégé d'histoire*, Ph.D. (Paris), is Professor of History at the new University of Arras and was formerly lecturer at the University of Paris-Sorbonne. He has published *La France, la Belgique et l'organisation économique de l'Europe, 1918–35* (1992) and *Paribas, Europe and the World, 1872–1992* (1992).

YOUSSEF CASSIS, Ph.D. (Geneva), F.R.Hist.S., teaches economic history at the University of Geneva and is a Business History Fellow, Business History Unit, London School of Economics. His major publications include *City Bankers, 1890–1914* (1994), and *La City de Londres 1870–1914* (1987). He has edited a number of books, including *Capitalism in a Mature Economy: Financial Institutions, Capital Exports and British Industry 1870–1939* (with J. J. Van Helten) (1990), *Finance and Financiers in European History 1880–1960* (1992), and *Business Elites* (1994). He is also joint editor, with P. L. Cottrell, of *Financial History Review*. He is currently completing a book on business leaders in twentieth-century Europe.

EMMANUEL CHADEAU, *agrégé d'histoire*, Ph.D. (Paris), is Professor of Economic History at Charles de Gaulle University, Lille. He is a graduate of the École normale supérieure de Saint-Cloud, and was formerly Chargé de recherche au CNRS (1981–8). In 1993 he became a Junior Member of the Institut Universitaire de France. Joint editor of the journal *Entreprises et histoire*, his publications include *Histoire de l'industrie aéronautique: de Blériot à Dassault, 1900–1950* (1987), *L'Économie du risque: les entrepreneurs, 1850–1980* (1988), *Latécoère* (1990), *L'Ambition technologique: naissance d'Ariane, 1970–1973* (1994). His next book will focus on the history of mass retailing in France.

FRANÇOIS CROUZET, Ph.D. (Paris), F.R.Hist.S., Hon. CBE, Doctor honoris causa of the Universities of Birmingham, Cambridge, Edinburgh, Kent, and Leicester, is Emeritus Professor of History at the University of Paris-Sorbonne (he was Professor of Northern European History, 1970–92). He is a graduate of the École normale supérieure and was a post-graduate student of the London School of Economics; he was formerly Professor at the Universities of Bordeaux (1956–8), Lille (1958–64), and Nanterre (1964–9). His publications include *L'Économie britannique et le Blocus continental* (1958), *Capital Formation in the Industrial Revolution* (1972), *The Victorian Economy* (1982), and *Britain Ascendant* (1990) (the last two appearing first in French), and *La Grande Inflation* (1993).

JEAN-PIERRE DAVIET, *agrégé d'histoire*, Ph.D. (Paris), is a graduate of the École normale supérieure and a former fellow of the Fondation Thiers. He is currently Professor of History at the École normale supérieure de Cachan. His publications include *Un destin international: la Compagnie de Saint-Gobain de 1830 à 1939* (1988) and *Une multinationale à la française: histoire de Saint-Gobain 1665–1989* (1989).

MARC DE FERRIÈRE LE VAYER, Ph.D. (Paris), was formerly curator at the Christofle Museum in Paris, and is now Maître de conférences at Charles de Gaulle University, Lille. A specialist in the history of the luxury industry, he is the author of a thesis on the firm of Christofle. His last publication was *L'Orfèvrerie* (1994).

ROBERT FITZGERALD, BA, Ph.D. (London), is a lecturer in the School of Management, Royal Holloway, University of London. His publications include *British Labour Management and Industrial Welfare, 1846–1939* (1988) and *Rowntree and the Marketing Revolution, 1862–1969* (1995), in addition to a number of edited volumes on the competitiveness of Far Eastern business, the origins of Japanese industrial power, and state–industry relations in East Asia. He is currently editor of the *Journal of Far Eastern Business*.

TERRY GOURVISH, BA, Ph.D. (London), F.R.Hist.S., is Director of the Business History Unit at the London School of Economics and Political Science. He was formerly Dean of the School of Economic and Social Studies, University of East Anglia (1986–8). His publications include *British Railways 1948–73: A Business History* (1986), and *The British Brewing Industry 1830–1980* (with Richard Wilson) (1994). He has edited a number of books including *Later Victorian Britain* (1988, repr. 1990) and *Britain since 1945* (1991) (both with Alan O'Day).

ANDRÉ GRELON, Ph.D. (Paris), is a fellow of the Centre National de la Recherche Scientifique who works at LASMAS-IRESCO (a research centre concerned with analysis and methodology in applied sociology). His main interest is the history of scientific and technical higher education in France, and the training of engineers; he has several publications in this field.

MARC MEULEAU, *agrégé d'histoire*, Ph.D. (Paris), is a graduate of the École normale supérieure de Saint-Cloud. He works currently with the Banque Indo-Suez. He has published *Des pionniers en Extrême-Orient: histoire de la Banque de l'Indochine 1875–1975* (1990).

MICHAEL SANDERSON, MA. Ph.D. (Cambridge), is Reader in Economic and Social History at the University of East Anglia. Among his writings are *The Universities and British Industry, 1850–1970* (1972), *Education, Economic Change and Society 1780–1870* (1991), *From Irving to Olivier: A Social History of the Acting Profession in England 1880–1983* (1984), and *The Missing Stratum: Technical School Education in England 1900–1990*

(1994). Dr Sanderson is editor of the Economic History Society's Studies in Economic and Social History published by Cambridge University Press.

CHRISTINE SHAW, MA, Ph.D. (Oxford), is a Senior Research Fellow at the European Humanities Research Centre, University of Warwick, and was formerly a Research Officer at the Business History Unit, London School of Economics. Her publications in business history include the *Dictionary of Business Biography* (ed. with David Jeremy) (1984–6). Currently, she is concentrating on research in Italian Renaissance political history; her publications in this field include *Julius II: The Warrior Pope* (1993).

NICK TIRATSOO, BA, Ph.D. (London), teaches social history at Warwick University and is a Visting Research Associate at the Rusuners History Unit, London School of Economics. His publications include *Reconstruction, Affluence and Labour Politics: Coventry 1945–60* (1990) and (with Jim Tomlinson) *Industrial Efficiency and State Intervention: Labour 1939–51* (1993). He is currently working on a history of British management in the post-1945 period.

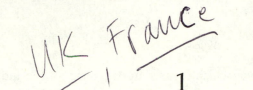
Divergence and Convergence in British and French Business in the Nineteenth and Twentieth Centuries

YOUSSEF CASSIS

For generations, the uneasy relationship between Britain and France has captured the popular imagination. From traditional enmity to ultimate alliance in major modern international conflicts, rivalry, in all sorts of matters, has remained its dominant feature.[1] Comparative studies between the two countries abound, from political systems to eating habits: they do not really extend to business history. In that particular field, comparisons with America, Germany, or Japan have taken precedence. This derives from the very logic of comparative analyses and their motivation. On the one hand, countries presenting a relative homogeneity offer the best prospects for fruitful comparisons—homogeneity in size, level of development, historical experience, etc. On the other hand, the temptation to compare one's country with the leading power of the day is difficult to resist, in order to measure the gap separating it from assumed best practices.

Comparative analysis will flourish when both conditions are met, as was the case for Britain and France from the beginning of the seventeenth to the end of the nineteenth century when, to use François Crouzet's words, the two nations were the 'guiding lights of Europe and the world'.[2] To a relative homogeneity in historical experience—the two first nation-states, the two pioneers of modern industrialization, the two major colonial empires of the modern era—was added the attraction, in particular from France's point of view, of comparing herself with the world leader both in technology and in parliamentary politics. Not surprisingly, this is the classical period of Anglo-French

I should like to thank François Crouzet and Terry Gourvish for their helpful comments on an earlier draft of this chapter. I have also benefited from François Crouzet's impromptu conclusion at the end of the Anglo-French business history conference from which this book has issued.

[1] For an overview of the subject see D. Johnson, F. Crouzet, and F. Bédarida (eds.), *Britain and France: Ten Centuries* (Folkestone, 1980).

[2] F. Crouzet, *Britain Ascendant: Comparative Studies in Franco-British Economic History* (Cambridge, 1990), 6.

historical comparison, one which focuses up the onset of the industrial revolution.[3]

Things of course changed after the first World War and even before, with the emergence of the United States in the world economy and of Germany in Europe. One of the motivations for Anglo-French comparisons—to measure up against the leader—was lost for ever, while the other—similarity between countries—has proved rather weak in the last two or three decades. Business history has suffered in particular from this diminished interest. Following the enormous influence of Alfred Chandler's work,[4] the major historiographical debates have centred around the emergence, development, and role of the large corporation, a phenomenon more characteristic of the period from the late nineteenth century onwards where, until the recent rise of Japan, the American model has acted as an irresistible magnet.

The object of this book is to explore the potential for comparisons in Anglo-French business history. The framework chosen is that of the nation, which remains dominant in comparative analysis. This is not to deny the importance of regional studies, which are growing alongside the rediscovery of the small and medium-sized firms' decisive contribution to economic development; or the fact that some aspects of business activity can to a certain extent transcend national characteristics, in particular in the large multinational companies. On the other hand, institutional factors such as legal constraints, state intervention, educational patterns, and so on are equally important. Moreover, competition between nations has increasingly been taking place at the economic and business levels, which are ultimately seen as a major determinant of a country's 'success' or 'failure'.

1. ECONOMIC DEVELOPMENT IN BRITAIN AND FRANCE

The economic position of Britain and France in the last quarter of the twentieth century appears basically very similar: a roughly equivalent total population of 55–7 million, and an insignificant difference in GDP, and consequently in GDP per head, of less than 5 per cent (see Table 1.1). Even such traditional structural differences as the share of agriculture

[3] Among the more important comparative studies see Crouzet, *Britain Ascendant*; C. P. Kindleberger, *Economic Growth in France and Britain 1851–1950* (Cambridge, Mass., 1964); D. Landes, *The Unbound Prometheus: Technological Change and Industrial Development in Western Europe from 1750 to the Present* (Cambridge, 1967); P. O'Brien and C. Keyder, *Economic Growth in Britain and France 1780–1914* (London, 1978); R. Roehl, 'French Industrialization: A Reconsideration', *Explorations in Economic History*, 13 (1976), 233–81; N. Crafts, 'Economic Growth in France and Britain, 1830–1910: A Review of the Evidence', *Journal of Economic History*, 44 (1984), 49–67.

[4] See A. D. Chandler, Jr., *Strategy and Structure* (Cambridge, Mass., 1962), *The Visible Hand* (Cambridge, Mass., 1977), *Scale and Scope* (Cambridge, Mass., 1990).

Table 1.1. *GDP and GDP per head in Britain and France, 1870–1989, in 1985 US prices ($m.)*

	Great Britain		France	
	GDP	GDP per head	GDP	GDP per head
1870	81,934	2,610	60,397	1,571
1913	183,707	4,024	108,738	2,734
1929	198,047	4,336	152,868	3,708
1938	234,507	4,938	147,523	3,516
1950	284,594	5,651	173,569	4,149
1973	565,655	10,063	537,997	10,323
1989	770,420	13,468	777,081	13,837

Source: A. Maddison, *Dynamic Forces in Capitalist Development* (Oxford, 1991), 6–7, 198–9. GDP per head for 1929 and 1938 calculated from the figures given by Maddison on pp. 198–9, 232–5.

have been greatly reduced: in 1987 only 7 per cent of the French work-force was employed in agriculture, as against 2.5 per cent in Britain. (The situation was in marked contrast to that of 1949, when 29.2 per cent of the French work-force was still on the land, corresponding to the situation in Britain in the first half of the nineteenth century.[5]) In a word, both countries exhibit the main features of an advanced industrial society. Furthermore, in recent years Britain and France have shared a similar path towards a post-industrial society. Although the phenomenon has been more pronounced in Britain, both countries have experienced a weakening of their traditional industrial base, a wave of consumerism, and an expansion of financial services following deregulation. They are also confronted with similar questions regarding on the one hand the new role of Germany in a unified Europe, and on the other hand the challenge posed to Europe not only by America and Japan but also by the newly industrialized countries of South-East Asia.

However, this late convergence should not conceal earlier divergence as well as more persistent differences between the two countries. An often forgotten difference is simply the size of the two countries' respective economies. From the mid-nineteenth to the mid-twentieth century, Britain was a significantly larger economy, measured in terms of GDP, than France: 30 per cent larger in 1870 rising to 69 per cent in 1913; 30 per cent again in 1929, but rising to 59 per cent in 1938 and 64 per cent in 1950. Britain's GDP was still 39 per cent larger than France's in 1960 before the

[5] A. Gueslin, *L'Économie ouverte 1948–90* (Paris, 1989), 99.

Table 1.2. *Percentage share of world manufacturing production, Britain and France, 1870–1980*

	Britain	France
1870	31.8	10.3
1913	14.0	6.4
1929	9.4	6.6
1938	9.2	4.5
1963	6.5	6.3
1980	3.8	7.0

Sources: League of Nations; World Bank.

two eventually converged some fifteen years later (Table 1.1). The same is
true of GDP per head, though to a lesser extent in the twentieth century,
as Britain has been a more populated country than France since about
1890; since the 1980s, however, the difference in total population between
the two countries has been minimal. Britain was also a larger producer of
industrial goods: having been treble that of France in the mid- to late
nineteenth century, her share of the world's manufacturing production
remained more or less twice as high in the first half of the twentieth
century, with the exception of the late 1920s, when the difference was less
than 30 per cent (Table 1.2).

These differences might well have had an impact on business organization and development, as will be discussed later. However, they must be
kept in perspective. First, apart from the level of industrial production in
the mid-Victorian period, when Britain's world supremacy was undisputed, the two countries were, together with Germany, basically in the
same league. Britain maintained her lead over her two European rivals
until the 1960s–1970s, but the similarities could well be seen as the more
significant aspect when judged against the United States of America. In
terms of mere size, the American economy was already more than two
and a half times larger than the British one in 1913, almost four times
larger in 1929, and almost five times larger in 1960. Secondly, these differences were accentuated in periods of economic depression, especially
in the late nineteenth century and the 1930s and 1940s, which affected
France more strongly than Britain and probably any other industrialized
country.[6] Conversely, France's sustained growth in the early twentieth
century—the *belle époque*—which continued in the 1920s, and even more

[6] See M. Lévy-Leboyer, 'La Décélération de l'économie française dans la seconde moitié
du XIXe siècle', *Revue d'histoire économique et sociale*, 49 (1971), 485–507; M. Lévy-Leboyer and
F. Bourguignon, *The French Economy in the Nineteenth Century* (Cambridge, 1990); M. Lévy-
Leboyer and J. C. Casanova (eds.), *Entre l'État et le marché: l'économie française des années 1880
à nos jours* (Paris, 1991), in particular part ii, pp. 189–410.

during the *trente glorieuses*—1945–73—brought her closer to her rival and eventually enabled her to overtake her.

Other indicators of economic performance show an earlier convergence between the two countries. Population growth explains for a large part Britain's faster economic growth in the nineteenth century (1.9 per cent as against 1.5 per cent for France between 1870 and 1913). On a per capita basis, however, France's growth rates were higher (1.3 per cent per annum against 1.0 per cent for Britain during the same period), a trend which continued during the twentieth century (1.1 as against 0.8 per cent between 1913 and 1950, 4.0 as against 2.3 per cent between 1950 and 1973).[7] From this perspective, France can be seen as sharing with Britain the label of early starter, or at least first follower, as opposed to late developers such as Germany in the Gerschenkronian model of analysis,[8] and as already displaying in the late nineteenth century many of the signs of economic maturity usually attributed to Britain.

French productivity in manufacturing industry has also been seen in very favourable terms, O'Brien and Keyder going so far as to claim that it remained higher than in Britain until the 1890s before falling somewhat behind.[9] Though almost certainly overestimated,[10] such figures are at least an indication that France's productivity levels in manufacturing industry were not far behind Britain's in the nineteenth century. French levels overtook those of Britain in the 1960s and have remained higher ever since, the actual difference separating the two countries varying according to calculations.[11] France's weaker economic performance until the mid-twentieth century could therefore be attributed to her lower level of productivity in a much larger agricultural sector. But French agriculture has also been rehabilitated, recent research having shown that small farmers were not particularly averse to change,[12] while others have drawn attention to the possibly better quality of life in the French countryside as compared with Britain's cities.[13]

The reassessment of the performance of the French economy has been undertaken in the last three decades by the 'revisionist' school, composed of both French and Anglo-Saxon historians. The results are by now fairly

[7] A. Maddison, *Dynamic Forces in Capitalist Development* (Oxford, 1991), 49–50.

[8] Roehl, 'French Industrialization'.

[9] O'Brien and Keyder, *Economic Growth in Britain and France*, 83–90.

[10] Crafts, 'Economic Growth in France and Britain', 59–67; Jean-Pierre Dormois, 'Des machines et des hommes: étude des différentiels de productivité entre la France et le Royaume-Uni avant la première guerre mondiale' (doctoral thesis, European University Institute, Florence, 1993).

[11] Comparative data in S. Broadberry, 'Manufacturing and the Convergence Hypothesis: What the Long Run Data Show', *Journal of Economic History*, 53/4 (1993).

[12] R. Hubscher, 'La Petite Exploitation en France: reproduction et compétitivité, fin du XIXe–début du XXe siècle', *Annales ESC* 40/2 (1985).

[13] O'Brien and Keyder, *Economic Growth in Britain and France*, 185–98.

well known and are well summarized in Rondo Cameron and Charles Freedeman's words:

In the 1940s and 1950s a number of scholars, mainly American, believed that the problem to be explained was French economic retardation in the nineteenth century . . . With the evidence now at hand . . . it is clear that the earlier discussions were based on a faulty premise. In fact, the French economy performed very well in comparison with other industrialised nations.[14]

However, as is often the case, revisionism has become a new orthodoxy and Nick Crafts has recently warned that some of the revisionist conclusions might be too optimistic, France appearing in his view as an average European performer, 'respectable but certainly not outstanding'.[15] Nevertheless, average is a far cry from backwardness, a concept almost totally discarded in the analyses of French economic performance and replaced by that of difference or, more recently, specificity.

This is in sharp contrast to the British historiography, where the concept of decline remains an analytical tool in most historical studies of British economic performance since the late nineteenth century. To what extent this is justified by the actual record of the British economy is probably as much a matter of point of view as of accumulated evidence. For, despite their far higher level of sophistication, British economic and business historians might well be in a position not very dissimilar to that of their French colleagues of a generation ago when, in the words of the late Jean Bouvier: 'For too long and with too much exclusiveness, the emphasis was put on our backwardness and slowness. Because France was a medium-sized country, her handicaps were overstated and her advantages neglected.'[16] It is also possible that writers do not sufficiently stress the difference between two separate facts: Britain's fall from her position of a dominant economy, which she enjoyed before 1914, and her comparatively mediocre performance after the Second World War. The mood, however, seems to be changing among British economic historians. Theories of economic growth emphasizing the effects of catching up with the leader and the convergence between industrialized countries are increasingly seen as providing a better explanation for Britain's disappointing—in comparison to her Western European neighbours—economic performance after the Second World War than all the shortcomings which have successively or simultaneously been invoked.[17] As Barry Supple recently commented:

[14] R. Cameron and C. Freedeman, 'French Economic Growth: A Radical Revision', *Social Science History*, 7/1 (1983), 3.

[15] Crafts, 'Economic Growth in France and Britain', 67.

[16] J. Bouvier, 'Introduction: libres propos autour d'une démarche révisionniste', in P. Fridenson and A. Strauss (eds.), *Le Capitalisme français 19e–20e siècle: blocages et dynamismes d'une croissance* (Paris, 1987), 13.

[17] The most recent examples are the contributions of C. Feinstein, 'Success and Failure:

The bedrock of the debate has always been the relative 'failure' of the British economy and its associated demotion from the leading ranks of industrial powers. In this respect it is, of course, possible that the historical perspective misleads us, and that we are witnessing a long-run tendency to convergence in the productivity and income levels of leading industrial societies.[18]

Nevertheless, the idea of decline remains widespread within and outside the academic world.

An Anglo-French comparison is a fitting place for a reflection on the implications of the French revisionism on British business history. They have so far been very limited. This is not really surprising, for comparisons with France have only played a marginal, and very recent, role in the perception, measurement, and analysis of the British decline, far less than comparisons with the United States, Germany, and Japan. Yet, because of the similarities between the two countries, in both their historical development and current position, the notions of backwardness and decline are strongly interrelated. It is for example significant that both countries have been at times described as the 'sick man' of Europe.[19] The ideas of decline and backwardness are best seen as reflecting a certain malaise at a particular stage of each country's history. The differences existing between the two economies in the nineteenth century were not sufficient to describe France as 'backward'. In the same way, for Britain to be on a par or even slightly behind France in the late twentieth century can hardly be considered as a sign of 'decline'.

It could of course be argued that the two countries, both old industrial nations, have been in decline. This is a complex and in many respects contradictory contention. On the one hand, it is difficult to see how it applies to the thirty years following the Second World War, when all indicators show France as one of the top performers. On the other hand, there is no doubt that a 'German complex' exists in both Britain and France. The British argue that they have fallen behind Germany, the French feel that they have not entirely caught up with her. This complex, mainly entertained by the media and by politicians, could also be seen as a variation on the old themes of French backwardness and British decline. This is not the place for a detailed comparison between French, British, and German economic growth since the Second World War. In many respects, Germany appears to have been the strongest performer. Before

British Economic Growth since 1948', and B. Supple, 'British Economic Decline since 1945', in R. Floud and D. McCloskey (eds.), *The Economic History of Britain since 1700*, 3 vols. (2nd edn. Cambridge, 1994), iii. 95–122 and 318–46.

[18] B. Supple, 'Fear of Failing: Economic History and the Decline of Britain', *Economic History Review*, 47/3 (1994), 443.

[19] Such a label has been less common for France, though it was used in the 1940s and 1950s, under the Fourth Republic. Rondo Cameron, in his article 'L'Économie française: passé, présent, avenir', *Annales ESC* 25/5 (1970), 1418, attributes it to the American economist Warren Baum in 1958.

unification, West Germany had the largest GDP, the lowest rate of inflation, the lowest rate of unemployment, and the strongest currency of
the three countries. On the other hand, on the basis of a simple indicator
giving an overall measure of economic performance, GDP per head,
Germany was only very fractionally ahead of France and Britain. According to Maddison's figures, in 1989 GDP per head in 1985 $US prices was
$13,989 in Germany, $13,837 in France, and $13,468 in Britain. (In 1913 the
figures were respectively $2,606, $2,734, and $4,024, and in 1950 $3,339,
$4,149, and $5,651.[20]) A third aspect of this contention reflects very
contemporary worries about the threat posed to Europe (including
Germany), and not only Britain and France, by the rise of the newly
industrialized countries.

Anglo-French comparisons should be particularly interesting in this
context. The homogeneity between the two countries, far greater than
with the United States or Japan, together with the lack of synchronization
in their periods of stronger or weaker economic performance, provides a
valuable ground for testing the validity of many explanatory variables of
economic performance, especially, in connection with this book, those
concerning business activity.

2. BUSINESS DEVELOPMENT IN BRITAIN AND FRANCE

Comparing business development in Britain and France is more difficult
than comparing their overall economic performance. In the first place,
data are not so readily available. Aggregate data—on production, exports,
employment, productivity, research and development, and so on—do not
reflect the complexity and diversity of business activity. At the micro-
economic level, business history, as a subdiscipline, is less advanced than
economic history, particularly in France. As François Caron points out:
'French enterprises are today discovering that they have a history. In their
overwhelming majority they had, until the 1970s, paid but scant attention
to this aspect of their identity.'[21] Direct comparisons at branch level are
also a rarity.

In addition, France tends to be on the fringes of international comparisons. She has, very unfortunately, been left out of the two most influential recent comparative analyses of the relationships between
business organization and economic performance, Alfred Chandler's *Scale
and Scope* and Michael Porter's *The Competitive Advantage of Nations*.[22]

---

[20] Maddison, *Dynamic Forces in Capitalist Development*, 6.
[21] F. Caron, 'L'Entreprise', in P. Nora (ed.), *Les Lieux de mémoire*, iii: *Les France* (Paris, 1993),
323.
[22] Patrick Fridenson has related these analyses, in particular Chandler's, to the French

David Landes's comparative analysis of Western Europe's industrial development was of course a notable exception.[23] Landes, however, was a leading protagonist of the backwardness thesis. With the loss of its backwardness, France might have lost some of its appeal to foreign, in particular American, business historians and analysts. The notion of French 'specificity' put forward by French historians does not easily fit into the general categories cherished by social scientists: Britain is a better example of early start, world dominance, and decline, Japan a better example of state-induced economic prowess, Germany a better example of a bank-dominated economy, and so on. The agenda for Anglo-French comparisons in business history is therefore particularly challenging. If the notions of backwardness and decline are to be replaced by those of difference or specificity, the object of a comparative analysis must be to establish what have been the main similarities and differences in the business development and organization of the two countries in the last hundred years and try to evaluate their real significance and impact.

Until the 1960s, the main difference lay in the scale of the two countries' business activities, both at the national and international levels. France might not have been 'backward' in comparison with Britain in the nineteenth century or the United States in the twentieth century. Nevertheless, as indicated above, she ranked behind Britain in terms of wealth and level of industrialization. Business activities, whether industrial, commercial, or financial, were more developed in Britain. The number of large manufacturing companies was much higher in Britain than in France: in 1929, for example, 39 companies employed 10,000 people in Britain as against 22 in France.[24] Big business had also, from an early stage, been more diversified in Britain, having penetrated a much wider range of industries and services, in particular those connected with consumers' demand. At the international level, the development of multinational enterprises had reached a higher level in Britain than in France and, until the Second World War, than in any other country in the world: in 1914 Britain held

case, in 'The Relatively Slow Development of Big Business in 20th Century France', paper presented to the Eleventh International Economic History Congress, Milan, 1994, session A2, 'Global Enterprise: Big Business and the Wealth of Nations in the Past Century, 1880s–1980s'.

[23] Chandler, *Scale and Scope*; M. Porter, *The Competitive Advantage of Nations* (London, 1990); Landes, *Unbound Prometheus*.

[24] See Ch. 13 by Y. Cassis in this volume. Whereas there is an abundance of lists of the British largest companies (L. Hannah, *The Rise of the Corporate Economy* (2nd edn. London, 1983); Chandler, *Scale and Scope*; D. J. Jeremy, 'The Hundred Largest Employers in the U.K.: 1907, 1935, and 1955', *Business History*, 33/1 (1991); P. Wardley, 'The Anatomy of Big Business: Aspects of Corporate Development in the Twentieth Century', *Business History*, 33/2 (1991)); such lists still hardly exist for France, the only available ones having been published in the 1950s by J. Houssiaux, *Le Pouvoir de monopole* (Paris, 1956).

some 45.5 per cent of the accumulated stock of foreign direct investment, France 12.2 per cent; in 1938 their respective share was 39.8 and 9.5 per cent.[25]

In terms of overall production, France lagged behind Britain in most, and at times all, major industrial sectors, from coal extraction (where France was at a strong disadvantage in terms of resource endowment), iron, steel, cotton (though not wool), and mechanical engineering in the nineteenth century; to oil, motor cars (from the 1930s), chemicals, and electrical engineering in the first half of the twentieth century, to which must be added traditional British strongholds such as the branded consumer goods industry, or banking, insurance, and other financial and commercial services, including shipping, where the City of London reigned supreme. Tables 1.3 to 1.6 illustrate the gap separating the two countries in some of these sectors.

The gap was often huge: between 1890 and 1940 the size of the French shipbuilding industry was about a fifth of that of the British, whereas it had been its most serious rival in the 1860s and 1870s;[26] in the second half of the nineteenth century the British consumption of raw cotton was between four and five times higher than the French: 492,000 tons against 115,000 in 1860, 788,000 against 159,000 in 1900.[27] But it was sometimes narrow if it existed at all: in motor cars, for example, where France had an early lead, or in steel, where she overtook Britain in the inter-war years. Some industries were particularly dynamic despite their disadvantage in size: coal extraction, for example, increased faster in the Nord-Pas-de-Calais, the country's main productive area, than in Britain as a whole between 1870 and 1914.[28]

The gap narrowed after 1918 and even more after 1945, and in a number of industries output has been higher in France than in Britain. Differences have persisted, however, at the business level, the number of large companies remaining higher in Britain than in France: among Europe's 500 largest companies in Europe in 1989, 130 were British and 72 French.[29] The same is true of multinational enterprises, the United Kingdom holding 26.1 per cent of the accumulated stock of foreign direct investment in 1988 against 5.9 per cent for France, despite the increase of outflows of French foreign direct investment in the late 1980s, which rose from 6

[25] G. Jones and H. Schröter, 'Continental European Multinationals, 1850–1992', in id. *The Rise of Multinationals in Continental Europe* (Aldershot, 1993), 10.

[26] S. Pollard and P. Robertson, *The British Shipbuilding Industry, 1870–1914* (Cambridge, Mass., 1979), 42–3. See also E. Lorenz, 'L'Offre de travail et les stratégies d'emploi dans la construction navale en France et en Grande-Bretagne (1890–1970)', *Le Mouvement social*, 138 (1987), 27.

[27] B. R. Mitchell, *European Historical Statistics* (London, 1980).

[28] M. Gillet, *Les Charbonnages du Nord de la France au XIXe siècle* (Paris, 1973), 82. On the British coal industry in the same period, see R. Church, *The History of the British Coal Industry*, ii: *1830–1913: Victorian Pre-eminence* (Oxford, 1986).

[29] Jones and Schröter, 'Continental European Multinationals', 23.

Table 1.3. *The iron and steel industry in Britain and France, 1880–1975: some comparisons*
(a) Output

	Great Britain		France	
	(1)	(2)	(1)	(2)
1880	7,873	1,316	1,725	389
1913	10,425	7,787	5,207	4,687
1928	6,716	8,657	9,981	9,479
1938	6,869	10,565	6,012	6,137
1955	12,670	20,108	10,960	12,592
1975	12,131	20,098	17,921	21,530

Notes: Col. (1): pig iron; col. (2): crude steel in thousand tons.

(b) *Largest firms (by work-force)*

	Great Britain		France	
	Firm	Work-force	Firm	Work-force
c.1910	Armstrong	25,000	Schneider	15,000[a]
	Vickers	22,500	Wendel	28,000[b]
	GKN	21,710	Marine Homécourt	13,200
	Bolckow Yaughan	18,000	Chatillon, Commentry	11,000
	John Brown	16,205	et Neuves-Maisons	
1929	Vickers	44,162	Wendel	33,000
	GKN	30,000	Schneider	
	United Steel	19,229	Marine Homécourt	
	Dorman Long	18,028	Longwy	9,724
1955	Vickers	70,000	Schneider	50,000
	GKN	62,000	Wendel	21,000
	Stewarts & Lloyd	42,000	Usinor	16,000
	United Steel	34,785	Sidelor	12,200
1973	British Steel	229,000	Usinor	46,828
			Creusot-Loire	41,500
			Vallourec	29,000
			Wendel-Sidelor	25,248

[a] Le Creusot only.
[b] Incl. German interests.

Table 1.4. *The motor industry in Britain and France*
(a) *Output (cars)*

	Great Britain	France
1929	182,000	211,000
1938	341,000	200,000
1955	898,000	560,000
1975	1,268,000	2,951,000
1985	1,048,000	2,817,000

(b) *Largest firms (work-force)*

	Great Britain		France	
	Firm	Work-force	Firm	Work-force
1929	Austin	19,000	Citroën	31,000
	Morris	10,200	Renault	25,500
	Ford	7,128	Peugeot	20,000
1955	Ford	24,773	Renault	28,000
	BMC	23,000	Citroën	17,400
			Peugeot	12,833
1975	BL	190,841	Renault	157,000
			Citroën	104,000
			Peugeot	90,276

per cent of total outflows in 1980–4 to 10 per cent in 1985–90.[30] However, this importance of large multinational companies has been a British particularity, France being much closer to Germany in that respect.

Beyond recent convergence, more deep-rooted similarities can be observed in the development of British and French business in the last hundred years, which would merit further investigation. This mainly concerns the two countries' respective competitive advantages, which have tended to lie in the same industries: the industries of the first industrial revolution before 1914, despite the 'decline' of the British steel industry, with a slower start than the United States and Germany in the 'new' industries. Within these new industries, there was a common strong development after the First World War leading to European prominence in motor cars, aerospace, oil (the latter especially in Britain but with a strong

[30] J. H. Dunning, *Multinational Enterprises and the Global Economy* (Wokingham, 1992), 17–18.

Table 1.5. *The largest firms in the British and French electrical industries*

	Great Britain		France	
	Firm	Work-force	Firm	Work-force
1929	Associated Electrical Industries	30,000	Compagnie Générale d'Électricité	15,000
	General Electric Company	24,000	Thomson	
	Callenders Cable and Construction Company	14,000	Alsthom	12,000
1955	Associated Electrical Industries	87,000	Compagnie Générale d'Électricité	18,000
	General Electric Company	60,000	Thomson	
	British Insulated Callenders' Cables	39,000	Alsthom	
	English Electric Co.	39,000	Jeumont	6,000
1975	GEC	201,000	Compagnie Générale d'Électricité	124,500
	Thorn	82,000	Thomson	84,657
	Plessey	77,000		
	EMI	40,300		

effort to catch up, at least for refining, on the French part), rather than chemicals or electrical engineering, where Germany maintained her advantage. The two countries also shared strong positions in the world of finance, especially before 1914 as leading foreign investors and home of major international financial centres. A subdivision of the SIC double-digit groups into three- or four-digit categories would no doubt present a more differentiated picture. In the textile industry, for example, the French silk industry was much more successful than its British counterpart, though it declined from the 1880s, as a result of strong German and Swiss competition. In the chemical industry France built a strong position in industrial gas with the company L'Air liquide.

The two countries' respective strengths and weaknesses continued to converge until the 1970s. Since then, 'deindustrialization' has proceeded faster in Britain, but France may well be following the same path. Some significant differences have appeared, the most spectacular being in the motor car industry, which has rapidly declined in Britain. France has also been able to hold her own in areas of the electrical industry such as

Table 1.6. *The largest firms in the British and French chemical industries*

	Great Britain		France	
	Firm	Work-force	Firm	Work-force
*c.*1910	United Alkali	12,000	Saint-Gobain	11,540
	Kynoch	8,000	Kuhlmann	2,000
	Lever Bros.	4,700		
	Brunner Mond	4,400		
*c.*1930	Unilever	60,000	Saint-Gobain	15,000
	ICI	49,706	Péchiney	9,000
	Reckitt	8,100	Kuhlmann	7,000
	Boots	7,129		
*c.*1953	ICI	115,306	Saint-Gobain	11,090
	Unilever	50,287	Rhône-Poulenc	9,706
	Boots	35,938	Péchiney	
	Beecham		Kuhlmann	
	Reckitt			
*c.*1972	ICI	199,000	Rhône-Poulenc	118,112
	BOC	40,600	PUK	95,000
	Beecham	25,200	L'Air liquide	24,000
	Reckitt	25,000	Roussel-Nobel	23,400

telecommunications and transportation. Britain remains stronger in oil and consumer packaged goods, as well as in financial services. For the rest, there is much in common: relative strength in defence, chemicals, and health-care; weaknesses in machine tools and electronics. Finer comparisons would be required, because of the increased specialization within branches through product differentiation. Nevertheless, there exists in both countries a common concern about a lack of competitiveness, an apparent fragility in export markets, in a number of industries, and the possible compensation offered by the development of services. The answers so far have somewhat differed. Despite the growth of foreign direct investment in the French economy since the 1950s,[31] France has tended to favour national solutions, while Britain has strongly encouraged foreign, and in particular Japanese, investments, in order to rebuild segments of her industrial base, in particular in motor cars, consumer electronics, and computers.[32]

[31] Abundance of figures in J. H. Dunning and J. Cantwell, *IRM Directory of Statistics of International Investment and Production* (Basingstoke, 1987).

[32] The phenomenon has been widely commented on in the media. See e.g. C. Rapoport, 'Japan to the Rescue', *Fortune*, 18 (Oct. 1993).

3. SECTORAL EXAMPLES

A number of major industries are discussed in some detail, though mostly in a national context, in the following chapters, in connection with the three main themes of the book: food and drink by Robert Fitzgerald and Terry Gourvish, food-retailing by Emmanuel Chadeau, motor cars by Nick Tiratsoo, chemicals by Jean-Pierre Daviet, and electricity by Eric Bussière. Seen in a comparative perspective, they provide further evidence of the main converging trends between British and French business outlined above. Given the space available, the following paragraphs can only be rough sketches of the development of these industries in the two countries.

Food, drink, and tobacco has been among the most successful industrial sectors in British business for over a century.[33] In France, however, it has hardly counted at all in the world of big business until the Second World War, despite the importance of the cognac and champagne industries, and of course wine-making, which is strangely ranked as agricultural produce rather than manufacture. Although this sector remains much stronger in Britain, with such industrial giants as Unilever, BAT, Grand Metropolitan, Allied Lyons, Gallaher, Bass, Guinness, Tate & Lyle, and Cadbury Schweppes among the top fifty British industrial companies in 1990, a few large French companies have emerged in the last two decades. These include in particular BSN, the glassmaker turned food conglomerate after its failed take-over bid on Saint-Gobain in 1969 and its take-over of Gervais-Danone, the dairy products manufacturer, in 1972 (its turnover was more or less the same as Allied Lyons in 1990 with over £5 billion); but also Beghin-Say, in sugar-refining; Louis Vuitton-Moet Hennessy (LVMH), in luxury products, including champagne and cognac; and Perrier of mineral water fame, which were all larger than any German group in the sector.[34] The links between Guinness and LVMH, though somewhat unstable, are another sign of convergence in the consumer goods industry.

Convergence also occurred in food-retailing, another area of British business success since the late nineteenth century which only emerged in France after the Second World War. Before 1914, Thomas Lipton and Home and Colonial Stores were already fully-fledged retailing chains, the former with 242 shops in Britain, 38 branches abroad, and £2.5 million

---

[33] Among the major studies are C. Wilson, *The History of Unilever* 2 vols. (London, 1954); B. Alford, *W. D. & H. O. Wills and the Development of the U.K. Tobacco Industry, 1786–1965* (London, 1973); P. Chalmin, *The Making of a Sugar Giant: Tate and Lyle 1859–1989* (London, 1990); T. R. Gourvish and R. G. Wilson, *The British Brewing Industry 1830–1980* (Cambridge, 1994); R. Fitzgerald, *Rowntree and the Marketing Revolution 1862–1969* (Cambridge, 1994).

[34] These companies still await their history. On BSN see F. Gautier, 'B.S.N.', in *L'Industrie française face à l'ouverture internationale* (Paris, 1991). On the French sugar industry, see J. Fiérain, *Les Raffineries de sucres des ports en France (XIXe–début XXe siècles)* (Paris, 1976).

capital in 1898, when it was converted into a limited company.[35] The
inter-war years saw the rise of Marks & Spencer and Sainsbury. It is true
that France had been a pioneer, with Britain, of the large department
stores, in particular with the Bon Marché, one of the oldest and largest in
the world in the late nineteenth century.[36] Mass retailing, however, took
off later; but the convergence with Britain is striking. In 1990 Sainsbury
and Carrefour were ranked respectively 48th and 49th in *The Times 1,000*
largest industrial companies in Europe with a turnover approaching £8
billion, and Tesco and Promodès respectively 66th and 74th. Differences
no doubt exist in the concept of mass retailing in the two countries:
hypermarkets have mainly remained a French phenomenon while the
growth of shopping centres has been particularly strong in Britain.
However, such a massive development of large groups in food-retailing
has had no parallel elsewhere in Europe, despite the existence of large
chains such as Migros in Switzerland, Ahold in Holland, or Metro in
Germany. In the same way, while opening hours remain tightly regulated
in Germany, France appears to be starting to follow Britain in a move
towards deregulation.

The chemical industries have followed a parallel path. Britain was
slightly ahead of France before 1914 in terms of both output (their production of sulphuric acid, for example, was respectively 1,082,000 and
900,000 tons in 1913) and number of large firms (Table 1.6). However, both
countries lagged well behind Germany, in particular in organic chemistry
and its application to synthetic dyes.[37] Similar attempts at developing an
autonomous dye industry were undertaken, with the encouragement of
the State, during the First World War, resulting in the creation of the
British Dye Corporation (merged in ICI in 1926) and the Compagnie
nationale des matières colorantes (taken over by Kuhlmann in 1924). A
significant divergence resulted from the merger leading to the foundation
of Imperial Chemical Industries (ICI) in 1926, which has never been entirely dissipated: creating a French ICI has always loomed large in French
political and business circles. Negotiations towards a merger between
Saint-Gobain and Kuhlmann failed in 1927, for reasons explained by Jean-
Pierre Daviet in Chapter 10. State-originated attempts in the 1960s to
concentrate the French chemical industry around two major companies,
Péchiney-Ugine-Kuhlmann (PUK) and Rhône-Poulenc, ended with mixed

[35] See D. Oddy, 'Lipton, Sir Thomas Johnstone (1850–1931): Grocer', in D. Jeremy (ed.),
Dictionary of Business Biography, iii (1985), 799–802; P. Mathias, *Retailing Revolution* (London,
1967).
[36] R. B. Miller, *The Bon Marché: Bourgeois Culture and Department Store, 1869–1920* (London,
1981); V. Bourienne, 'Boucicaut, Chauchard et les autres: fondateurs et fondation de grands
magasins parisiens', *Paris et Île de France: mémoires publiés par la fédération des sociétés
historiques et archéologiques de Paris et de l'Île de France* (Paris, 1989), xl. 257–335.
[37] See L. F. Haber, *The Chemical Industry, 1900–1930: International Growth and Technical
Change* (Oxford, 1971).

success, as the former firm eventually divested itself of chemicals while the latter never quite managed to match ICI's achievements.[38] Comparisons should be made at the level of each of the major products making up the chemical industry, which would reveal more subtle differences. It is interesting to note, however, that the same broad trends are discernible in the pharmaceutical industry, with Britain enjoying a slightly larger share of world exports (16.8 as against 13.9 per cent in 1967, 12 as against 11.5 per cent in 1990), but having a clear advantage in terms of both innovation capacities and large firms; in 1991 four British companies were among the world top twenty (Glaxo, SmithKline Beecham, ICI, and Wellcome) as against a single French one (Rhône-Poulenc).[39]

A similar pattern is observable in the electrical industries: a slower start than in Germany, early dependence on foreign technology, stronger development in Britain from the 1930s to the 1960s, and eventual convergence, France being this time ahead of Britain, Alcatel-Alsthom (formerly the Compagnie générale d'électricité) and Thomson having become substantially larger companies than the British General Electric Company.[40] However, the convergence between the two countries, and indeed between all European countries, lies in the loss of competitiveness to the United States and Japan, in particular in computers, despite massive government aid in France.

The contrast is starker in the motor car industry, particularly since the 1970s. Before this, the industry had also run a similar course in the two countries, with France's early advantage switching in favour of Britain from the 1930s. In any case, demand conditions were similar in the two countries, offering few possibilities for mass production on American lines.[41] The position has changed, however, in the last twenty years. While Peugeot (which took over Citroën in 1974) and Renault have maintained their position among the top six European companies, the British-owned component of the country's motor car industry has almost completely

[38] For the history of the major firms in each country see W. J. Reader, *Imperial Chemical Industries: A History*, 2 vols. (London, 1970–5); A. Pettigrew, *The Awakening Giant: Continuity and Change in Imperial Chemical Industries* (Oxford, 1985); J.-P. Daviet, *Un destin international: la Compagnie de Saint-Gobain de 1830 à 1939* (Paris, 1988) and *Une multinationale à la française: Saint-Gobain 1665–1989* (Paris, 1989); P. Cayez, *Rhône-Poulenc, 1895–1975* (Paris, 1988); J. F. Léger, *Une grande entreprise dans la chimie française: Kuhlmann 1825–1982* (Paris, 1988).

[39] G. Owen, 'Nations, Industries and Firms: British Manufacturing and World Competition between the 1960s and the 1990s', paper presented at the Centre for Economic Performance, London School of Economics, 21 June 1994.

[40] The major works on this sector are P. Lanthier, 'Les Constructions électriques en France: financement et stratégies de six groupes industriels internationaux, 1880–1940' (thèse de doctorat, Université de Paris X, 1988); A. Broder and F. Torres, *Alcatel-Alsthom: histoire de la Compagnie générale d'électricité* (Paris, 1992); F. Caron and F. Cardot (eds.), *Histoire générale de l'électricité en France*, i (Paris, 1991); R. Jones and O. Marriott, *Anatomy of a Merger: A History of G.E.C., A.E.I. and English Electric* (London, 1970).

[41] There are interesting comparisons in S. M. Bowden, 'Demand and Supply Constraints in the Inter-war UK Car Industry: Did the Manufacturers Get it Right?', *Business History*, 33/2 (1991).

disappeared since the take-over of Rover by BMW in 1994. This is not the place to compare the development of this industry in the two countries, which could have easily made up a full section of this book.[42] Among the reasons for such a divergence is the managerial failure which occurred in the British but not in the French motor industry. Nick Tiratsoo's analysis of Standard Motors strongly emphasizes this explanation and, while it might be difficult to generalize over British industry as a whole, it appears well suited to the motor industry.[43] The diverging evolution of the motor industry in Britain and France was also affected by their respective export markets. French producers had to compete from an early stage in the Common Market, and this was a stronger incentive for modernization than the Commonwealth, which absorbed the bulk of British exports. State intervention and industrial policy, on the other hand, appear to have mattered less. There were nationalizations in the two countries, and, despite differences in the type of relationships between government and business, government policy seems to have played only a marginal role in the success of the French motor industry, while some ill-judged state interventions in Britain were compounded by more fundamental management weaknesses.[44] The question remains, however, whether Britain will be the *first* or, at least in the foreseeable future, the *only* major industrial country to surrender a significant domestically owned motor car industry.

4. ENTREPRENEURSHIP AND BUSINESS ORGANIZATION

The various factors affecting business performance might present sharper contrasts between the two countries. This book examines in more detail three of them: ownership and control, with particular reference to the family firm; education and training; mergers and business concentration. They encompass most determinants of business activity, although some themes would certainly deserve a specific discussion, for example state

---

[42] There is a huge literature on the subject. From a business history perspective see in particular J. M. Laux, *In First Gear: The French Automobile Industry to 1914* (Liverpool, 1976); P. Fridenson, *Histoire des usines Renault*, i: *Naissance de la grande entreprise* (Paris, 1972); S. Schweitzer, *André Citroen* (Paris, 1992); J. L. Loubet, *Automobiles Peugeot: une réussite industrielle* (Paris, 1990); G. Maxcy and A. Silberston, *The Motor Industry* (London, 1959); R. Church and M. Miller, 'The Big Three', in B. Supple (ed.), *Essays in British Business History* (Oxford, 1977); R. Church, *Herbert Austin: The British Motor Car Industry to 1941* (London, 1979); W. A. Lewchuck, *American Technology and the British Motor Vehicle Industry* (Cambridge, 1987); R. J. Overy, *William Morris, Viscount Nuffield* (London, 1976); S. Tolliday and J. Zeitlin (eds.), *The Automobile Industry and its Workers: Between Fordism and Flexibility* (Cambridge, 1987); N. Tiratsoo, 'The Motor Car Industry', in H. Mercer, N. Rollings, and J. Tomlison, *Labour Governments and Private Industry* (Edinburgh, 1992); R. Church, *The Rise and Decline of the British Motor Industry* (Basingstoke, 1994).

[43] See the recent study by Church, *Rise and Decline of the British Motor Industry*.

[44] Owen, 'Nations, Industries and Firms'.

intervention, industrial relations, or the role of the banks and capital markets. The individual essays dealing with these three problems are case-studies rather than overviews of the global issue. Such an approach has the advantage of providing a thorough analysis of at least some aspects of the issue, thus avoiding the necessary simplifications of general surveys. The disadvantage is the well-known difficulty of generalizing from case-studies. The remainder of this introduction will therefore be devoted to a comparative discussion of the major issues raised by the family firm, education and training, and mergers and survival in Britain and France.

Ownership and control: the family firm

In both Britain and France, the role of the family firm has been at the core of most debates about business organization and its effect on the two countries' general economic performance. The role ascribed to the family firm appears in many respects highly contradictory. Early analyses of France's economic backwardness in the nineteenth century put a strong emphasis on entrepreneurial failure: in an age dominated by the family firm, France's weakness derived from her lack of development of large enterprises on the British scale. With the advent of managerial capitalism, both France and Britain have been seen as remaining for far too long committed to 'family capitalism'. For Alfred Chandler, for example, French enterprises, like their British counterparts, failed to develop the 'organizational capabilities' in the basic industries of the second industrial revolution during the crucial period from the late nineteenth to the mid-twentieth century.[45] In this perspective, Britain and France appear as the two early industrialized countries, dominated by the family firm and the industries of the first industrial revolution and quickly losing ground to their more dynamic American and German competitors.

In fact, recent research has shown that in all European countries, including Germany, family ownership has persisted in enterprises large and small well into the twentieth century.[46] Here the dividing line is not so much between Britain and France on the one hand and the United States and Germany on the other, as between Europe and America. Although the trend towards a functional and later a multidivisional structure is clearly discernible, the adoption of such forms of organization in European enterprises has been at best patchy and cannot be readily seen as a primary factor of business success or failure.[47] In addition, small and medium-

---

[45] Chandler, *Scale and Scope*, 596.

[46] There is a good recent overview of the question in R. Church, 'The Family Firm in Industrial Capitalism: International Perspectives on Hypotheses and History', *Business History*, 35/4 (1993).

[47] See the essays on Britain, France, and Germany in A. D. Chandler and H. Daems (eds.), *Managerial Hierarchies* (Cambridge, Mass., 1980).

sized family firms have recently been rehabilitated.[48] The huge conglomerates issued from the waves of merger frenzy which took place in the last three decades have often proved disappointing in terms of both performance and innovative capacity. Germany's economic strength has increasingly been seen as resting on her *Mittelstand*, her medium-sized family firms excelling in occupying 'niches' in high-quality products, in particular in the machine tools industry. If anything, Britain and France are now considered as lacking succesful medium-sized companies and are attempting to encourage their development.

The persistence of family ownership and control is thus no more considered as having had a negative effect on economic growth. Such a revision has proceeded faster in France: Maurice Lévy-Leboyer showed some twenty years ago that businessmen's attachment to small-scale industrial production was a rational choice well adapted to the country's comparative advantage in quality production.[49] In Britain, Alfred Chandler's condemnation of the attachment of British industry to 'personal capitalism' remains a powerful voice, despite strong reservations expressed by British historians.[50] William Lazonick in particular, building on Chandler's work, has persisted on this path, suggesting that Britain's loss of world economic supremacy derived from her outdated form of business organization,[51] while Donald McCloskey's earlier rehabilitation of the Victorian entrepreneur had not met with unanimous agreement.[52]

The essays in the first section of this volume go a step further and emphasize the positive contribution of the family firm. That family ownership is not incompatible with strong business performance is a case which hardly needs to be made. The food companies Rowntree and Cadbury in Britain, studied by Robert Fitzgerald, where the family maintained managerial control until the 1930s in the former case and as late as the 1960s in the latter, are good examples, as are the more recent French hypermarket and supermarket chains—Carrefour, Promodès, Centres Leclerc, Intermarché, Casino—studied by Emmanuel Chadeau: all, with the exception of Casino, were founded after 1948. Christofle, the famous

---

[48] See e.g. M. J. Piore and C. F. Sabel, *The Second Industrial Divide: Possibilities for Prosperity* (New York, 1984); M. Muller (ed.), *Structure and Strategy of Small and Medium-Size Enterprises since the Industrial Revolution* (Stuttgart, 1994).

[49] M. Lévy-Leboyer, 'Le Patronat français a-t-il été malthusien?', *Le Mouvement social*, 3 (1974).

[50] See R. Church, 'The Limitations of the Personal Capitalism Paradigm', contribution to 'Scale and Scope: A Review Colloquium', *Business History Review*, 64/4 (1990); L. Hannah, 'Scale and Scope: Towards a European Visible Hand?', *Business History*, 33/2 (1991); B. Supple, 'Scale and Scope: Alfred Chandler and the Dynamics of Industrial Capitalism', *Economic History Review*, 44/3 (1991).

[51] William Lazonick, *Business Organization and the Myth of the Market Economy* (Cambridge, 1991).

[52] D. McCloskey and L. Sandberg, 'From Damnation to Redemption: Judgments on the Late Victorian Entrepreneur', in D. McCloskey, *Enterprise and Trade in Victorian Britain* (London, 1981).

silversmiths studied by Marc de Ferrière, is a rare example of the survival of a *medium-sized* family firm over five generations, although it has run into serious difficulties in the last couple of years and might well end under the wing of a larger group. Family firms can show a high degree of managerial flexibility. Robert Fitzgerald shows that there existed a diversity of alternatives to Chandler's model of managerial capitalism: for example, the effectiveness of links between firms, which also characterize the much praised family-owned *zaibatsu* of pre-war Japan, a point which also applies to the organization of several sectors of French industry. Moreover, family ownership did not stunt managerial development. Cadbury believed that industrial management was a highly skilled profession, while in 1917 Seebohm Rowntree was investigating the 'ideal structure' for a modern business. The management of French hypermarkets has also been highly flexible, as shown by Emmanuel Chadeau in Chapter 3. As is often the case in new industries, the impetus was given by individual entrepreneurs coming from outside the business establishment. As they have progressively grown into giant firms, however, they have been capable of decentralizing and recruiting salaried managers while ultimate control has remained in the hands of members of the founding families. Christofle's longevity has no doubt been due to its capacity to exploit the full potential of a niche market. However, according to Marc de Ferrière, its strategic decisions—opening a shop in New York as early as 1848 and a subsidiary company in Karlsruhe in 1856— and the adaptability of its management structures should not be underestimated even within the framework of a medium-sized company.

A major problem associated with the running of family firms is the unchecked dictatorial power of the boss. This is not, however, a privilege of the family firm. Nick Tiratsoo's analysis of the failure of Standard Motors puts a strong emphasis on the responsibility of its managing director in the late 1940s, John Black, who, according to a journalist, had 'personal and centralised control' reminiscent of 'the almost patriarchal . . . old family business'; and yet he only held about 1 per cent of the company's stock. Indeed Tiratsoo's more general considerations about the shortcomings of British management in the late 1940s have not so much to do with family capitalism as with socio-political attitudes such as a strong belief in leadership qualities rather than technical competence, and a profound distrust of all initiatives taken by the Labour Government.

Family ownership and control of large corporations has dramatically declined in both Britain and France since the Second World War. Family firms are mostly associated with small and medium-sized companies, their major problem being survival into the second, let alone the third, generation. In their overwhelming majority they are either liquidated or taken over by larger companies. A handful of such firms has grown into large companies in the second half of the twentieth century; family ownership, however, has proved difficult to maintain (as is already apparent in some of the French hypermarket chains), while old-established large family companies, such as Michelin or Peugeot, are notable exceptions.

Education and training

There are, apparently, more divergences in the debates surrounding the role of education and training in British and French economic and business performances. Despite dissenting voices,[53] the French educational system is usually considered to have played a positive role.[54] This is a point of view shared by Michael Sanderson, who shows in Chapter 6 that, despite the many prejudices against France, educational experts inquiring in France were usually favourably impressed, particularly in the areas of technical, vocational, and managerial education. Britain, however, was selective in her imitation of the French model, rejecting in particular the concept of the *grandes écoles* as superior to the universities, although the foundation of the London School of Economics was partly influenced by French ideas.[55]

English education, by contrast, has consistently been blamed for its contribution to the country's economic decline.[56] Education of businessmen is of course the crucial issue. In that respect, the French system appears superior on two counts. First, higher education has mattered more to the French than to the British business élite: statistical analyses have consistently shown that the percentage of businessmen with university education was higher in France than in Britain and indeed any other European country.[57] And secondly, the French have favoured a scientific type of higher education while the British have for a long time stuck to the humanities.

---

[53] See in particular R. Locke, *The End of the Practical Man: Entrepreneurship and Higher Education in Germany, France and Great Britain 1880–1940* (Greenwich, Conn., 1984), who condemns the French *grandes écoles* for being excessively theoretical.

[54] See e.g. C. P. Kindleberger, 'Technical Education and the French Entrepreneur', in E. C. Carter *et al.*, *Enterprise and Entrepreneurs in Nineteenth- and Twentieth-Century France* (Baltimore, 1976).

[55] M. Sanderson's chapter in this volume.

[56] The literature on the subject is extensive. Two recent condemnations of the English educational system are M. J. Wiener, *English Culture and the Decline of the Industrial Spirit, 1850–1980* (Cambridge, 1981) and Locke, *End of the Practical Man*. Two opposite views, dealing with Wiener's rather than with Locke's thesis, are H. Berghoff, 'Public Schools and the Decline of the British Economy 1870–1914', *Past and Present*, 129 (1990) and W. D. Rubinstein, *Capitalism, Culture and Decline in Britain, 1750–1990* (London, 1993).

[57] Comparative statistics in H. Kaelble, 'Long-Term Changes in the Recruitment of the Business Elite: Germany Compared to the U.S., Great Britain and France since the Industrial Revolution', *Journal of Social History*, 13/3 (1980). See also the studies gathered in M. Lévy-Leboyer (ed.), *Le Patronat de la seconde industrialisation* (Paris, 1979).

This at least is reflected at the institutional level. As is well known, élite education consisted of the *grandes écoles* in France, and of the public schools and Oxford and Cambridge in Britain. Several *grandes écoles* are engineering schools, in the first place the most prestigious of them, the École polytechnique, where a fair share of the leaders of France's largest companies has consistently been educated. Graduates from the École polytechnique usually perfect their education in the various *écoles d'application*, the most prestigious of which are the École des mines and the École des ponts et chaussées, and through them gain entry into the famous *grands corps*. Centrale, which has ranked since its foundation in 1829 among the top *grande écoles*, is also an engineering school, as are the less prestigious *écoles des arts et métiers*, which have mostly catered for middle management. Outside science and engineering, three major institutions have also, and increasingly in the last three decades, contributed to business leaders' education: the École libre des sciences politiques (since 1945 the Institut d'études politiques) or Sciences-po, the École des hautes études commerciales (HEC), studied by Marc Meuleau in Chapter 7 of this volume, and the École nationale d'administration (ENA), established after the Second World War to provide the State with top-level civil servants. Finally, graduates from the École normale supérieure, whether in arts or science, had kept in their majority outside the business world; but the trend has recently been reversed.[58]

The two chapters by André Grelon and Marc Meuleau analyse the development of two major French *grandes écoles*, the École supérieure d'électricité (Supélec) and the École des hautes études commerciales (HEC), thus covering both the technical and the commercial ends of businessmen's education.[59] In an Anglo-French comparative perspective, a few points deserve particular attention. The first one concerns the role of the State, which has played a decisive role in shaping the French educational system. Yet Supélec and HEC were both founded by private interests. The second point is that the achievement of the French *grandes écoles*, which strongly impressed many British obervers, must be put in perspective. Marc Meuleau clearly points out that, until the 1960s, the HEC curriculum had only limited value as a business education. Thirdly, André Grelon reveals that even in France employers often preferred poorly qualified engineers. And despite a wealth of engineering schools, engineering has remained one of the endemic weaknesses of French industry. The *grandes écoles* have also been criticized for producing an arrogant business élite—in particular the *polytechniciens*—and of depriving

---

[58] See A. Peyrefitte (ed.), *Rue d'Ulm* (new edn. Paris, 1994).

[59] Other *grandes écoles*, in particular Centrale and Polytechnique, have already been studied. See in particular J. H. Weiss, *The Making of Technological Man: The Social Origins of French Engineering Education* (Cambridge, Mass., 1982); T. Shinn, *Savoir scientifique et pouvoir social: l'École polytechnique 1794–1914* (Paris, 1980). Several books have been published in 1994 for Polytechnique's bicentenary.

business of valuable men unfortunate enough to have failed the entrance *concours*.

In contrast to the *grandes écoles*, the public schools are secondary school institutions. And yet, for a long time, they have been considered sufficient, if not more important than university education, to ensure entry not only into the social but also into the professional élite. This is, at least formally, an important difference from France. Oxford and Cambridge have enjoyed a reputation at least as high as that of the French *grandes écoles*, including in scientific subjects which, after a long neglect in the nineteenth century, came strongly to the forefront first at Cambridge and then at Oxford.[60] However, top businessmen educated at the two ancient universities seem to have preferred to study arts or the humanities, although it must be said that the statistics available are not sufficiently precise on this particular aspect.

But were the two systems as different as they appear at first sight? Yes and no. They did share an essential common feature which set them apart from the German system: their élitism. Both the *grandes écoles* and Oxbridge aimed at producing a national élite, self-conscious of its status and recognized as such, with strong leadership qualities and a wide network of relationships encompassing the political, administrative, and business worlds. The fact that the French business leaders were trained as engineers did not in the end matter so much. As Christine Shaw clearly points out in Chapter 9, they were recruited by large companies as *polytechniciens*, with all the prestige, relationships, etc. going with the title, not as engineers. As far as the latter were concerned, that is, those really in charge of technical matters and in their majority graduates from the lesser *grandes écoles*, their professional status was no less subordinate than that of their British counterparts, with the difference that the words engineers and *ingénieurs* did not, and still do not, have the same meaning in English and French. Whereas in England the notion usually extends to manual workers, in France it is reserved to middle managers, or *cadres*, which may explain the complex from which British engineers seem to have been suffering.[61]

Despite this common élitism, there has been an important difference in the career pattern deriving from each educational system. In contrast to Britain, and to all other advanced industrialized countries, French business leaders start their career in the Civil Service. They enter business either at about 40 years of age, at a middle rank, or later in life, in a senior managerial position, sometimes directly as 'PDG' (*président directeur général* or chairman and managing director).[62] This type of recruitment of

    [60] M. Sanderson, *The Universities and British Industry 1850–1970* (London, 1972).
    [61] See A. Thépot (ed.), *L'Ingénieur dans la société française* (Paris, 1985); R. A. Buchanan, *The Engineers: A History of the Engineering Profession in Britain 1750–1914* (London, 1989).
    [62] M. Bauer and B. Bertin-Mourot, *'Les 200' en France et en Allemagne: deux modèles de détection-sélection-formation des dirigeants des grandes entreprises* (CNRS et Heidrick and Strug-

top managers has been widely discussed, and most often criticized, in recent years. Not only does politics play a major role in such appointments, but the *grandes écoles* have also been accused of producing administrators, nay bureaucrats, rather than entrepreneurs, and this has been seen as one aspect of the *mal français*. It should not be forgotten, however, that the passage from public administration to business (known in France as *pantouflage*) has been the rule in large public companies since the late nineteenth century, but was less discernible nation-wide because of the lasting importance of family firms. In Britain, by contrast, corporate careers have become the norm in large companies since the 1960s, or even earlier, even though the cases of passage from senior Civil Service to top business positions have increased in the last few decades.

Many studies have pondered the impact of these differences and similarities and have compared France and Britain with other countries. The importance of education to economic performance is unanimously recognized, but there is not much agreement about the way they interact.[63] The relationship becomes less clear when considering advanced industrial societies, and even less so in the particular instance of managers' education and training. The issue is likely to remain contentious for some time to come.

Mergers and survival

Strong divergences can also be observed in the degree of merger activity and business concentration in Britain and France for most of the period under review. Comparisons are difficult, in particular before the 1960s, as the data available are incomplete and not necessarily compatible between the two countries. It is clear, however, that both merger activity and industrial concentration were more intense in Britain. Between 1900 and 1909, for example, the total value of firm disappearances reached £55 million in Britain as against £1.76 million in France, the number of companies absorbed being respectively 659 and 23.[64] The figures might be underestimated for France, but the gap is too wide not to reflect a substantial difference. It had narrowed, however, eighty years later: in 1988 there were 537 domestic mergers in France, worth £7.3 billion, as against 937 in Britain with a total value of £16.9 billion.[65]

---

gles, n.d.). On the historical background to this phenomenon see C. Charle, 'Le Pantouflage en France (vers 1880–vers 1980)', *Annales ESC* 42/5 (1987).

[63] There is a useful survey of the debate in D. H. Aldcroft, *Education, Training and Economic Performance 1944 to 1990* (Manchester, 1992).

[64] Hannah, *Rise of the Corporate Economy*, 212; Houssiaux, *Pouvoir de monopole*, 340. Further data on French industrial concentration can be found in F. Braudel and E. Labrousse (eds.), *Histoire économique et sociale de la France*, iv: *L'Ère industrielle et la société d'aujourd'hui* (Paris, 1979–80).

[65] J. Franks and C. Mayer, 'Capital Markets and Corporate Control: A Study of France, Germany and the UK', *Economic Policy* (Apr. 1990), 198, quoted by L. Hannah, 'International

Industrial concentration was also higher in Britain: before 1914 the share of manufacturing net output of the 100 largest firms was respectively 15 and 12 per cent, rising to 26 and 16 per cent in 1929, and to 38 and 26 per cent in 1962–3.[66] Britain had in fact reached American levels in the mid-1920s and achieved the most highly concentrated industry in the world by the 1960s. There were, of course, exceptions, for example in the brewing industry which, as indicated by Terry Gourvish in Chapter 10, is today more concentrated in France. It is, however, a much smaller industry than in Britain. Not only are individual firms smaller than their British counterparts, but the size and nature of the market does not allow for the emergence of 'niche' players.

Whether high levels of industrial concentration have had a positive effect on business performance remains a matter of contention. Britain's poor economic performance in the late nineteenth century has been attributed to the atomistic character of its industry.[67] Many observers, on the other hand, have noticed that another period of comparatively poor economic achievement, the 1970s, coincided with Britain's highest levels of industrial concentration. In the same way, increased concentration and the promotion of 'national champions' have not met with unanimous approval in France. Generalizations at this level are meaningless. For if the trend for ever-increasing concentration and the formation of huge conglomerates appears to have been reversed, the rationale behind most mergers—reaching economies of scale and increasing market share—is unlikely to disappear. Michael Porter has recently drawn attention to the decisive importance of strong competition between firms on the domestic market, as a necessary step towards international competitiveness.[68] If this analysis seems to rule out the strategy of national champions, it does allow for a high level of concentration.

The situation has to be judged in the specific context of each industry and each country. The failure of the major French chemical industries to merge in 1926–7, on the model of ICI in Britain or IG Farben in Germany, has generally been seen as a serious blow to the industry, depriving the country of a major player on the international scene and reducing the scale of investment in major research and development projects. Jean-Pierre Daviet takes a different view. There were undoubtedly good reasons for a merger, and personal and firm rivalries could have been overcome.

Comparisons of Big Business 1880s–1980s: A Descriptive Statistical Essay', paper presented at the Eleventh International Economic History Congress, Milan, 1994, Session A2, 'Global Enterprise: Big Business and the Wealth of Nations in the Past Century, 1880s–1980s'.

[66] Hannah, *Rise of the Corporate Economy*, 180; J. P. Daviet, 'Some Features of Concentration in France (End of the 19th Century/20th Century)', in H. Pohl (ed.), *The Concentration Process in the Entrepreneurial Economy since the Late 19th Century* (Stuttgart, 1988), 73.

[67] See in particular B. Elbaum and W. Lazonick (eds.), *The Decline of the British Economy* (Oxford, 1986).

[68] Porter, *Competitive Advantage of Nations*.

Nevertheless, Daviet considers that the merger would not have been a success: given the weaknesses existing in French management methods, the new firm would not have been able to manage its strategic resources satisfactorily. As for the British brewing industry, Terry Gourvish provides a measurement of the merger movement, showing both the industry's transformation since the 1950s and the limits of its concentration compared with other countries. Mergers were the result of a number of factors—new market conditions, technological changes, government attitudes—to which the industry was able to respond adequately.

Banks are usually involved in merger negotiations, not necessarily for the better. The failure of the merger in the French chemical industry in 1927 was at least partly a result of the distrust of bankers. Recent transactions, in particular take-over bids, have never failed to benefit bankers, who are paid high fees; they have not always worked in the merged firms' best interests. The role of banks has been a controversial issue in Britain and France: they have been accused of neglecting industry in favour of foreign investment, and of refusing to take long-term financial commitments. Such criticism has been rejected by recent research: in both countries external finance, whether provided by the banks or by the capital markets, appears to have been adequate to complement what was, as everywhere else, the major source of funds for industrial firms: self-finance.[69]

Another criticism, the lack of entrepreneurial leadership, in particular in the question of the rationalization of industry, has been stronger in Britain, reflecting in a way the difference between the merchant banks and the *banques d'affaires*. While the former have their origins in the financing of world trade, the latter are the heirs to the Crédit mobilier, and direct control of industrial companies has from the start been an essential part of their strategy. However, this major difference between these two types of banks might well have been, at times, more formal than real. Paribas has been since its foundation in 1872 the prototype of the French *banques d'affaires* and, as Eric Bussière reveals in Chapter 12, its industrial policy was dictated by caution. Although the bank was involved in industrial finance, its prime considerations were financial, which meant divesting when necessary and frequent changes in the composition of its portfolio: in the early 1920s, plans to reorganize the French and Belgian electrical industries in order to compete more efficiently with Germany proved too ambitious and ended in the bank's withdrawal. The merchant banks never entertained such plans; however, they increasingly moved into domestic issuing after the first World War.

[69] The most recent discussions are for France A. Plessis, 'Les Banques, le crédit et l'économie', in Lévy-Leboyer and Casanova (eds.), *Entre l'État et le marché*, and the special issue of *Entreprises et histoire*, 1/2 (1992), and for Britain M. Collins, *British and Industrial Finance before 1939* (London, 1990).

This difference of degree continues to separate the two countries. France has somewhat oscillated between the so-called German and Anglo-Saxon financial systems, the former dominated by the banks, the latter by the capital markets. This duality is especially visible in the *banques d'affaires*, with their roots in both international and industrial finance, the deposit banks having been more tempted, sometimes at their own peril, by the universal bank model.

5. CONCLUSION

There has been clear convergence between British and French business in the last hundred years, deriving in large part from the French economy catching up with, and eventually overtaking, the British one in the 1970s. There cannot be convergence, however, without divergent initial starting-points. Although she was not 'backward', France was clearly 'behind' Britain in terms of overall wealth and level of industrialization. This was particularly the case in the scale of business activities, which was altogether of another order of magnitude in Britain. Has this convergence been a result of British decline? Answers to this question will greatly vary. The point of view developed in this introduction is that, if a degree of decline cannot be ruled out, convergence with France appears to be in the norm of the two countries' long-term development.

At the beginning of the period under review, Britain and France were already losing their position as the two leading industrial nations. This does not mean that comparing the two countries has lost its significance and that the relevant benchmark must be the United States, Germany, or more recently Japan. Whatever the strength of the American model, European comparisons are more meaningful. Within the European context, a tripartite comparison with Germany would of course be most welcome, and is attempted by Cassis in Chapter 13. However, such a comparison should from the start avoid the trap of the 'German complex'. Taking a long view shows that each country had areas and periods of relative strengths and weaknesses, that the order of the ranking occasionally changed, but that convergence has been the dominant feature. This is why comparative analyses based on the superiority of one model of business organization have proved sterile.

PART I

THE FAMILY FIRM

2

Ownership, Organization, and Management: British Business and the Branded Consumer Goods Industries

ROBERT FITZGERALD

1. MANAGERIAL ENTERPRISE AND BRITISH FAILURE

The failings of British management have been the target of prolonged adverse criticism, and this respectable and in many ways justifiable practice has recently been bolstered by the powerful assault of an authoritative source. It would be a revisionist, and undoubtedly foolhardy, historian who could dismiss the existence of some link between Britain's relative economic decline, the loss of competitiveness, and the inadequate decisions and capabilities of business leaders, managers, and firms. Chandler's *Scale and Scope: The Dynamics of Industrial Capitalism* has a more ambitious objective than this acknowledgement of managerial weakness as one contributory factor amongst many. In relating national economic success to a particular form of capitalist enterprise and organizational structure, specifically the multidivisional corporation, it places the principal blame for British failure on the nature and composition of its industrial management. In order to illustrate the force of his thesis, Chandler directly criticizes a group of British industries which, as counterpoints to descriptions of decline in textiles, steel, shipbuilding, and engineering, have been distinguished as examples of sectoral competitive achievement.[1] In his criticism of the failings of British management, specifically the continuance of business dynasties into an era when other forms of ownership and control were supposedly more appropriate, he is joined by Lazonick.[2] In specifically detecting the existence of managerial failure and missed opportunities in the branded consumer goods industries, Chandler is seeking to undermine one of British industry's strongholds, and, with the fall of this redoubt, his thesis of widespread, almost national managerial failure would be secured. *Scale and Scope* has attracted world-

---

[1] A. D. Chandler, *Scale and Scope: The Dynamics of Industrial Capitalism* (Cambridge, Mass., 1990).

[2] W. Lazonick, Business Organisation and the Myth of the Market Economy (Cambridge, 1991).

wide attention precisely because its discussion of national economic success is rooted in the micro- or meso-economic analysis of real companies and industries. It shares this approach with Michael Porter's *The Competitive Advantage of Nations*,[3] and both works have received international acclaim because, as every business historian knows, there is a self-evident reality in looking beyond aggregate macro-economic statistics. Per capita economic growth and rising living standards depend on increases in value-added which result from the exploitation and efficient organization of market knowledge, research, products, technology, or some other form of competitive advantage at the level of businesses and their networks and institutional couplings. Chandler and Porter's use of evidence and case-studies is not, on the other hand, devoid of workable hypotheses, and their books do offer distinctive explanations of national economic success. By employing historical and geographical comparisons, the overview to be found in *Scale and Scope* has the potential to elucidate reasons for similarities and differences between nations. The book outlines the rapid expansion of electricals, chemicals, automobiles, machinery, and packaged consumer goods in the twentieth century, arguing that industrial leadership passed to those companies and economies which effectively organized and managed the growing size and complexities of manufacturing. The thesis holds great explanatory power for the period of study between 1880 and 1950, when technological imperatives and the arrival of mass markets encouraged returns to scale and the internalization of markets within the visible hands of managerial hierarchies. His three chosen countries, during these years, accounted for at least 50 per cent of world industrial production.[4] In a book of this size, some debate about the thesis and its supporting evidence is inevitable, but we should always remember that any perceived conceptual and methodological problems are more than compensated by unique and obvious strengths.

Chandler's description and explanation of British managerial failure have been the subject of scepticism and criticism.[5] Continental European historians have also questioned the starkness with which he has differentiated family businesses from the managerial enterprise,[6] but it is British business historians who have been notably reticent. Such a response, coming from some that have worked conscientiously on the inadequacies

---

[3] M. Porter, *The Competitive Advantage of Nations* (London, 1990).

[4] Chandler, *Scale and Scope*, 3–4. The figures, from W. W. Rostow, *The World Economy: History and Prospect* (Austin, Tex., 1978), 52–3, are 68% in 1870, 66 in 1913, and 52 in 1936–8.

[5] See L. Hannah, 'Scale and Scope: Towards a European Visible Hand?', *Business History*, 33/2 (1991), 297–309; R. Church, 'The Limitations of the Personal Capitalism Paradigm', *Business History Review*, 64 (1990), 703–10; B. Supple, 'Scale and Scope: Alfred Chandler and the Dynamics of Industrial Capitalism', *Economic History Review*, 44/3 (1991), 500–14.

[6] See P. Fridenson, 'Business and the Shopfloor', *Contemporary European History*, 2 (1993), 81–5.

of British managers, was not simply an expression of hurt national pride. Chandler notes that the country's largest 200 companies were located in several key sectors, and that they differed from their United States counterparts in important ways. There were fewer in the technologically advanced, faster-growing sectors such as electrical equipment; a greater number could be located in the traditional fields of brewing, textiles, or the older branches of the chemicals industry; and a bigger proportion of British enterprises produced consumer and not industrial goods. Chandler mentions and seemingly criticizes their average size,[7] but some contrast is unsurprising when the top 200 companies in the United States operated in a domestic economy that, becoming four to five times larger, offered greater opportunities. The size of the home market, as well as the extent to which demand is differentiated by product, may influence potential returns to scale in some sectors, although it is difficult to state the exact level of influence.[8] Chandler is right to emphasize the degree to which Britain's industrial production became concentrated in the first half of the twentieth century within its largest firms. It follows that the quality of their decisions and actions would have important repercussions for the wider British economy, although Chandler's specific interest in manufacturing does not take account of the contemporaneous expansion and role of service sectors. Ultimately, Chandler fails to say what the average size of the top 200 British industrial enterprises should have been between 1880 and 1950, and a more direct comparison of Britain's biggest companies with those at the lower end of the USA's largest 200, as cited in *Scale and Scope*, might have been illuminating, if not conclusive. The link between market size, potential returns to scale, and the magnitude of companies is a debating point because it is directly related to the managerial demands and the type of organizational structure that is required in any given case. It is too broad an assumption to claim that the managerial enterprise as defined by Chandler, and as possibly evidenced in so many large US companies, is universally appropriate. In addition to the dimensions of the domestic market, the flexibility and efficiency of market relationships, the provision of basic infrastructure, the availability of finance or technology, cultural attributes, product specificities, and marketing requirements will affect transaction cost calculations and the degree to which activities are internalized within single enterprises. They will therefore affect choices of optimum company size, ownership, and organizational structure, and, just as alternative arrangements are available, they are not always a source of national disadvantage.

Yet Chandler's comparative method, looking at the extent to which enterprises in the United States, Britain, or Germany conformed to a

[7] Chandler, *Scale and Scope*, 239–40.

[8] R. Fitzgerald, *Rowntree and the Marketing Revolution 1862–1969* (Cambridge, 1995), 190–1; Hannah, 'Scale and Scope', 297–309.

particular set type, does not allow the possibility of 'substitute' pathways and institutions in economic development, an approach which is notably characteristic of Gerschenkron.[9] To forward his discussion of British management, Chandler reverts to stating that, even if Britain's largest companies were smaller than those in the USA, they were nevertheless large corporations, so hinting that they should be judged by the same standards. Unfortunately, this assumption is a significant denial of the comparative method. By making it, he is able to criticize Britain's biggest firms, arguing that they were, in contradistinction to United States companies, inappropriately managed on the basis of 'personal capitalism'. Chandler has previously described how, in the decades after 1880, many family-owned businesses in the United States were replaced by large-scale enterprises that were financed by outside shareholders and controlled by professional executives through managerial hierarchies. It was these changes in ownership, size, personnel, and organizational structure which enabled a range of companies to gain first mover advantages, and success in rapidly expanding industries secured US economic leadership during the twentieth century. Increasingly capital-intensive processes could be funded; as the scale and complexities of production and distribution intensified, full-time, professional managers were needed; and formal organizational procedures assisted decision-making, monitoring, and the allocation of resources. Britain, as the designated home of personal capitalism, offends against Chandler's view of the modern large-scale business, characterized by its 'extensive managerial hierarchy' and the presence of professional executives having no connection with the founding family or little or no equity in their company. By personal capitalism, Chandler is referring to enterprises run without the benefit of an extensive managerial hierarchy, or to companies where founders and their families continued to be executives or influential shareholders. British managerial teams were smaller than their US or even German counterparts, argues Chandler, and executives, chosen for their personal connections or family ties, were relative amateurs. To apply the well-known, probably overused cricketing analogy, they were 'gentlemen' rather than 'players',[10] and British managerial culture was inadequately visionary, more traditional, and less technically competent in relation to their major international rivals. As a result, British enterprises were smaller, less capital-intensive, insufficiently structured, poorly managed, and concentrated in sectors which made limited technological and organizational demands. Founding families being in a position to secure high dividend returns for personal consumption, the survival of joint ownership and control is seen as a drain on corporate resources and investment.[11]

---

[9] A. Gerschenkron, *Economic Backwardness in Historical Perspective: A Book of Essays* (Cambridge, Mass., 1966).

[10] D. C. Coleman, 'Gentlemen and Players', *Economic History Review*, 26 (1973), 92–116.

[11] Chandler, *Scale and Scope*, 239–42, 390.

2. BRANDED GOODS AND CRITICAL SUCCESS FACTORS

In *Scale and Scope* Chandler seeks to strengthen the force of his argument by attacking the management and record of a sector that has been widely viewed as a source of national competitive advantage. Even those relatively successful industries that made branded, packaged goods are viewed as reflecting, perhaps magnifying, the larger British experience. The manufacture of these products, it is argued, was dependent on comparatively uncomplicated production processes, and product-specific distribution facilities or specialized marketing services were not required. Capital and managerial demands were low enough to allow the continuation of the founding business dynasties. None the less, Chandler states that British food-producers were slow to adopt canning technology, and that, by relying on independent wholesalers, the branded goods sector as a whole spent too little on distribution facilities. Given the prominence, average size, and particular nature of the British branded goods sector, functionally departmentalized organizations were common within its large-scale enterprises. Due to the culture of personal capitalism, family members were usually appointed as departmental heads, although Lever Brothers is quoted as the only exception to this particular practice in the years before the First World War. Britain's companies failed to match the investments of overseas rivals in management, manufacturing plant, and marketing channels, but there were fewer implications for the branded goods sector than the technologically and organizationally more complex engineering, electricals, or motor car industries. This factor, says Chandler, explains comparative British success in consumer products, and the presence of so many branded goods companies in the nation's top 200 manufacturing concerns. He admits that the early development of mass consumer markets in Britain also encouraged the growth of companies in foods, soaps, or tobacco. British enterprise could be expected to respond to the opportunities presented, and Chandler accepts that the branded goods sector, having gained first mover advantages, consolidated its market position and its profits. But, because this large and available home market remained unchallenged, management is still seen as a hidden weakness, and it is not until the arrival of US competitors in the inter-war period that some improvements occurred. Once again, Lever Brothers is depicted as an exception amongst British branded goods companies because of its commitment to expansion overseas.[12]

Chandler is able to explain the concentration of the branded goods companies to be found in Britain's top 200 firms, whilst indicating their organizational weaknesses. He looks at British managerial failure as a general phenomenon which afflicted even its most successful industries and companies, so becoming the central cause of long-term economic

[12] Ibid. 262–6, 268, 367–8, 389.

decline. If, on the other hand, the British domestic market encouraged the growth of consumer goods firms possessing different organizational requirements, there are potentially a large number of causal factors to be considered, as well as the possibility that variations in the size and governance of enterprises might have been effective substitutes for one another. The size of any market and the existence of artificial, national, or institutional barriers placed limits on scale economies and a firm's optimum level of internalization, and the British economy was smaller than that of the United States. The effectiveness of links between smaller, even family-owned firms—as a result of proximity, experience, available infrastructure and transport, religious affiliation, shared background, and the nature of trust relationships—would favour a reliance on market mechanisms, and alter the balance of transaction costs against the formation of larger enterprises and the visible hand of managerial hierarchy. Chinese capitalism, for example, is dependent on small-scale firms and market mechanisms, its success being based on accepted confidence in personal, family relationships,[13] and it is worth exploring the nature and value of established inter-firm couplings in pre-war Britain and Europe to see if they help elucidate variations from models of US managerial enterprise. Differences in national and business cultures may be an additional consideration in the nature of trust relationships between companies and in the appropriateness of personal management over formal systems within firms. In the branded goods sector, marketing reasons must receive prominence. The very success of these industries in Britain—the early development of the consumer market noted by Chandler—rested to some extent on product differentiation, and entrenched brand loyalty would have hindered any subsequent rationalization of lines and companies. US companies like General Foods and Borden would eventually have benefited from the greater returns to scale that a larger domestic market would have made possible, and they would have found it easier to standardize consumer preference. The advantages of later development may apply to demand as well as supply-side factors, and, given the long-term success of branded goods production in Britain, differing circumstances may simply have required different choices and substitute economic pathways. Considering the prevalence of holding company and network structures, it is hard to justify Chandler's preference for unified managerial hierarchies in all circumstances. He is highly criticial of holding companies in Britain, but the much-praised family-owned *zaibatsu* of pre-war Japan also adopted this form, as have the competitive and modern-day Korean *chaebol*.[14] It is perhaps not so much the organizational structure that is

---

[13] S. G. Redding, *The Spirit of Chinese Capitalism* (Berlin, 1990); S. G. Redding, 'Competitive Advantages in the Context of Hong Kong', in R. Fitzgerald (ed.), *The Competitive Advantages of Far Eastern Business* (London, 1994), 71–89.

[14] G. G. Hamilton and M. Orru, 'Organisational Structure of East Asian Companies', in

critical but the extent to which it restrains competition, necessary rationalization, or returns to scale. In Japan, interconnected firms could share funds, personnel, technology, and knowledge between separate units, so optimizing factors and resources that were in short supply in an industrializing country. Linkages and not unitary corporate structures facilitated Chandler's investment in management, manufacturing, and marketing.[15] Within the British consumer goods industries, product differentiation, consumer loyalties, even technology may have limited the benefits to be gained from the amalgamation of production units amongst subsidiaries or affiliated firms. Advantages can be found in internal network structures that are less hierarchical than Chandler's model. The multidepartmental and the multidivisional form developed in order to facilitate the flow of goods along the production process, but networked chains of command and communication allow companies to address functional and locational as well as product and production considerations.[16] Within the branded consumer goods industries, the integration and role of the marketing function with every other department has to be fully considered within any organizational structure. Overseas operations and sources of supply forced companies to incorporate the geographical dimensions of their business, and, within consumer goods industries, responsiveness to demand and national preferences have often favoured multidomestic production and control.

In any case, Chandler's view of strategy as a highly planned, long-term process and his emphasis on formal systems rather than vision, informal relationships, personal qualities, and individual creativity do appear rather old-fashioned. Business strategy can be seen as adaptive and opportunistic, the building of organizational capabilities and systems depending on and varying with circumstances and initial competencies. Company size, managerial organization, and overall objectives will reflect the unique quality of each company's competitive position. Chandler believes that personal capitalism created a lack of formal strategy formulation at the very top of British firms, but that absence is not in itself

K. H. Chung and H. K. Lee (eds.), *Korean Managerial Dynamics* (New York, 1989); T. Kikkawa, 'Kigyo Shudan: The Formation and Functions of Enterprise Groups', in E. Abe and R. Fitzgerald (eds.), *The Origins of Japanese Industrial Power: Strategies, Institutions, and the Development of Organisational Capability* (London, 1995); P. O'Brien, 'Industry Structure as a Competitive Advantage: The History of Japan's Post-war Steel Industry', in C. Harvey and G. Jones (eds.), *Organisational Capability and Competitive Advantage* (London, 1992), 128–59; H. Morikawa, *Zaibatsu* (Tokyo, 1992); Y. Suzuki, *Japanese Management Structures, 1920–80* (London, 1991); C. Johnson, *MITI and the Japanese Miracle: The Growth of Industrial Policy 1925–1975* (Stanford, Calif., 1982).

[15] H. Morikawa, 'Managerial Enterprise in the Economic Development of Post-war Japan', in Abe and Fitzgerald, *Origins of Japanese Industrial Power*.

[16] C. A. Bartlett, 'Building and Managing the Transnational: The New Organisational Challenge', in M. E. Porter (ed.), *Competition in Global Industries*' (Cambridge, Mass., 1986), 367–404.

evidence of a strategic vacuum.[17] The stress upon individual creativity and opportunism may be critical in our evaluation of the consumer goods sector, where marketing—the process of product development, branding, and advertising—may have been more determinant of the profitability and growth of firms than issues of managerial organization. A good marketing idea may prove to be a more important critical success factor than managerial organization; in other words, the emergence of one type of organizational capability will act as a substitute for the absence of another. So, it is revealing that, when Chandler talks of marketing, he seems in the main to be referring to the organization of distribution, in many ways a branch of operations management. In detecting a general, national failure in the management of Britain's large-scale companies, Chandler is creating a parallel and perhaps equally sterile debate to the one that raged over the decline of British entrepreneurship between 1870 and 1914, the consequence of an emerging anti-business culture, when differences between companies and industries within single countries were clearly evident. Variations in the competitiveness and commercial success of sectors, and coincidently in the effectiveness of management, are to be expected within any economy. National achievement rests upon a corps of competitive industrial clusters, and it could be argued that the branded goods sector has made a positive contribution to British economic growth, even if the number of successful clusters has continuously declined.[18] The case of managerial failure and the importance of ownership and organization as critical success factors in the British branded goods sector needs to be reassessed.

3. FAMILY ENTERPRISE AND THE CASE OF CADBURY

Chandler begins his detailed analysis of British managerial enterprise with a close investigation of two well-known firms, the chocolate-makers Cadbury Brothers and Imperial Tobacco. The Quaker firm of Cadbury is chosen because it epitomizes the retention of family control within large companies, and because Chandler wants to demonstrate his thesis by undermining its reputation for effective management. If Cadbury should fall to his most damaging assaults on British management practice, very few others could justify their own, more evident shortcomings. Imperial Tobacco illustrates British business's tendency to adopt holding company structures: horizontal mergers of convenience protected members from competition; they prevented the process of rationalization and the development of managerial hierarchies which could extract scale economies;

---

[17] See e.g. J. Kay, *Foundations of Corporate Success* (Oxford, 1993); H. Mintzberg, *The Rise and Fall of Strategic Management* (Princeton, NJ, 1993).

[18] Porter, *Competitive Advantage of Nations, passim*.

and they maintained family control, a desired aim, in the affiliated units. Chandler's negative view of Imperial Tobacco makes many justifiable points, but his case-study of Cadbury is, arguably, a significant misinterpretation of the available evidence and of the character of the company. He notes that Cadbury has 'long been considered one of the nation's best-managed companies'. In 1930, it was the 28th largest British enterprise,[19] and the prolific Cadbury family filled every important position within its functionally departmentalized structure. Chandler is critical of the lack of budgetary control, appropriation procedures, and other capital-allocation techniques, and, as a result of family members being preoccupied with departmental matters, he perceives an absence of strategic, board-level decision-making. Its governance structure is compared unfavourably to Borden and General Foods in the United States, and to Stollwerck in Germany.[20] The poverty of Chandler's case against Cadbury is quickly evident, and it is largely dependent upon his analytical approach and on the assumptions inherent to it. He believes that his chosen examples of personal capitalism failed to develop the inherent capabilities of 'extensive managerial hierarchy', but the exact meaning of 'extensive' is hard to validate, and, as we have noted, the appropriateness of his model ignores the contingency of 'optimum' organizational forms within a variety of national circumstances. The concept of personal capitalism, moreover, is ultimately vague, since, within Chandler's schema, it refers to a dominant management style or culture, in which blood relationships and personal contact serve as inadequate replacements for formal, professionalized systems.[21] This does not necessarily undermine its usefulness in explaining complex historical, economic, and sociological phenomena, but any set of circumstances is potentially open to wide interpretation, and a re-examination of the data's quality and quantity in any specific example may produce different conclusions. As we shall see, some caution in the case of Cadbury is deserved.

In *Scale and Scope*, Chandler describes Cadbury's ownership and organization structures and sees in them an absence of strategic direction, while the company's dominant culture is portrayed as amateur and introspective. In addition to being the cause of high dividends and low investment, personal capitalism prevented the evolution of a managerial hierarchy. Family members continued to rely on personal, established authority rather than objectively determined systems and enhanced organizational capabilities, and able managers and technicians were largely barred from promotion to the board. The case of Cadbury, however, seems to contravene this central tenet of *Scale and Scope*. Family ownership and control remained a potent force at Cadbury and only slowly dissolved after 1962,

---

[19] As measured in terms of the market value of shares.
[20] Chandler, *Scale and Scope*, 242–6.
[21] Ibid. 240.

yet the firm had been an active recruiter of managerial talent and operated
a clearly understood multidepartmental structure. Family control of the
board did not hinder the development of the managerial hierarchy under-
neath it. The most ambitious career managers might have felt ultimately
frustrated, but generation on generation continued to demonstrate high
levels of motivation and loyalty.[22] As has been noted elsewhere, family-
owned firms account for some 75 and 99 per cent of all companies in the
European Community, and for some 65 per cent of its GDP and employment.[23] Given the scale of their importance, diversity in the control,
management, and organization of these enterprises should not be surprising. While some families have proved a drain on investment resources—
as the Mackintoshs, owners of the chocolate and toffee firm, did in the
1960s—others have demonstrated a commitment to the success of their
firms, the Cadburys and the Rowntrees being two notable examples.
If the Frys confronted the problems of succession just after the Great War,
the Cadburys produced a number of talented and respected business
leaders who carried forward the benefits of inherited experience and a
powerful, beneficial business culture.[24] Although the United States is
quoted in *Scale and Scope* as the very bastion of managerial capitalism, the
fact that about one-third of the largest United States firms, those quoted in
the *Fortune 500*, are family-owned cannot be ignored.[25] If the continuance
of the Cadburys in their business is to be criticized, then it is worth
remembering that Milton Hershey remained influential in his company
until his death in 1945, and that Mars is still one of the world's largest
family concerns.[26]

Cadbury is rightly seen as important to British business history, and
many details of its development are well known, but we do not yet
possess a comprehensive, up-to-date business history, and the company's
extensive archives deserve thorough researching. Chandler obtains most
of his information on the company's management and structure from a
document published by Cadbury in 1943, which he terms a 'report'.[27] This
document was a contribution to contemporary business literature, and is
closer to a public relations document than a detailed, internal investigation of company procedures. Although accurate, it should not be used as

[22] Cadbury Brothers, *Industrial Record, 1919–39: A Review of the Inter-war Years* (London,
1944), *Industrial Challenge: The Experience of Cadburys of Bournville in the Post-war Years*
(London, 1964); Fitzgerald, *Rowntree and the Marketing Revolution*, chs. 7 and 11. See also
I. O. Williams, *The Firm of Cadbury, 1831–1931* (London, 1931).
[23] G. Jones and M. B. Rose, 'Family Capitalism', *Business History*, 35 (1994), 1.
[24] Fitzgerald, *Rowntree and the Marketing Revolution*, 185–216. See also C. Dellheim, 'The
Creation of a Company Culture: Cadbury's, 1861–1931', *American Historical Review*, 92 (1987),
13–44.
[25] Jones and Rose, 'Family Capitalism', 1.
[26] Fitzgerald, *Rowntree and the Marketing Revolution*, 186–214; K. Shippen and P. A. W.
Wallace, *Milton S. Hershey* (New York, 1959), *passim*.
[27] Cadbury Brothers, *Industrial Record*.

a definitive and fulsome statement of the many business issues which it addresses. The retention of family control is undeniable, but there is no clear evidence of undesirable consequences, such as a shortage of capital or a stunted managerial structure. By 1900 Cadbury Brothers had a basic multifunctional organization, and each department was led by a director, appointed from the family. Policies were co-ordinated through the Committee of Management, but decisions tended to be taken by individual directors. As a result, the departmental management staff had an executive role, and in the following years their numbers greatly expanded alongside the scale of Cadbury's organization.[28] There was, possibly, a weakness in top-level decision-making, yet the lack of formal consultation may not have been essential to a company of Cadbury's size, culture, and methods. This business already had an established reputation for factory organization and personnel management, and in the 1900s it was able to respond flexibly and effectively to market opportunities. Two of its most successful products—Cadbury's Dairy Milk chocolate and Bournville cocoa—were launched in 1905 and 1906 respectively, and, contrary to Chandler's description of a domestic market dominated by uncompetitive British firms, these two products were developed as a direct response to highly successful imports. The British confectionery industry finally secured its answer to Dutch alkalized cocoa essence and Swiss milk chocolate, which had dominated the domestic market for decades.[29]

Moreover, a combination of shortages and rising sales during the Great War induced Cadbury to undertake organizational reform, for it had to solve new difficulties in the anticipation, planning, and meeting of consumer demand. In order to implement centrally agreed objectives, the independence of the departments was gradually curtailed. In an effort to reduce waste, co-ordinate production programmes, and improve the flow of goods between process stages, further centralization was effected in 1919. The large-scale building programme instituted at Bournville after the war and the increasing mechanization of processes between 1926 and 1935 multiplied the scale of Cadbury's operations. Chandler links the commitment of US companies to management, manufacturing, and marketing investment with their eventual success, and associates personal management in Britain with ultimate competitive failure. But there is no doubting the commitment of Cadbury to manufacturing processes, the achievement of returns to scale, and product and price competitiveness, nor the contribution of technical and managerial skills to this increase in organizational capabilities. Its transport and distribution system was also developed during the inter-war years, a timely response to the possibilities of lorries and a result of increasing per capita consumption.

[28] Cadbury Brothers, *Industrial Challenge*, 9; E. Cadbury, *Experiments in Industrial Organisation* (London, 1913), 1–2, 13.

[29] Fitzgerald, *Rowntree and the Marketing Revolution*, 1–42, 75–126, 183–216.

Cadbury's distribution system was highly planned and systematized, but, like all confectionery companies, its sales continued to depend on impulse purchases within countless newsagents, kiosks, and tobacconists, and a reliance on multi-purpose wholesalers was rational and economical. Business policy continued to be co-ordinated through board meetings, but directors and top management also formed board committees as a means of improving and facilitating decision-making. They were further assisted by both the Planning and the Cost Office, and Chandler's claim that the company paid inadequate attention to costing and investment procedures is hard to justify. Although a family business, Cadbury believed 'Industrial management is a highly skilled profession involving careful recruiting and training', and in the inter-war years it adopted a positive approach to the recruitment of university-educated staff. A managerial hierarchy was created and systematically graded, and Cadbury's multidepartmental structure was consequently deepened. It is hard to measure definitively the extent to which managerial organization provided for its size and characteristics, although Chandler admits that makers of branded, packaged goods had fewer opportunities for growth and oversaw less technologically complex processes.[30] Cadbury did, to use Chandler's terminology, attend to the issues of management, manufacturing, and marketing, and this family-owned, multidepartmental business does meet the test of profitable longevity in a way that the much-praised Stollwerck does not. Cadbury's particular organizational capabilities are demonstrated by its transforming influence upon Fry, to which it was formally linked under the British Cocoa and Chocolate Company. Chandler makes some telling points about the failures of holding company structures in Britain, but perhaps some qualifications are needed in this specific case. Despite a joint board, the two firms continued to operate separately, but they did employ for a while very different marketing and production policies, Cadbury concentrating on quality milk chocolate, cocoa, and assortments, Fry on low-priced goods and chocolate-enrobed count lines.[31] The advantages of joint distribution were exploited, and, just as Japanese network structures helped the transfer of capital and expertise between companies, Fry imitated Cadbury's experience in factory organization when it moved to its new works in the 1920s. Cadbury's leadership of British Cocoa and Chocolate was finally confirmed in 1935 when the two firms were effectively joined.[32] There is no indication that Cadbury suffered from a lack of capital or managerial talent, despite remaining a family concern, and, when issues of size, ownership, and financial restructuring did become problematic, change was effected. After 1962 it evolved into a publicly owned company in which the family influence slowly

---

[30] Chandler, *Scale and Scope*, 168–70.
[31] A count line is a product sold by the unit rather than by weight.
[32] *Fry's Works Magazine: Bi-Centenary Number* (1928), 74–80.

diminished, especially after the merger with soft-drinks manufacturers Schweppes in 1969.[33] It is, in short, possible to review the history of Cadbury and conclude that the founding family did not prevent the development of a managerial hierarchy, nor did it hinder the upgrading of products and production processes.

4. ROWNTREE AND EXEMPLARY PRACTICE

As far as Cadbury's great competitor and fellow Quaker firm Rowntree is concerned, managerial failure is even less likely. There are strong parallels in the evolution of management between these companies, but, by the inter-war period, Rowntree had absorbed the organizational lessons to be learnt from the United States and applied them systematically. Its attention to structure and procedure helped create a whole pantheon of acknowledged management experts, including Sheldon, Urwick, Northcott, and Seebohm Rowntree himself, and it won the company a reputation for exemplary practice. During the early 1900s Rowntree was run by departmental directors who were in the main family members. Policy was co-ordinated through an executive board, called the Directors' Conferences, but Seebohm Rowntree, with some exaggeration, believed that they were running their product-based departments as if they were independent businesses.[34] Supply and demand difficulties in the First World War, as at Cadbury, forced Rowntree to consider organizational questions, and it was Seebohm who undertook a personal initiative. One key issue was the improvement of strategic decision-making through the creation of board subcommittees, although, for a while, only weekly Directors' and Managers' Conferences were established. By October 1917 Rowntree was investigating the 'ideal' structure for a modern business.[35] To improve efficiency and the flow of goods, certain functions—including costing and budgetary control—were centralized in 1919, and from May 1920 a central planning department began apportioning raw materials to the production units. Wages, too, became a matter of single, company-wide policy. Reaction from once independent managers was expected, just as it was accepted as part of the process of change.[36] A subcommittee system was finally founded in January 1920 with the precise aim of giving the executive board adequate time and information to consider strategic issues. All directors, both family as well as non-family members, continued to be

[33] Fitzgerald, *Rowntree and the Marketing Revolution*, 422–3.

[34] Management Research Group No. 1 Papers, W/2/32/5 (307), Staff Initiatives, 25 May 1932.

[35] Rowntree Archives, Directors' Conferences, xxv, 1 Oct. 1917.

[36] Organization Dept., ii, A/1337, Memo, 'Function: Comparison/Subject: Costing'; Managers' and Directors' Conferences, i, A/−, Planning Dept., 12 Jan. 1922; Directors' Conferences, xxvii, 25 Mar. 1919, 7 Apr. 1919; xxxi, 16 Aug. 1921.

executives, and a Finance Committee concentrated on the drawing up of capital budgets several years ahead.[37]

The commercial difficulties of the post-war slump encouraged the Management Committee to look for economies, not to increase dividends but to invest in new machinery and processes. Rowntree was committed to organizational as well as production-line efficiency, and a Business Organization Committee with Oliver Sheldon as its secretary was appointed to consider recommendations. By September 1921 central policy formulation through the board was deemed inadequate, and a co-ordination director and a headquarters staff were created to assist the chairman in the management and monitoring of other departments. One board member, indeed, wondered if the company was 'going report mad', the imposition of intricate systems and procedures arguably hindering effective decision-making and consequent action. Seebohm Rowntree had just returned from a tour of factories in the United States, and he rightly concluded that its administrative methods would shape the world. He noted how most large-scale companies in the USA possessed organization charts and planning departments, and that these were generally missing in Britain. Seebohm was struck by an insistence, notable at International Harvester and Proctor and Gamble, on the need to build a cadre of educated management personnel, and this conclusion and others soon proved influential at Rowntree.[38] From October 1921 it was decided to end any reliance on informal authority relations at the company. Orders had been previously implemented by people accepting orders from family directors or respected individuals, with little notion of their being 'under' a superior within a determined hierarchy. The company's organization, it was now held, had just 'grown' around particular personalities, and the quality of management rested on their continuation in office. Again, there is probably some exaggeration in the strength of this statement, but the declaration of future intent and the assessment of modern company organization are revealing. The Business Organization Committee became concerned with the structure of control, effective co-ordination, and the formal allocation of responsibilities, and authority relations were clearly defined through the publication of an organizational chart. The headquarters staff was expanded to co-ordinate with the key line functions of distribution and production, as well as the staff functions of labour, finance, technical assistance, and co-ordination. This new structure of headquarters, functions, and departments sought to establish the correct balance

[37] Directors' Conferences, xix, 6 and 13 Jan. 1920, 20 Feb. 1920; xxx, 18 Jan. 1921.
[38] Directors' Conferences, xxx, 14 Sept. 1920; xxxi, 3 Feb. 1921, 26 Apr. 1921; xxxii, 26 July 1921, 10 Oct. 1921, 6 Dec. 1921; *Cocoa Works Staff Journal* (Mar. 1922), 182–4, B. S. Rowntree, 'Impressions of Management in Britain'; Newspaper Cuttings, i, A/790, L. Urwick, 'How We Reorganised an Old Business', *Business*, 54 (Nov. 1928), 255–8, 298; Organization Dept., A/652, Job Analysis File, *c.*1927–33, letter from O. Sheldon; Board Papers, i, A/888, B. S. Rowntree and J. S. Rowntree's Visit to the USA, 1921.

of responsibilities between directors and managers. The company created a series of managerial grades to meet its organizational needs, and it began a policy of recruiting well-educated or graduate personnel. Directors were 'thus relieved of a great deal of the pressure of day by day administration', being freed to concentrate on long-term decisions, corporate strategy, and the role of subsidiaries. A Works Organization Committee was charged with the task of continuously improving the organization chart, procedures, and authority relations.[39]

Rowntree was determined that it should be run according to international best practice. Indeed, its approach formed the background to Sheldon's *The Philosophy of Management*, whose anonymous descriptions and well-considered recommendations were highly influential amongst thinkers on business organization in Britain, the United States, and Japan. Seebohm Rowntree became convinced that up-to-date British employers followed the example to be found at his factory,[40] although the direct nature of this trend, its scope and depth, and the obvious difference between management thinking and practice cannot be easily disaggregated. But Rowntree is a well-attested example: the company's organizational structure and managerial hierarchy were defined; responsibilities and authority relations were allocated, and board-level activities were differentiated from those of middle management; planning, including the determination of capital and current budgets, was formalized and centralized; and every procedure, including product mixes, departmental relationships, and the ordering of raw materials or office stock, could be found in the handbook of standard practice instructions.[41] Seebohm Rowntree was able to introduce his ideas on the nature and organization of management after assuming the role of acting chairman in 1921, and his formal appointment two years later confirmed the permanence of his changes. Seebohm recognized that only an extension and systematization of management could accommodate the growth in the scale of industrial enterprise. But Rowntree remained a family concern. He associated family control with the continuation of a particular business culture, and Christian stewardship, industry as a communal service, co-operative work methods, thrift and efficiency, and the manufacture of competitive, quality products were highly inculcated values. In a statement resonant of the industrial organization to be found in Japan, there was a suspicion of

---

[39] Organization Dept., ii, A/1392.

[40] L. F. Urwick, *The Golden Book of Management: An Historical Record of the Life and Work of Seventy Pioneers* (London, 1956), 155–61, 279–81; O. Sheldon, *The Philosophy of Management* (London, 1923); *Cocoa Works Staff Journal* (Mar. 1922), 192–4.

[41] Newspaper Cuttings, i, A/866, O. Sheldon, 'Standardised Management Procedure', paper to the 4th International Congress on Scientific Organization of Work, Paris, 1929; Organization Dept., ii, A/1345, Board Minute, 18 Oct. 1921; Management Research Group No. 1 Papers, W/2/32/5 (307), Staff Initiatives, 25 May 1932; Manufacturing Confectioners' Association 1932.

outside shareholders who were devoid of a genuine commitment to the long-term welfare of the company, just as executives and managers had to show a lifetime loyalty.[42] Rowntree's lack of competitiveness compared to its vigorous rival Cadbury was quickly exposed after the Wall Street Crash, and, in response to pending collapse of the business, further reorganization occurred after 1931. It was stipulated that every director had to have an executive, full-time post, and family members who were semi-retired or burdened with other interests or public duties soon left. They would no longer have automatic preference when appointments were made to the board, and candidates would in future be selected according to merit and their ability to fulfil demanding, professional roles.[43]

The Rowntrees remained influential, but during the 1930s the company ceased to be a family concern in any meaningful sense. George Harris, who came to dominate the firm in the 1930s, and finally succeeded Seebohm as chairman, was married into the family, but he was explicit in his determination to oust the Rowntrees and replace their amateur approach. Paul, Edward, and Lawrence Cadbury continued to be in charge of their company because, as a successful enterprise, it did not undergo Rowntree's corporate crisis, or the sense of internal dissipation which had previously overtaken Fry. They were, moreover, respected and talented individuals, whose attention to factory organization, production methods, and management maintained Cadbury's competitiveness. Interestingly, Harris's perception of a professionalized Rowntree was only incidentally associated with managerial organization. The company had adopted in the 1920s a well-documented structure and a set of formal procedures, but none of these innovations nor Seebohm's total commitment to them had improved its competitive position against Cadbury. Harris placed his trust in the quality of key individuals, in creativity, and in a strategy predicated on market research, product development, branding, and advertising. He had learnt these techniques of the 'marketing orientation' first hand, whilst seeking and ultimately failing to launch Rowntree products in the United States. His insights into American business were different from those of Seebohm Rowntree, the organizational systematizer. Harris led and encouraged opportunism, entrepreneurship, and relentless activism, and he was often frustrated and critical of the company's intricate procedures. The value-added to be found in detailed systems and planning mechanisms seemed small compared to a good marketing idea, and, in a decade which saw the development of Black Magic, KitKat, Aero, Dairy Box, Fruit Pastilles, and Fruit Gums, it was Harris that spurred Rowntree's renaissance. The creation of an organizational capability in marketing emerged as a more critical success factor

---

[42] Sheldon, *Philosophy of Management*.

[43] Directors' Conferences, xxxiv, 27 Jan. 1931; York Board, 1, 21 Apr. 1931; Newspaper Cuttings, ii, A/469, Yorkshire Gazette, 1 Apr. 1932.

than Rowntree's strength in managerial organization. From the 1930s the family exerted some influence over the company through its controlling trusts, but there was never direct interference in management.[44] There are parallels to these shareholding arrangements with Cadbury, but also with US chocolate manufacturer Hershey. Personal capitalism, therefore, does not usefully divide British and American confectionery firms, and this point is reinforced if we remember that Mars remains one of the world's largest family concerns and that it operates with a culture that stresses informality and individual creativity rather than hierarchial systems.

5. THE MANAGERIAL REVOLUTION IN BRANDED GOODS

An optimistic revision of the case against Cadbury and the supporting evidence of Rowntree do not by themselves mean that the management of the British branded goods sector was generally 'sound'. One of Britain's most important concerns, the soap, chemicals, and foods manufacturer Lever Brothers, is accepted by Chandler and others as a managerial enterprise. Organizational reforms were implemented in 1921, during the depths of the post-war slump and contemporaneously with Cadbury and Rowntree. Francis D'Arcy Cooper's system-building replaced Lord Leverhulme's more personal approach, and further reorganization followed the merger with the Dutch Margarine Unie in 1929, the formation of Unilever, and the Great Depression of 1929–32. Chandler believes the approach, unlike that at ICI, was unplanned and responsive,[45] but Lever Brothers in the 1920s and Unilever in the 1930s were undoubtedly companies with extensive managerial hierarchies. His view seems a harsh judgement, based on his own particular interpretation and on the notion of strategy and organization-building as formally-implemented grand schemes. As well as bringing two large companies together during depressed economic conditions, Unilever had to evolve a hybrid or network structure that took account of both products and the geographical difficulties of international source supply and marketing. The company may not have had the perfect multidivisional organization, but its structure may have suited its specific operational needs.[46] By emerging as Britain's biggest advertiser, Unilever was a formative power within the nation's

---

[44] Fitzgerald, *Rowntree and the Marketing Revolution*, 277–85.

[45] Chandler, *Scale and Scope*, 368, 378–89.

[46] C. Wilson, *The History of Unilever*, i (London, 1954), 213–15, 244, 246–7, 266, 269–73, 276, 296, 299–300, 302, and ii (London, 1954), 307–11, 381; 'Management and Policy in the Large-Scale Enterprise: Lever Brothers and Unilever, 1918–38', in B. Supple (ed.), *Essays in British Business History* (Oxford, 1977); P. Mathias in Supple, *Essays in British Business History*; D. F. Channon, *The Strategy and Structure of British Enterprise* (London, 1973), 172–3; Unilever Archives, BB6, 'Rationalisation', 'Lever—Management and Labour', 'Reorganisation of Top Management, 1925'.

branded goods sector, as was the company which by the 1960s spent the second largest annual sum on the promotion of its products, the pharmaceuticals- and foods-maker Beecham.[47] There is some evidence that this concern began attending to matters of management and organization in the late 1930s, and the formation of product divisions occurred soon after 1950, further structural developments continuing into the 1960s as a response to diversification, internationalization, and increasing size (see Table 2.1). But, as in the case of Rowntree, it might be said that its adoption of a modern marketing philosophy, during the 1950s, may have been more critical to its long-term success.[48]

On the other hand, criticisms of another giant business, Imperial Tobacco, are harder to deflect, and its component firms were even in the post-war years family-dominated and operationally uncoordinated, despite some aspects of purchasing and finance becoming centralized.[49] Nor does the record of brewers, millers, and biscuit manufacturers, as related by Chandler, appear at first sight creditable, even if Spillers moved towards a multidivisional form by 1939.[50] The managerial revolution in Britain occurred after its occurrence in the United States, and one of *Scale and Scope*'s problems is a terminal date of about 1950. Imperial Tobacco, for example, instituted a multidivisional structure in 1964, by which time the company was seeking to accommodate continuous product diversification, and family representation on the board was minimal. Of the branded household goods producers to be found amongst Britain's 100 largest manufacturers, some nineteen companies—in many cases following the recommendations of management consultants McKinsey & Company—had multidivisional structures by 1970. Two, British Sugar and Watney Mann, had a multifunctional organization, and seven were holding companies.[51] In Chandlerian terms, the 'managerial revolution' occurred throughout Britain's largest companies during the period of 1950–70, and organizational change may have been responding to the quickening pace of business activity and corporate growth. Were multidivisional structures or even the extensive managerial hierarchies advocated by Chandler only suited to the dimensions and nature of the

[47] Fitzgerald, *Rowntree and the Marketing Revolution, passim*.

[48] Chandler, *Scale and Scope*, 370–1; BLPES, Seminar on Problems in Industrial Administration, 1959/60, No. 252, H. G. Lazell, 'Development and Organisation of Beecham Group Ltd'; BLPES, Joint Seminar on Problems in Industrial Administration, 1968–9, No. 394, H. G. Lazell, 'Marketing in a Competitive Economy'; H. G. Lazell, *From Pills to Penicillin: The Beecham Story* (London, 1974); Channon, *Strategy and Structure*, 147–8.

[49] Channon, *Strategy and Structure*, 100–1; Chandler, *Scale and Scope*, 246–9.

[50] Chandler, *Scale and Scope*, 262–8, 368, 370; L. Hannah, *The Rise of the Corporate Economy* (London, 1983), 85; L. Hannah (ed.), *Management Strategy and Business Development: An Historical and Comparative Study* (London, 1976), 185–6.

[51] Channon, *Strategy and Structure*, 52–63, 92–103, 163–73, 191–2; T. R. Gourvish, 'British Business and the Transition to a Corporate Economy: Entrepreneurship and Management Structures', *Business History*, 29 (1987), 18–45.

Table 2.1. *British-owned branded household goods producers amongst the largest 100 manufacturers, 1970*

	Sales (1969–70) (£m.)
Multidivisional structure	
British American Tobacco[a]	1,467
Unilever[b]	1,145
Imperial Tobacco	1,120
Associated British Foods[c]	503
Rank Hovis McDougall	359
Allied Breweries	346
Bass Charrington	315
Unigate	301
Cadbury-Schweppes	262
Tate & Lyle	228
Brooke Bond Liebig	209
Spillers	174
Whitbread	174
Beecham	161
Reckitt and Colman	157
Lyons	155
Courage Barclay	115
Rowntree Mackintosh	113
Fisons	82
Multifunctional structure	
Watney Mann	144
British Sugar	64
Holding company structure	
Distillers	382
Guinness[d]	163
Glaxo	140
Scottish & Newcastle	117
International Distillers & Vintners	100
United Biscuits	83
Wellcome Foundation	75

Note: The list is taken from Britain's 100 largest manufacturing companies, as cited in D. F. Channon, *The Strategy and Structure of British Enterprise* (London, 1973), 52–63.

[a] British American Tobacco produced mainly for export markets, and its largest subsidiary was a US firm, Brown and Williamson.

[b] Unilever was, of course, an Anglo-Dutch company.

[c] Associated British Foods was part of the Weston conglomerate. Garfield Weston, a Canadian, settled in Britain in the 1930s.

[d] Guinness was well known for its Anglo-Irish connections.

post-war economy? For readers of *Scale and Scope* this seems an irresolvable problem of cause and effect, and casts doubt on the criticisms levelled at British business in the inter-war years. As we have noted, we must be careful in our attribution of any managerial failings merely to the inherent problems of family businesses or holding companies, which may indeed have particular strengths. After all, the decline of the nation's competitiveness was accelerated rather than halted between 1950 and 1970, despite the adoption of the multidivisional structure. Were the right lessons being learnt from the McKinsey 'experts', or were other aspects of strategy and management being ignored? Imperial Tobacco's multidivisional structure did not save it some twenty years later from corporate failure, take-over, and the sale of its assets. Although it is not conclusive, there is some evidence that in these years British companies and notably those making branded household goods absorbed the attitudes and methods of the marketing orientation.[52] This trend, a response to the arrival of widespread 'mass consumption', may have been more beneficial to this industrial sector than adjustments in managerial organization. It is self-evident that many of the circumstances which drove forward the USA's domestic economy favoured the development of household packaged goods with unique product differentiation and the capability for potent promotion. The consequences of successful internationalization in the post-war years are revealed by the place of six US companies amongst Britain's twenty biggest advertisers in 1960 (see Table 2.2), a presence that continued to grow.[53] But the internationalization of the world economy is not itself proof of failings amongst Britain's household branded goods sector, and British soap, chemical, food, and tobacco firms continued to vie for a share of home and overseas markets. Both Rowntree and Cadbury remained dangerous competitors of Mars, and, although it achieved an unrivalled position in the confectionery industry world-wide, it did so despite being a predominantly family firm. No one denies the comparative success of the US economy in the thirty odd years after 1945, but explanations remain complex, and not every part of the British industrial scene can be fairly categorized as a 'failure'. Perhaps history is the one social science where it is commendable to reserve judgement and express caution, and there is evidently a case for further research which incorporates the perspective of *Scale and Scope*, whilst looking at a broader range of issues. For the mean time, the record of Britain's branded household goods companies may be, as one might expect, a mixed one, but it is safe to say that overall they do constitute a

---

[52] British Institute of Management, *A Survey of the Functions of Marketing, Branding and Product Awareness* (private publication, 1961); *Marketing Organisation in British Industry* (private publication, 1970). See Fitzgerald, *Rowntree and the Marketing Revolution*, esp. 9–42.

[53] In 1990 nine subsidiaries of US companies were listed amongst the largest twenty advertisers. The Swiss-owned Nestlé was 8th in the rankings. See Advertising Association, *Advertising Statistics Yearbook* (1991).

Table 2.2. *Britain's twenty largest advertisers, 1960*

	Advertising expenditure (£000s)
1. Unilever	13,136
2. Beecham Group	6,340
3. Thomas Hedley	5,225
4. Imperial Tobacco	5,000
5. Cadbury	3,172
6. Mars	2,925
7. Rowntree	2,818
8. Nestlé	2,243
9. Reckitt and Colman	2,117
10. Shell-Mex and BP	1,674
11. Gallaher	1,595
12. J. Lyons	1,368
13. ICI	1,346
14. Kellogg	1,313
15. Colgate-Palmolive	1,308
16. Associated Electrical Industries	1,154
17. Alfred Bird	1,125
18. Dunlop	1,114
19. British Motor Corporation	1,047
20. Cooperative Wholesale Society	981

Source: *Financial Times*, 18 Aug. 1961.

successful industrial cluster. An analysis that so resolutely sees the British branded goods sector as competitively weak must need adjustment, and, in looking again at the importance of family enterprise and managerial organization, we must account for the broad nature of organizational capabilities and the reality of 'substitute' economic institutions.

3

Mass Retailing: A Last Chance for the Family Firm in France, 1945–90?

EMMANUEL CHADEAU

1. THE RETAILING REVOLUTION IN POST-WAR FRANCE

The emergence of mass retailing was a comparatively late development in France. At the end of the 1940s it accounted for only 8 per cent of retailing, and 7 per cent of food products. Forty years later, the figures were about 45 and 55 per cent respectively, while the volume of domestic final consumption had increased fourfold.[1] At the beginning of the process, organized retailing prevailed only in Paris or in provincial cities where large department stores had been established between the reign of Napoleon III (1852–70) and the outbreak of the First World War, and in some less urbanized districts in the provinces, where pioneers had created a few chains of food shops (especially between 1890 and 1920), or set up co-operatives accessible to affiliated semi-independent shopkeepers (between 1925 and 1939). But at the end of the 1980s 22.5 per cent of retailing was controlled by chains of supermarkets and hypermarkets ('giant stores') located for the most part in the suburbs and at main crossroads, while city-centre retailing experienced a major transformation.[2]

This tremendous change emerged from two processes: on the one hand a real revolution in consumption habits; and on the other an 'Americanization' of the French 'way of life'. The first of these processes has often been described as a consequence of the long period of rapid growth experienced by France from the end of the 'age of reconstruction'.[3] But the

---

[1] For these figures and for detailed data for intermediate years see: Ministère du commerce et de l'artisanat, Direction du commerce intérieur, *La France des Commerces* (Paris, 1991), 50–4; C. Desaegher, 'De la boutique à l'hypermarché: le commerce de détail en France, 1945–90' (dissertation, Université Lille III, June 1992); Institut du commerce et de la consommation (ICC) et Bureau d'information et de prévision économique (BIPE), *Canaux de distribution et consommation en Europe* (Paris, 1989); A. Lancelot and D. Parisot, *Les Canaux de distribution 1962–1983* (Paris, 1984). General information computed by the National Administration for Statistics begins in 1974 with the data for 1973: INSEE, *Comptes commerciaux de la nation* (1973 ff.).

[2] INSEE, *Comptes commerciaux*. See also J. du Closel, *Les Grands Magasins, 100 ans après* (Paris, 1989).

[3] See the most recent books of collected essays: M. Lévy-Leboyer and J. C. Casanova (eds.), *Entre l'État et le marché: l'économie française des années 1880 à nos jours* (Paris, 1991); J. M.

second process has until recently been underestimated by popular opinion, especially outside France. Though the country has been for some time a 'hypermarket- or supermarket-land', foreign popular novels and movies have regarded it as dominated by independent shops and shop-keepers selling traditional baguettes and litres of red wine to homogeneous consumers wearing Basque caps and carrying their dairy purchases from one village shop to another in an old basket. The fact that even small groceries or cheese-shops were now mainly part of large franchises was disregarded.[4]

For their part, historians have focused on the strong contrast between an alleged economic stagnation in the inter-war years and the visible and intense post-war market-pulled and state-pushed changes in French industry.[5] Consequently, the part played by retailing firms in the French economic revolution from the 1950s to the 1980s has been more or less ignored by current academic literature.[6] The facts are these, however. The 'retailing revolution' has produced large firms each employing first thousands and later tens of thousands of employees. For example, at the beginning of the 1990s the largest groups of hyper- and super-markets (the firms Carrefour, Promodès, Centres Leclerc, Intermarché, and Casino-Rallye) each operated hundreds (and in one case thousands) of outlets, with an annual turnover ranging from £7 billion to £12 billion, and an annual value-added of between £1 billion and £1.5 billion.[7] All these firms became multinationals from the late 1960s—with Promodès making 30 per cent of its annual turnover in foreign countries—expanding both in Europe and in the United States. Twenty years later some of them had signed trading agreements with European competitors (for example Casino with Argyll in Great Britain and Ahold in the Netherlands).[8]

The French commercial revolution was not confined to food-retailing. Larger firms began to distribute domestic equipment (Darty SA, £1.5 billion in turnover in 1991) or clothing (Groupe André, £1.1 billion)

Jeanneney (ed.), *L'Économie française depuis 1967* (Paris, 1989); and the classic J. J. Carré, P. Dubois, and E. Malinvaud, *La Croissance française* (Paris, 1972).

[4] See e.g. Patricia Highsmith's *Ripley under Water* (international copyright, 1991) where characters buy only in small shops, though living 50 miles south-east of Paris in an area where official data show that 65% of daily purchases take place in super- and hypermarkets.

[5] Cf. Institut d'histoire industrielle, *L'Industrie française face à la compétition internationale* (Paris, 1991); Philippe Mioche, 'La Sidérurgie française 1945–1982' (unpublished thèse d'État, Paris-Sorbonne, Jan. 1992). As is well known, in France the word 'industry' means only mining, steelmaking, metalwork, and manufacturing.

[6] However, the Nov. 1993 issue of *Entreprises et histoire* deals with 'Le Commerce: révolutions, rénovations'.

[7] Ministère du commerce, *La France des commerces*, 64–5; Ministère du commerce et de l'artisanat, Direction du commerce intérieur, *La Grande Distribution en France: 48 monographies de groupes* (Paris, 1993 edn.).

[8] J.-F. Jourdan, 'Promodès' (unpublished dissertation, Institut européen des affaires, Jan. 1992); Groupe Casino, annual reports, 1988–91.

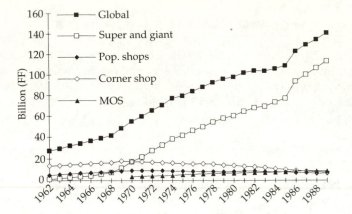

Fig. 3.1. *Corporate mass retailing: annual turnover by enterprise type, 1962–89*

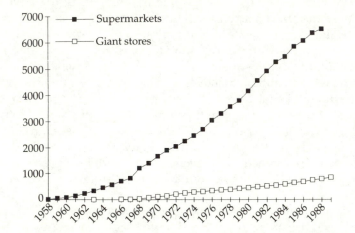

Fig. 3.2. *Supermarkets and giant stores in France: number of locations, 1958–89*

through a large network of shops. Some of the hypermarket firms (for example the Auchan group from northern France) undertook complementary activities alongside a large hypermarket in suburban areas, for instance car- or tool-hiring, car-spares, sports clothing and equipment, knitting-wool franchised shops, fast-food, etc. All of them sell petrol (10 per cent of the domestic market in 1970, 40 per cent in 1991), most of them control or are partners in chains of self-service restaurants and cafeterias located both in city centres and in the suburbs or on motorways. Until the middle of 1992 one of them, the Groupe Casino, was also a large food-manufacturer involved in grocery, biscuits, drinks, and ready-to-eat

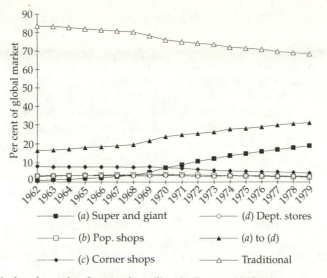

Fig. 3.3. *Market share of each type of retailing in France, 1962–79*

meals. And, following the American and German model, others (La Redoute, Les Trois Suisses, for example) developed as mail-order selling (MOS) companies, delivering to millions of customers inside and outside France, and applying early computing technology and mainframes to their production and marketing policies.

In spite of their influence over French consumption and their linkage with productive activities, almost all these leading firms were created after 1948—with the exception of Casino, Docks de France (chain stores), André (shoe-shops), and the MOS companies. The first Leclerc's shop opened in 1949, the first Carrefour supermarket in 1960, and the Carrefour company itself only in 1961 (the year Promodès was created), two years before Auchan. The firms Rallye and Intermarché appeared only in 1969 and 1971, and Cora in 1975.[9] More striking is the fact that these firms were all (and almost all remain) family firms, in spite of the fact that they became large companies and extended all over the country and abroad. And since they had to organize to meet the challenges of increasing size and of fierce competition, it may be interesting to study what kind of strategy(ies) and structure(s) they developed first to cope with rapid growth and then to remain familial.[10]

[9] *La Grande Distribution* (1992 edn.); Jourdan, 'Promodès; J. J. Villermet, *Au Carrefour d'une révolution: la naissance de l'hypermarché* (Lisses, 1991); E. Leclerc, *Ma vie et mon combat* (Paris, 1974).

[10] In addition to the literature quoted earlier, this chapter is based upon corporate sources (referred to in footnotes) and a series of interviews organized by the author and a small

2. THE FOUNDERS OF MULTIPLE STORES

The men who created modern retailing firms in France were all born in the provinces. Their names were unknown to the Parisian establishment of banking and industrial interests and managers. They often began as local retailers or wholesalers. They lived in middle-sized or small towns or cities, owned and managed small family businesses, and their influence, fame, and credit was limited to their immediate neighbourhoods. Promodès, for example, was created by the Halley family of Cherbourg in Normandy, a dynasty of local wholesalers in grocery. Carrefour was founded by the merging of two family businesses. The first was led by the Badin-Defforey family of Bourgoin and then Lagnieu, small towns north-east of Lyons at the foot of the Jura mountains, the second by the Fourniers, who were haberdashers and then clothiers and retailers in Annecy, one of the quietest cities of the central French Alps. Before they launched their first hypermarket under the name of 'Auchan', the Mulliez of Roubaix, a town 7 miles north-east of Lille, headed small spinning-mills that had extended their sales through a network of franchised knitting-wool shops. The Pollets also came from Roubaix. 'Wool-spinners since 1822'—as they liked to advertise in their letter headings—they were first merchants, then manufacturers. In 1922 they began to sell knitting wool and woollen clothing from a warehouse under the name 'La Redoute Spinning-Mills'. Customers were attracted there by low prices advertised in local newspapers, a magazine for families (1926), and a fifteen-page catalogue promoting local mail-order sales (1929). The Bouriez family, who came late to mass retailing, was a dynasty of traders and manufacturers well known in Nancy, and also involved in local politics.[11]

Besides these heirs of small businesses, there were a few absolute newcomers to business. One should note the example of Édouard Leclerc, son of a retired teacher, who in 1949 created his first discount shop in a small Breton town, or Jean-Pierre Le Roch, originally one of Leclerc's partners, who in 1969 founded a rival food-shop chain under the name 'Ex-Leclerc'—later called 'Intermarché'.[12] And finally, in non-food products there was Jean-Louis Descours, who in the 1960s rose to the top of 'Chaussures André' (later 'Groupe André'), a small chain of shoe-shops. Founded in the 1900s by a family of manufacturers, the firm had recruited Descours in 1947 for his financial ability (he was formerly an employee in tax and duty administration). Descours subsequently transformed André

research team. Among those interviewed were: two generations of the partners of Casino; M. Bon (Carrefour's CEO 1988–92); J.-L. Descours (Groupe André's CEO); R. Seynave (MOS firm Quelle's CEO, former manager of the head office at La Redoute).

[11] *Who's Who in France*, 1975–90; Villermet, *Au Carrefour*; Jourdan, 'Promodès'; F. Petit, J. Grislain, and M. Le Blan, *Aux fils du temps: La Redoute* (Roubaix, 1985); *La Grande Distribution* (1987–92).

[12] Leclerc, *Ma vie*, ch. 1.

into a large group of several hundred shops selling shoes or clothes under various brand names.[13]

Of course, some large retailing firms existed when the commercial revolution began. But of these, only one, the 'Établissements économiques du Casino—Guichard Perrachon' of Saint-Étienne, was innovative when as early as 1948 it created some of the first self-service shops in France. Indeed, its age (it was founded in 1898 as a large city-centre grocery), its size (with 1,587 affiliated or owned chain stores and shops in 1934), its turnover, and its influence as a grocery manufacturer made it unique in France. At this time, however, it had only a regional presence, in the Massif Central and part of the Rhône valley, its headquarters remaining in Saint-Étienne, a city with a manufacturing and mining hinterland unable to compete seriously with Lyons, France's second city, 50 miles to the east. And the 'provincial' features of Saint-Étienne's Casino business were reinforced by a tradition of local family alliances and by the recruitment of its leading managers from among the sons or sons-in-law of its founder Geoffroy Guichard (1867–1940).[14] Far beyond Casino in the small world of chain stores and shops came Docks de France, also provincial, also family-owned (by the Toulouses), also ignored in Paris, though it had, like Casino, introduced self-service in its shops in 1948.[15]

The last to join the general movement towards new forms of mass retailing were the large firms who owned the famous Parisian department stores and their subsidiaries or affiliates in the provincial 'metropolises' or middle-sized cities. Most of them—even the only one to remain family-owned, the Galeries Lafayette group (founded in 1895)—had been operating for some time on a national scale, with operational and top-management structures of a 'managerial' type. Indeed, they were also the largest commercial French firms in terms of capital, number of employees, purchasing power, and cash flow. Were these advantages handicaps to the pursuit of rapid economic growth and responsiveness to sudden changes in consumer demand? Some writers have asserted that the most innovative of these firms experienced disappointingly poor results and heavy political pressure in the 1930s when they attempted to reach low-income urban consumers through chains of 'popular stores' promoting cheap grocery and miscellaneous goods. These same writers note that their 'business culture' was directed to the traditional needs of the middle class rather than the new working class, so in the 1950s and 1960s they developed middle-sized city-centre shops selling everyday food, dairy, and household goods to middle-class families who were also customers of their big prestigious premises on the largest avenues. In fact, it was not until the 1970s that department store firms began to change

[13] *Who's Who in France*, and interview with Descours by IEA's students in Paris, 1991.
[14] C. de Suyrot, 'Geoffroy Guichard (1867–1940)' (unpublished dissertation, Lyons, 1990).
[15] *Who's Who in France*.

their strategy, entering the field of hypermarket and suburban commercial centres, while they reshaped their traditional stores in city centres.[16]

3. EDUCATION AND TRAINING

The men who led the commercial revolution were also non-typical of the French business élite, as regards their training. Édouard Leclerc (born in 1926) left the Grand Séminaire which he had joined two years earlier to become a priest, and became a discount shopkeeper in the small Breton town of Landerneau. Among the four men who founded the Carrefour Co. at the beginning of the 1960s, only one, Jacques Fournier (born in 1928), had experienced a prestigious graduate training at the École des mines de Paris. But he was the last of the four to enter the company after its creation. The enterprise had in fact been inspired by his brother Marcel (1914–85), fourteen years his senior, who invented the hypermarket concept. Marcel Fournier spent some time at the École de tissage (Weaving School) of Lyons, but he really learnt the job in his father's haberdashery shop. Taking over the management in 1945 he transformed it into a clothing store supported by a wholesale firm and a small clothing manufacture. When he created his first supermarket in Annecy in 1960 he entered a partnership with the Defforey brothers, Denis (born in 1925) and Jacques (born in 1929). Both ended their education at the *baccalauréat* (secondary school) stage and learnt the job in the family firm, the first as retail inspector and food-purchasing manager, the second as manager in the head office of the Établissements Badin-Defforey in Lagnieu.[17]

Family and corporate training was also a well-established tradition in the Établissements économiques du Casino. From the end of the Second World War to the 1960s it was led by Pierre Guichard (1906–88), son of the founder Geoffroy, with the help of some of his brothers and brothers-in-law. Pierre was educated at a prestigious private school in Normandy, the École des Roches at Verneuil, where he received a general education until he was 18 years old. He then joined his father in the family firm. In the 1950s he recruited his own son Yves (born 1934), who had also been educated at the École des Roches, and gave him a retailing apprenticeship in the company. As early as 1953 one of Pierre Guichard's nephews, Antoine (born in 1926), made his appearance. He was the only one in the family with a graduate qualification in Business Administration gained at the École des hautes études commerciales (HEC).[18]

---

[16] Du Closel, *Les Grands Magasins*; C. Brosselin, *La Distribution: croissance et concentration* (Paris, 1985); S.-F. Careil, *Le Grand Magasin: baromètre et conjoncture* (Paris, 1955); DAFSA/ Conseil et analyses stratégiques, 'Les Grands Magasins' (Paris, 1991); M. Dasquet, *Les Grandes Réussites françaises: Le Bon Marché* (Paris, 1955); M. Heilbronn, *Galeries Lafayette, Buchenwald, Galeries Lafayette* (Paris, 1989).

[17] Villermet, *Au Carrefour*, pt. i.

[18] De Suyrot, 'Geoffroy Guichard'; interviews with partners in Groupe Casino, 1992.

Family training is of course of long tradition among northern French textile dynasties. From the opening of its first warehouse in 1922 to the closing of its spinning workshop in 1959 and the nation-wide success of its MOS catalogue in the first half of the 1960s, La Redoute was run by three cousins. Henri, Joseph, and Charles Pollet were sons of three brothers with the same names, who were recruited between the wars by their fathers in the family spinning-mill, then in the warehouse, and finally in the commercial branch of the family firm. They themselves installed their heirs early in the 1960s. Patrick (born 1947), Joseph, and Francis (both born in 1921) had all followed undergraduate courses, in efficient but non-prestigious schools: the École de commerce of Reims in Champagne; the École d'administration des affaires of Lille; and the Institut Technique Roubaisien. From this last technical school—familiar to the sons of textile manufacturers—there also came Gérard Mulliez (born 1932), founder of the Auchan group in 1964, but mainly trained by his father and uncles in the family plant as foreman in the dye workshop (1954), manager of the machinery department of the spinning-mill (1956), and then sales manager of a subsidiary promoting franchised knitting-wool shops (under the name of 'Phildar'). Turning to Normandy, Paul-Louis Halley (born in 1934) had a very brief education at the City of London College. He then joined his father Paul-Auguste, a prominent local wholesaler. Acting as a commercial traveller for the firm in 1959–61 he then became development director of the newly established Promodès, a post similar to that held by Jacques Fournier at Carrefour.[19]

Does this mean that practical experience and training was the only route to innovation and business success in reshaping and expanding retailing firms in the 1950s and 1960s, even among undergraduate and graduate managers? Until a larger collection of case-studies is assembled to challenge this conclusion, we must accept it.

4. BUSINESS STRATEGY

All the entrepreneurs mentioned above were trained within the family firm during a period when economic prospects seemed bleak. The great period of urban development and the rapid growth of urban middle-class incomes, which began in the time of Napoleon III, ended in the 1880s or 1890s. Once ended, new avenues for success and fortune had to be found by ambitious small or middle-sized wholesalers or retailers. Unable by themselves to persuade peasants to become urbanites, or to promote a significant increase of wages among the working class, they adapted to the market. To sell more, they had to sell cheaper, and to sell cheaper, they had to purchase basic goods such as food, clothing, and ironmongery at

---

[19] *Who's Who in France*, passim; Petit, Grislain, and Le Blan, *Aux fils du temps*; Jourdan, 'Promodès'.

lower prices. They also had to bring these goods closer to low-wage customers—i.e. in small towns, in working-class districts in larger towns, in poor suburban areas, and in the large cities. City-centre department stores were able to reduce margins because they bought large batches of selected clothing and semi-luxury goods (including furniture) which attracted additional customers. They accumulated profits by responding quickly to seasonal changes in taste. New ways of attaining this strategy had to be deployed by promoters of chain stores: the choice of specific ranges of household goods (whether groceries, drinks, or ironmongery, etc.); a simultaneous distribution through the largest number of shops at prices determined centrally; the reduction of wholesale and retail margins by the use of corporate warehouses, manufacturing subsidies, or long-term contracts with wholesalers or manufacturers; the establishment of brand names to win customer loyalty. To succeed in such a task, retailing entrepreneurs had to be strongly involved on the ground. This explains why the chain stores and co-operatives of the 1890s–1930s came from the provinces, especially from parts of France where cyclical industrial crises often hit real wages and employment (for example the area of the Loire around Saint-Étienne and Champagne), or from districts which were left out of the economic prosperity enjoyed by Paris and Lyons in the inter-war years (e.g. the Loire basin, the Jura, and the central Alps). In larger towns, especially in the densely populated districts of Paris, 'commodity shops' or 'five-cents shops' were established by department stores such as the Galeries Lafayette. The promoters claimed they were the 'shops for basic needs', contrasting them with the large city-centre department stores, which were 'the stores for pleasure'.[20]

French consumption remained stagnant until the late 1940s, influencing entrepreneurial responses. Docks de France and Casino established self-service in their shops in order to reduce running costs in a period of high inflation and scarcity of basic household goods. Modern cash registers appeared in the same chain stores by 1952 (the first of them being paid for with Marshall Plan funds) to cut accounting costs under an 'anti-inflation' and 'price-freezing' government led by the pessimistic right-wing representative of the Loire, Antoine Pinay. In 1949, when Édouard Leclerc opened his first discount warehouse in Brittany, he hoped as an ardent Christian to get his main flow of customers from low-wage-earning 'workers'. In this he was mistaken, however, his success coming from lower middle-class Parisians on holiday. Marcel Fournier turned the family shop into a clothing store, offering the women of his small city cheap clothing, an opportunity provided by the disappearance of dressmakers working at home.[21]

[20] Heilbronn, *Galeries Lafayette*, quoting Bader, his father-in law.

[21] Leclerc, *Ma vie*, 39 and *passim*; Villermet, *Au Carrefour*, pt. i; Desaegher, 'De la boutique', ch. 2; on cash registers note the oral evidence of Y. Lapalu, general secretary, ICC, Paris, 1991.

The economic climate changed in the mid-1950s. For the first time real disposable incomes grew steadily and rapidly. In that climate, new paradigms of corporate growth appeared. Prosperity encouraged an acceleration in the turnover of retailing stocks and an increase of the firms' self-financing capability. Additional profits and cash flow were now used to enlarge shops or stores and widen the range of goods offered to consumers. This greater range, and the added turnover it produced, made the firm more profitable, increasing cash flow and the ability to expand. The co-operative and the multiple store gave way to the supermarket (from 1957), a commodity discount store ten or twenty times larger than the traditional chain store. Then the supermarket, following Carrefour's innovation, gave way to the hypermarket, a giant one-level store with a car-park, ten to twenty times bigger than a supermarket. Of course, those concerns whose cash was most quickly centralized—pioneering supermarket operators such as Leclerc and Carrefour—were the first to introduce hypermarkets, chain-store operators such as Casino or Docks de France being latecomers.[22]

In the same period, mail-order selling (MOS) firms applied the size and the 'all under the same roof' concept to their catalogues, with more varied collections and an increased number of pages and references. This increase in initial investment, in the production of the seasonal catalogue, was rewarded with higher margin earnings provided by additional customers.[23] It seems that, in both commercial and financial matters, the pioneers of the new retailing, if unwittingly, were prepared by a traditional family business culture to meet the challenge of expanding wages and mass consumption. Of course, most of them were helped by favourable market conditions. Over the entire post-1954 period, they benefited from creeping inflation (receiving payments in cash but paying suppliers on thirty to sixty days' credit), from large state- or local authority-financed housing schemes, from state-funded road and motorway construction, from the birth in the mid-1950s of nation-wide consumer credit institutions and commercial radio stations.[24] And, finally, they also benefited from the rapid development of computer sciences and business comput-

[22] The first supermarket chain to copy Carrefour's introduction of the hypermarket was a newly founded company, 'Auchan', followed by Leclerc; Docks de France and Casino followed only in 1968 and 1970. All the oral evidence collected during our inquiries shows that the creation of stores of 5,000–6,000 sq. metres devoted mainly to food inspired more scepticism than admiration at first.

[23] La Redoute data, collected by the company at Roubaix, show that annual turnover grew by about 12% per year in real terms from 1960 (the year following the closing of the spinning-mill and the reshaping of an extended catalogue) to 1972 (the year the company, helped by its computerized files of customers, moved from a 'production strategy'—i.e. adding new customers to its files—to a 'marketing strategy'. Interview with Robert Seynave, 1992.

[24] The nation-wide programme of popular suburban housing was launched in 1953; VAT was introduced in 1954; a twenty-year national motorway programme was agreed in 1960; the Parisian surburban development plan was first passed in 1960 and reshaped in 1965, the

ing machines, since the American firms, as early as 1954, readily reduced prices and adapted their mainframe computers in order to gain a new market.[25]

5. MANAGEMENT AND CONTROL

With this rapid increase in the scale of the business operations, the organization and structure of the firms had to change from a family to a managerial type. Once again, pioneers were able to build on their inherited business culture. In France, department stores and later the multiples had devised a typical managing organization combining a small headquarters staff and a large number of semi-autonomous specialized field managers. The nineteenth-century department store saw the emergence of the department 'supervisor' who enjoyed a high degree of autonomy. The supervisor himself recruited his assistants (salesmen or saleswomen, storekeepers, etc.). He chose the range of goods, was responsible for his inventory, established prices, and could offer discounts. He was supported by horizontal divisions for each department, which were also staffed by managers in charge of their own budgets, work-force, and who were assigned annual goals in terms of growth and efficiency: supply managers (one for each type of product), department designers, and personnel managers. In such a system, the top management of a large store and even of a multiple store company was based on centralized commercial and financial information, on the inspection and control of a few employees whose status, like that of the supervisor, was somewhere between that of a salaried manager and a managing partner.[26]

The management principles of multiple store companies were similar. From the 1900s to the 1930s Casino's shops were run by partners who provided both the premises and the goodwill, while the chain brought them a brand name, a selection of goods, price guidelines, management advice, delivery services, and sales promotion campaigns. Decisions and information circulated from top to bottom. A corporate newspaper en-

year in which a nation-wide programme of 'new cities' around Paris and near Rouen, Lyons, Nice, Marseilles, and Lille was passed. The right to broadcast nation-wide was given to the commercial radio corporations RTL and Europe 1 in 1954.

[25] First contacts between IBM and La Redoute were established in 1954 and the MO firm received its first mainframe panel in 1958, four years having been spent to shape it to commercial requirements: interview with Seynave. The idea of electronic price stickers was developed as early as 1968 by two leaders of mass retailing, Étienne Moulin (Galeries Lafayette) and Jacques Pictet (Paridoc), and its design began in 1972: GENCOD, *Hommage à Jacques Pictet* (Paris, 1991).

[26] V. Bourienne, 'Boucicaut, Chauchard et les autres: fondateurs et fondation de grands magasins parisiens', in *Paris et Île de France: mémoires publiés par la fédération des sociétés historiques et archéologiques de Paris et de l'Île de France* (Paris, 1989); du Closel, *Les Grands Magasins*.

sured the horizontal transmission of information from shopkeeper to shopkeeper. General control was in the hands of inspectors, who also tried to recruit new affiliates. Since Casino was also a manufacturing firm, industrial control was subordinated to the commercial side, but its factories could also supply competitors, whether multiples or independent retailers, as well as its own shops.[27] This type of firm was managed by a combination of owner-managers and salaried managers. At the Galeries Lafayette, in the 1920s and 1930s, the founder, Théophile Bader, controlled the entire business organization. He also took all decisions relating to promotional campaigns and the selection of products. He was assisted by his two sons-in-law. One of them managed the giant store in Paris, the second was in charge of purchasing and also ran the popular 'five-cents' stores and controlled all the branches or affiliated stores in the provinces. Lower down, salaried managers, recruited either internally or externally, shared the day-to-day management of operations, sales, and personnel.[28] In the same period Geoffroy Guichard took as partners his sons Mario (1891–1976), Jean (1892–1961), Georges (1894–1971), Paul (1900–82), and Pierre (1906–88), and one of his sons-in-law, François Kemlin (1892–1965). Each of them managed a branch of the firm: manufacturing, supplies, distribution, shop inspection, personnel, and sales promotion.[29]

This type of organization was extremely effective. It gave a certain degree of autonomy to junior and local managers (departmental supervisors, shopkeepers), who were interested in the profits of the company and on whom commercial decisions and the day-to-day relationship with customers ultimately depended, while it eased the burden on the senior executives. Non-food multiples, smaller department stores, and clothing chain stores in the provinces copied this form of organization, mainly because it was well adapted to their activities in which the need for working capital was greater than that for fixed capital, and also to a seasonal or a cyclical demand, where customers could be reached either by personal contact at shop level or through advertising or promotional campaigns orchestrated from the centre. This explains why this type of organization was adopted by newcomers in mass retailing in the 1950s and 1960s, and why inheritors of department stores and multiples were able to combine new commercial strategies (self-service, supermarkets, hypermarkets, and the integrated shopping malls) with their usual methods of management.

This adaptation process followed two paths. When Édouard Leclerc

[27] De Suyrot, 'Geoffroy Guichard'; newspapers and collection of circulars from Casino's archives, Saint-Étienne.

[28] Heilbronn, *Galaries Lafayette*. Solidarity between appointed managers and managing shareholders, after Heilbronn, was fully demonstrated under the German occupation of France, when both the Germans and the Vichy government prosecuted the Bader-Heilbronn family for its activity in the Resistance.

[29] De Suyrot, 'Geoffroy Guichard'.

decided in 1953 to expand his discount warehouses throughout France, he had no inherited management structure, and his capital was too small to allow him to increase the number of outlets and still remain independent from his suppliers—whom he hated—and from his bankers—whom he believed to be prejudiced. Consequently he gave up any idea of creating a corporate business and created what he himself called a 'progressive movement', i.e. a society of independent retailers who wanted to shift from small shopkeeping to larger operations. By paying him a nominal fee, the retailers benefited from the 'Centre Leclerc' brand name (which was associated with low prices) and from management guidance. They provided the premises, goodwill, and capital for the initial stocks. They were all married couples, because Leclerc believed that unmarried people had no interest in increasing their estate. In 1957, when supermarkets first appeared, Leclerc and his retailers established a new Society to manage large warehouses and a purchasing group jointly owned by its members. In 1963 a third company was founded which, for a percentage on turn-over, supplied members with management help, computerized control of stocks, prices, and capital, and professional training. Year after year, dozens and then hundreds of independent retailers entered the Leclerc Societies, creating the largest chain of food-retailing in 1970s and 1980s France, a chain that with its unique brand name appeared to be a highly integrated concern. In reality it was a loose federation of retailers who applied in their supermarkets and discount stores the management methods inherited from the department stores: autonomous departmental supervisors, paternalistic management of personnel (between 20 and 150 people according to store size), financing, etc. This style of running mass retailing was of course copied, for example by Intermarché (established in 1969), and sometimes perfected (Intermarché introduced its own fleet of lorries delivering to its associates and advertising its name on French roads).[30]

Elsewhere, the existing family management and control had to adapt to the new techniques and market conditions. Following a well-proven tradition in family firms, the younger members were put in charge of the modernization process under the supervision of their seniors. As we have noted, in 1961 Paul-Louis Halley was entrusted by his father Paul-Auguste with the task of creating supermarkets under the name 'Promodès', a forward diversification from the family wholesale business. In 1969 he became 'executive manager' of the new firm, and finally became its chairman and managing director, his father remaining chairman of the group for a few years.[31]

A similar but more complex evolution may be observed in the mail-order firm La Redoute. The founder, Henri Pollet, died in 1967 aged 77. Although his son Henri Jr. (born in 1915) had had the title of chairman and

---

[30] Desaegher, 'De la boutique'; Leclerc, *Ma vie*.
[31] Promodès, *Rapport annuel d'activité* (1960–72).

managing director for many years, his father retained *de facto* control until 1964. After his father's death Henri Jr. took charge of three departments: purchasing, personnel, and stores. One of his brothers, Philippe, was in charge of the mail-order department (first run manually, then by computer). Francis, one of Henri Sr.'s nephews, was in charge of both sales and internal communication. Another of the founders, Joseph, also installed his two sons in the family business: both Jean and Joseph Jr. were directors and branch managers. Each of these members of the Pollet family appointed salaried departmental managers recruited on the basis of their diplomas and professional expertise. The data-processing department was headed by a graduate from the École polytechnique, and the computerized order department by a science graduate. The purchasing and sales departments benefited from the abilities of graduates from business schools such as the Hautes études commerciales (HEC) and the ESSEC. The chairman and managing director was assisted in his daily activities by a company secretary, who was formerly a Civil Servant trained at the prestigious École nationale d'administration (ENA). Each of the senior salaried managers received from the owner-managers a set of annual goals for his department. The manager could seek help and a larger budget from 'his' member of the Pollet family, who would plead his cause at the partners' meetings. The Pollets controlled every division by paying occasional visits to all the outposts of the firm and talking to the staff, both junior and senior. They determined the firm's overall strategy at board meetings. Originally a partnership, La Redoute was converted into a private limited company in 1959, and a public company in 1964, when 30 per cent of its shares were listed on the Paris Bourse. With 70 per cent of the share capital the family was entitled to five seats on the board, the other places being taken by sleeping partners (a commercial bank, the investment bank which advised on the flotation, and a friend of the family involved in politics and in lobbying).

In the case of Casino, growth consolidated family control. In 1970, when the company acquired a smaller competitor, it had 2,056 shops, 52 supermarkets, and 2 hypermarkets; four years later, it had 2,025 shops, 60 supermarkets, and 8 hypermarkets. It also operated subsidiaries for catering, wine-making and bottling, coffee-roasting, chocolate manufacture, and abattoirs. It employed 11,000 people (excluding shopkeepers), of whom 11 per cent were skilled clerks, and more than a hundred were senior managers. But the general management still remained in family hands. Casino was a private limited company. In 1974 the executive board comprised two generations of the Guichard and associated families. Five grandsons of the founder Geoffroy Guichard were managing partners, supported by one of his surviving sons, Pierre (aged 68), and by a son-in-law, Freddy Pinoncély (aged 64). The supervisory board was made up of Geoffroy's sons and sons-in-law (one of them aged 85), together with a few 'notables'. In the same way, the subsidiaries of Établissements economiques du Casino were led by members of the family.[32]

6. MERGERS AND DIVERSIFICATION

From the mid-1970s to the mid-1980s things began to change. First, from 1972, the rate of growth of mass retailing fell to only 2–5 per cent per annum, whereas it had previously been twice as high as that of French GNP. Gains in market share fell threefold, and in some years—1972, 1973, and 1982–3—sales fell in absolute terms. In 1973 an Act limited the number and size of new locations. After a long period when popular consumption attempted to reflect middle-class standards, new tastes and needs developed, in particular an awareness of quality, while after 1975 local authorities favoured the regeneration of city centres rather than the development of new suburbs.[33]

Large firms had to reshape their strategy. In 1969 Promodès pioneered an expansion abroad, followed in 1973 by Carrefour and Casino. All firms also experienced external growth by taking over smaller competitors weakened by the new domestic conditions. In the 1970s retailers pursued a new strategy. They encouraged affiliated store-holders to break with their parent-firm and brand dealerships. At the same time, they helped small traders or local multiples to expand, in order to challenge their own competitors in traditional markets. After 1983, the merger wave intensified, the largest firms competing strongly with each other to become the largest purchasers of the new French integrated agro-businesses and catering firms. And, in the 1970s as well as in the 1980s, diversification was sought by every brand-owner as the best way to increase profits and finance growth in both domestic and foreign markets. Led by the food-retailer Carrefour, retailer-brands were developed after 1976 in co-operation with agro-businesses in order to build customer loyalty. In the late 1970s the Casino group expanded its catering lines and introduced new methods to dairy products in order to satisfy new demands for quality and freshness. Multiples also tried to increase the turnover per square metre of their large suburban sites, establishing around their hypermarkets new facilities such as restaurants, cafeterias, tool- and car-hiring centres. After 1977 they introduced corporate credit cards through joint ventures with commercial banks. Mail-order firms began to promote lotteries and opened retail shops in city centres. Non-food retailers began

[32] R. Priouret, *La France et le management* (Paris, 1967); Petit, Grislain, and Le Blan, *Aux fils du temps*; La Redoute SA, *Rapport annuel d'activité* (1964–73); de Suyrot, 'Geoffroy Guichard'; interviews with partners and senior partners, Groupe Casino and Casino SA, 1992.
[33] Long-term context analysed in Desaegher, 'De la boutique'; INSEE, *Comptes commerciaux de la nation* (1973 ff.).

to locate their stores in the large shopping malls located in city-centre redevelopments, and to assist in the financing of office-blocks.[34]

Diversification and external growth strategies implied heavier logistic and operating costs, larger corporate assets, and new capital inflows. It also meant a more intricate structure; the most aggressive firms frequently diversified backwards as manufacturers or property developers, and forwards as credit institutions. By the 1970s all of them had already moved from a conventional sales policy to new strategies based upon lavish marketing divisions. In the same period—especially in the 1980s—a new generation of business leaders took over from the pioneers.[35]

How did business organizations adjust? Did family control and management survive? Some cases may be pointed out. In 1981, La Redoute, with a mail-order subsidiary in Italy and another for city-centre stores in France, had 5 million loyal customers and files containing 10 million names, a 1,000-page biannual fashion catalogue, and an advanced data-processing order system (including phone orders and experimental 'minitel' facilities). It had become the second largest MOS firm in Europe, world-famous for its giant computer-processing warehouse in Roubaix. In 1982 Redoute adopted a new structure, when it became a listed holding company. The mail-order activity became a subsidiary company, 'La Redoute Catalogue', itself being the parent-firm for smaller more specialized subsidiaries and affiliates (for instance in children's mail-order clothing etc.). The Pollet family maintained a firm control over the holding company, while the main group operator, La Redoute Catalogue, was run by a salaried manager who had been recruited in 1965 by the data-processing department; he became marketing manager in 1970, then Charles Pollet's deputy as vice-managing director in 1972, and finally managing director in 1974. The holding company itself was quickly led by an outsider, a former sales assistant who then became the sales department manager. Eventually, in 1988, the bulk of the Pollet family's shares in the holding company was purchased on the Stock Exchange by the large department store company Le Printemps. Managers remained in charge, while family interests disappeared.[36]

At Casino, the new strategies initiated in the 1970s had no discernible effect on the management structure for some time. As late as 1982, following a reshaping of the company's partnership chart, the third generation

[34] INSEE, *Comptes commerciaux*, and Ministère du commerce, *La Grande Distribution* (1987, 1989, 1991).

[35] INSEE, *Comptes commerciaux*, and Ministère du commerce, *La Grande Distribution*. We also acknowledge our debt to a large panel of DAFSA/EUROSTAFF confidential studies on these firms for 1985–91 which we were given during our inquiry by professional associations.

[36] See n. 32 and interview with Seynave, 1992. The La Redoute group was eventually rebuilt in 1993 by the financier François Pinault after his take-over of Le Printemps group. In 1994 Le Printemps and La Redoute merged to form a new public company, owned by Pinault's private partnership.

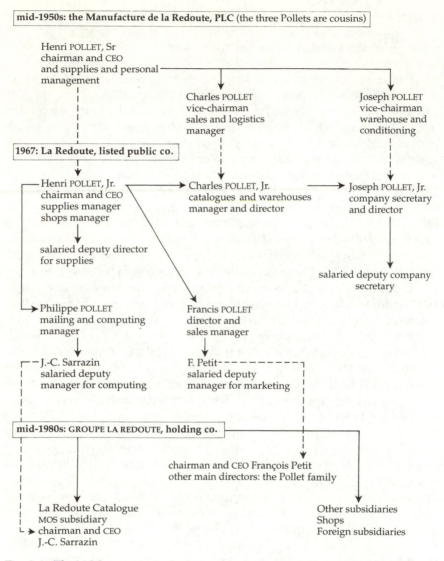

Fig. 3.4. *The MOS company La Redoute: managing organization, mid-1950s–mid-1980s*

was clearly in command, because notwithstanding the composition of the supervisory board all powers were transferred to the five cousins who were acting as managing partners, following a modification of the articles of association. A more important reform took place only after the death of Pierre Guichard, the former chairman of the supervisory board. The number of managing partners was reduced from five to three, and they managed the operating branches and exercised control over strategic

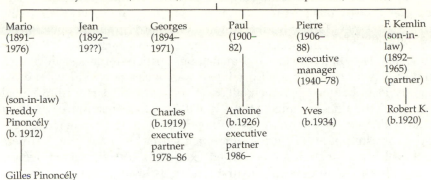

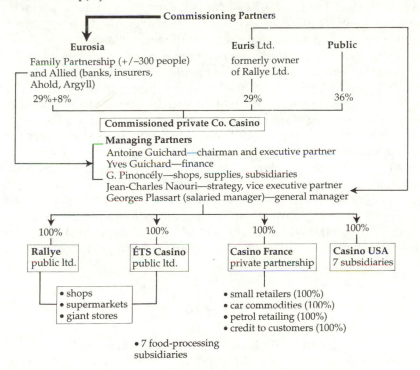

Fig. 3.5. *Members of the Guichard family and others involved in the Casino partnership from 1892*

direction and planning (commercial, finance, development). In the following year (1989) the company's rules were further modified. The Casino partnership became a holding company, whose main subsidiaries were: a smaller recently acquired retailer; a property company; the American subsidiaries; food-processing and catering; and Casino France, a general partnership responsible for all commercial activity in France. Eventually, in 1990, the new family leader, Antoine Guichard, grand-nephew of the founder Geoffroy, introduced a new organization which set aside family interests. The three cousins and managing partners remained in charge, but the power of the supervisory board was once again reduced and the family shareholders and their allies formed a new partnership called 'Eurosia'; the allies included Argyll, Royal Ahold, the insurance company Axa-Midi, and the pharmaceutical Rhône-Poulenc. The top management now consisted of an executive committee led by the managing partners but which also included the salaried executives of the various departments. In the same year, for the first time in its history, the listed Casino Co. issued convertible bonds. And two years later it changed its capital structure when it offered 29 per cent of its shares in exchange for a majority holding in Rallye, a major competitor which had previously been controlled by a bank-owned investment fund. A new partner, a 'foreigner', entered the board as member of the 'Eurosia' partnership.[37]

Other firms tried to maintain family influence by splitting their main interests into smaller subsidiaries linked to each other by private limited companies or partnership holding companies (Promodès, Groupe André). In 1986 Édouard Leclerc used his charismatic power over his network of companies to install his son Michel-Édouard. In 1986 also, a year after the death of the founder Marcel Fournier, the Carrefour company recruited a high-ranking manager, a former Inspecteur des finances with experience of ministerial cabinets and a state-controlled bank. First trained by Jacques Fournier with the position of deputy chief executive, he became Carrefour's chairman and chief executive in 1988. Unfortunately, the shareholders found his vigorous policy of growth too costly; annual turnover increased almost threefold in three years (from £4.5 billion to £11 billion) but the outsider was sacked in June 1992, before the firm was converted into a private limited company with family control over salaried managers reinforced.

7. CONCLUSION

Some forty years after the French 'commercial revolution' began, the changing scale of business and competition, extended to the twelve EC states, provides little scope for the survival of the small independent

---

[37] Éts. économiques du Casino, Groupe Casino, Casino SA, *Rapports annuels d'activité* (1974–90); French business newspapers and magazines, 1991–2, partner and senior partner inverviews, 1992. In Oct. 1994 the Casino partnership was reorganized as a public company, and Eurosia sold its shares to the new Casino company. The Guichard family lost its controlling interest, and a new executive board was installed.

family firm in a mass-volume activity such as retailing. In France, the pioneers had enjoyed favourable market conditions. For a considerable time, the French business establishment despised retailing (men such as Simon Marks were frequently dismissed as 'grocers'), and in consequence its members neither believed nor invested in the sector. Feelings of inferiority in relation to British banking and German manufacturing focused the attention of the business élite on finance and heavy industry. Such a climate provided much scope for individualistic pioneers who emerged from provincial trade and small-scale retailing. As pointed out here, most of them, already accustomed to local needs, and knowledgeable about price-cutting and the management structures appropriate for light industry, were able to meet the changing challenges of the market. Of course, the long period of growth which began in c.1950–4 provided an opportunity which they seized with remarkable success. Their earlier experience and inherited culture reaped unexpected dividends and considerable profits. Naturally, the scale of their success produced a limit to their power over market or technology. Retailing operations had to become standardized; firms had to insert themselves into a common economic landscape; higher financial risk now demanded stable and carefully formulated long-term strategies. The pioneering firms had to mature, individual efficiency and charisma had to be replaced by business administration and individuals by committees. In an economy dominated by large corporate business, mass retailing was perhaps one of the last areas open to the family firm in twentieth-century France.

4

Christofle: A Family Firm

MARC DE FERRIÈRE LE VAYER

1. INTRODUCTION

Since its foundation in 1845, Christofle, the firm of silversmiths, has been managed successively by five generations of Charles Christofle's descendants.[1] This enterprise, with its obvious familial character, is representative of a kind of company which is often viewed as being typically French, i.e. one specializing in luxury production.[2] In this chapter we will explore the way in which the family managed Christofle. Consequently, we will study the origins of capital at the time of the firm's foundation and examine the mechanisms by which funds were raised for its further development. This point is a crucial one, especially as the family—even in a broad sense—did not hold a majority of the capital before the 1940s. Another key element to understand is the capital structure and the importance of the various alliances among the different shareholders. It is apparent that successive generations of shareholder proved to be very faithful to the company.

To study the familial structure of the company is not enough to explain its functioning. In this instance, to define Christofle as a family firm is to assume that the family manages the firm and does not share control with an external team of professional non-family managers. Nevertheless, the significant growth of the company during the nineteenth and second half of the twentieth centuries, together with the diversification of the many crafts and the localization of its industrial plants, soon necessitated the creation of a numerous and highly competent management team. To understand its functioning also means looking at the way in which a family firm was able to maintain its existence for almost one and a half centuries.

2. AN OMNIPRESENT FAMILY

A family firm—and in particular a middle-sized firm—is frequently the achievement of a single entrepreneur. The attainment of success permits

---

[1] This chapter on the evolution of the firm is derived from Marc de Ferrière, 'Christofle: une aventure industrielle, 1873–1940', 3 vols. (unpublished Ph.D. thesis, University of Paris-Sorbonne, 1991).

[2] Marc de Ferrière, 'L'Industrie du luxe en France depuis 1945: un exemple d'industrie compétitive?', *Entreprises et histoire*, 3 (May 1993), 85–96.

the founder to pass on control to his or her heirs. In fact, Charles Christofle played a most prominent part both as the founder of his company and as its first successful manager. However, the case of Christofle is peculiar inasmuch as the founder's achievements were not the only cause of its success. The role of the family proved to be just as important. While the firm experienced the famous 'Buddenbrooks' syndrome,[3] there was an important difference. Here, the third generation neither let the firm disappear nor surrendered family control over it.

The Founder

Charles Christofle (1805–63) was a typical entrepreneur of the nineteenth century. Like many entrepreneurs at that time, he used to allege that he had started from nothing and was 'le fils de ses œuvres' (a self-made man).[4] In fact, he came from a family of small traders in Paris. The family circle was the perfect place for Charles to undertake his professional training. This family circle also provided him with the financial means required (although these were limited) to create his firm.[5]

The oldest records of members of the Christofle family involved in some sort of manufacturing activity show that they were established as makers of gold paillettes and spangles in Paris in 1793.[6] For almost half a century—until the creation of the silversmith's—the family owned several small enterprises located in the Marais in Paris, making products associated with luxury articles. In fact, Charles Christofle's mother and three of his uncles were button-makers and Hugues Calmette, his brother-in-law, managed a jewellery workshop which specialized in gilded copper jewels.[7] In 1830 Charles Christofle was entrusted with managing Calmette's jewellery workshop. This opportunity was to prove very important as he could apply—on a small scale—the managerial methods and principles which led to his future success in management.[8]

Charles Christofle insisted upon three main principles:

1. to ensure the best quality in order to maintain the customer's confidence;
2. to attach importance to exports so as to develop the enterprise;

[3] Peter L. Payne, 'Family Business in Britain: An Historical and Analytical Survey', in A. Okochi and S. Yasuoka (eds.), *Family Business in the Era of Industrial Growth: Its Ownership and Management* (Tokyo, 1984).

[4] A. Plessis, *La Banque de France et les 200 actionnaires* (Geneva, 1982).

[5] The myth of Christofle as a self-made man was established by Charles himself at the Industrial Exhibition of 1839, and later reproduced in the reports of Juries of International Exhibitions.

[6] Information on Christofle's family derives entirely from notarial drafts of the Minutier central of the Archives nationales in Paris.

[7] See Fig. 4.1.

[8] This was the subject of several publications by Charles Christofle, who insisted on being the propagandist of these ideas among the public.

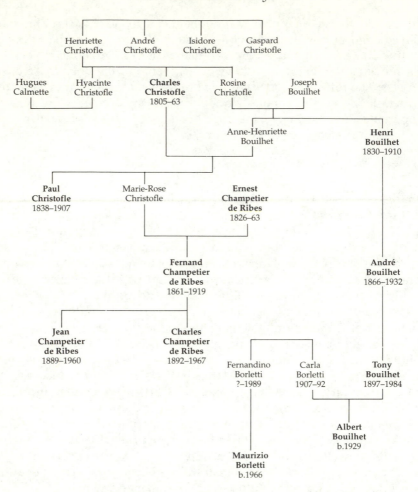

Fig. 4.1. *Simplified genealogy of the Christofle family*

3. not to hesitate to make investments in technical innovations.

He put his theories into practice when he founded his own silversmith's company in 1845. The firm was established to apply and commercialize a major technical innovation in the history of science and technology: the electroplating process. As early as 1842 Charles Christofle bought the patent from the French chemist Henri de Ruolz. He also entered into partnership with the two Elkington cousins from Birmingham who had registered similar patents in the United Kingdom.[9] The initial name of the company was 'Société Charles Christofle pour l'exploitation des brevets

---

[9] The issue of who had a prior claim to the discovery of electro-deposition will not be reopened here.

de dorure et d'argenture par la pile de Ruolz-Elkington'. Then, in order to retain the customer's confidence in the new products, i.e. gilded and silver electroplated items, Charles Christofle decided to transform his firm. In 1846 Christofle became industrial silversmiths, but the original jobbing activity was maintained. This enabled Charles to control the quality of the articles he manufactured. Action was also taken on the exports front. As early as 1848 Charles opened a shop in New York and before long he conquered important markets in South America and Italy and was able to open a subsidiary company in Karlsruhe in 1856.

Christofle had certainly gained his knowledge within a family business environment. However, he had also acquired an education outside the family, at Sainte-Barbe College.[10] This produced a circle of friends who might become potential business contacts. This point is developed later since this 'circle' was to play a prominent part in the development of the firm.

The Second Generation

The second generation included Charles's son Paul Christofle and his nephew and brother-in-law Henri Bouilhet.[11] Both continued the founder's work and developed it, with the result that his strategic options were maintained. Exports remained essential. The Karlsruhe subsidiary company was developed, and it opened its own subsidiary company in Vienna. Commercial travellers were regularly sent by Charles Christofle throughout the whole Mediterranean basin. This area became a very important market for Christofle, and this was particularly true of Italy, the Ottoman Empire with Constantinople and Egypt, and North Africa. South and Central America also remained preferential outlets. Christofle was established in the Russian Empire as well, and made attempts to supply the Transvaal, Australia, and even Japan.

Charles Christofle's successors transformed Christofle into a vertically integrated concern. In the 1870s, through several management decisions of primary importance, the firm created and integrated new trades and, after having invented the process for refining nickel ore (discovered in New Caledonia some years earlier), the managers decided to exploit their patents. Consequently, a factory was built in 1878 at Saint-Denis in the northern suburbs of Paris. This produced nickel mattes and also transformed nickel which was either sold directly or used by Christofle to manufacture different types of nickel silver. Following the same vertical integration scheme, the Saint-Denis factory also started to produce Christofle flatware. This is to be emphasized because it was Christofle's most profitable product, and had been subcontracted since

[10] Sainte-Barbe College was a most prestigious school in Paris in the 19th cent.
[11] See Fig. 4.1.

1854. Moreover, the vertical integration was achieved almost entirely by self-financing.

Henri Bouilhet and Paul Christofle contributed to the development of the firm through a strategy of external growth. They took over some of their main competitors: the Cheron company, well established in the 'Limonadiers' trade (retailers of soft drinks, wines, and spirits) and the Alfenide company (1888), their biggest competitor in flatware. Trade marks were meanwhile maintained, giving Christofle the opportunity to gain new markets. In addition, in 1900 the firm launched a new trade mark: Gallia.[12] With this they could satisfy customers looking for less expensive but comparatively high-quality hollow-ware.

The Third and Fourth Generations

The 'Buddenbrooks' syndrome was not surmounted without crisis. In fact, Charles Christofle's grandson Fernand Champetier de Ribes was well suited to the position of manager, but unfortunately he died in 1919, shortly after he had started running the firm. His cousin André Bouilhet did not possess the required capabilities for this task and took little interest in the business. Thus the fourth generation had to take charge of the company. Because they were young and had limited experience this generation found it difficult to cope with the economic hardships assailing the firm after the First World War. And, after piling one poor management decision upon another, Christofle was led into a critical financial situation.

The basis of Christofle's success, which had been established in the mid-nineteenth century, was effectively ruined by the war. Most foreign markets were lost. The Karlsruhe factory, sequestrated in 1916 by the German government, was liquidated in 1920. During the 1920s financial problems increased to such a point that outside capital became necessary. This predicament was due to external circumstances and also because, for the very first time in Christofle's familial history, the succession had not been prepared. This caused a split in the family. When Tony Bouilhet, the only representative of the fourth generation, took over the enterprise there was substantial recovery. The family was able to cope with its internal difficulties, but not without a high cost.

We now examine how power was transmitted within the family.

A Succession under Control

The family's endogamous character was observable from the foundation of Christofle. Charles, like two of his uncles, married his niece. The

---

[12] See *Catalogue Gallia*, reprint by Ketterer Kunst Verlag, Munich, with an introduction by Marc de Ferrière (forthcoming).

purpose of such customs was to ensure the maintenance of capital or possible fortune in the family.[13] In addition the Christofle family was a rather small one until the beginning of the twentieth century. After Charles, the following generations raised families of only two or three children. This facilitated (though it also limited) the choice of a successor. The three earlier generations insisted upon good training for their heirs. Paul, Charles's appointed successor and son, was sent to the chemist Wohler in Germany to prepare his thesis. Charles's other successor, his nephew and brother-in-law Henri Bouilhet, graduated as an engineer from the École centrale de Paris. As regards the next generation, Paul's adopted son Fernand Champetier de Ribes was also an engineer from the École centrale.

The family also tried to control the succession to the enterprise. Charles Christofle counted on his son-in-law to succeed him, but after the latter died in 1863 he designated his son and nephew as successors in his will. They in turn identified their sons as successors as soon as was possible. This strategy was disturbed only twice. Charles Christofle's successor, Ernest Champetier de Ribes, died before his father-in-law and Fernand Champetier de Ribes died suddenly when he was just taking control of the firm. However, the tradition of preparing the succession predominated until very recently.

Albert Bouilhet, the current president of Christofle, was prepared for his future responsibilities through his studies and training at several foreign silverware manufacturers. He entered the firm in 1954 and occupied different decision-making posts for almost fifteen years, before becoming director in 1968. In the same way, his younger brother and appointed successor Marc Bouilhet studied at the École des hautes études commerciales and worked in a few enterprises in France and abroad before assisting him as co-manager. However, this managerial training did not prevent the enterprise from encountering difficulties. Faced with a decline in its traditional markets, Christofle has delayed a necessary diversification and experienced a deteriorating financial situation in the 1980s.[14] In order to maintain the familial character of the firm, the Bouilhet family was compelled in September 1993 to place Christofle under a new management. The new chairman, Maurizio Borletti, aged 27, is a descendant of Tony Bouilhet's family-in-law. This branch keeps the enterprise within the family tree, but is not related to the founders.

The fact that only family members controlled the management of Christofle is all the more remarkable because they did not hold the major-

---

[13] Such customs were not unusual—cf. Lévy-Leboyer's reference to the Rothschild family. M. Lévy-Leboyer, 'The Large Family Firm in French Manufacturing', in Okochi and Yasuoka, *Family Business.*

[14] For more information on today's silversmiths' market see Roland Barois, Marc de Ferrière, and Jacques Mouclier, *Le Cristal, l'orfèvrerie* (Paris, 1994), 180–7.

ity of the capital before the 1940s. Therefore it is important to study the relationship between the family and Christofle's successive shareholders in order to understand how Christofle has remained a family company until the present day.

2. THE SHAREHOLDERS

Charles Christofle attended the Collège Sainte-Barbe in Paris. He was later among its administrators. There he formed long-lasting acquaint-anceships with men who were able, through their position in society, to give Charles strong support in his enterprise: for example the aides-de-camp of both Louis-Philippe and Napoleon III. There were also political personalities such as the deputy Vavin, who liquidated the civil list after the Revolution of 1848, and some Ministers, including A. Bixio from the *Gouvernement provisoire* in 1848. In addition to this support in politics, Charles established relationships in business. Among Christofle's first shareholders were bankers who had attended the same college as Charles. He was able to form a friendship with many scientists also, men such as C. Becquerel, J. B. Dumas, H. Sainte-Claire-Deville, and also, but most significantly, the chemist Henri Regnault who directed the Sèvres porcelain factory. He remained one of Christofle's shareholders until his death. Moreover these circles of acquaintances survived through generations and were observable up to the Second World War; this was the case for instance with the Dubufe family.

We will study the relations between the shareholders and the family over three definite periods:

- from the foundation of the firm to 1930;
- from 1930 to 1940;
- from 1940 to the present day.

From the foundation of the firm to 1930

For most of the firm's first century, the relationship between the managing family and the shareholders was a special one because of the legal form of the firm. In fact from its foundation the firm was a *société en commandite par actions* (joint-stock limited partnership). Charles Christofle, in accordance with the statutes, appointed his successors. The successive *gérants* (managers) were on the whole faithfully supported by the shareholders. They were able to develop the enterprise according to their wishes especially as regards achieving vertical integration and ensuring commercial expansion, by means of self-financing. The shareholders' attitude was not solely one of sleeping partners inasmuch as they were in fact totally supportive of the *gérant*, except on two occasions.

Table 4.1. *Christofle's return on invested capital*

	Annual percentage return
1849–70	18.20
1871–1914	14.25
1918–27	16.36
1928–40	0.00

Table 4.2. *Five periods of earnings under 10 per cent*

	Earnings (%)
1877–8	9.60
1884–6	8.70
1894–7	7.85
1901–3	8.95
1924–5	0.60

This support may be explained by the fact that the return on invested capital was sufficiently high to prevent any sort of resistance (Table 4.1). Charles Christofle often laid stress on this point: 'Je suis profondément convaincu que si nous étions en Angleterre cette question ne serait pas longue à decider et comme j'ai conduit notre affaire comme un manufacturier anglais, j'ai bien droit d'espérer que mes actionnaires se conduisent avec moi en actionnaires anglais.'[15] This extract dates back to the first years of existence of the firm and emphasizes the fact that shareholders regarded themselves as co-founders of the firm with the *gérant* and estimated that they were entitled to exercise a close control over its management. We may even say that Charles Christofle's management was permanently supervised.

This supervision produced strained relations between the *gérant* and the shareholders on at least two occasions. In 1848 the committee of surveillance complained that 'la gestation de M Christofle présente au point de vue de l'irrégularité de certains de ses actes relatés plus haut un danger pour la société et qu'il faut attribuer l'état des choses actuel à une mauvise administration générale'.[16] Ten years later the committee

[15] 'I am deeply convinced that were we in the United Kingdom it would not be long before this question were settled, and as I directed our business like a British manufacturer, I am entitled to believe that my partners are to behave as British shareholders would towards me.' Letter to the Committee of Shareholders sent out as a circular to all shareholders, 21 Mar. 1853, Christofle archives.
[16] 'Mr Christofle's management—with regard to the irregularity of certain above mentioned acts—is hazardous for the company and the present state of affairs results from

Table 4.3. *Christofle's capital, 1846–1936/7* (francs)

Year	Share capital	Debentures
1846	1,600,000	250,000
1847		250,000
1853	2,000,000	
1854		200,000
1856		400,000
1858	2,400,000	
1861	3,000,000	
1875/6		500,000
1876/7		500,000
1877/8		1,000,000
1888/9		1,000,000
1912/13	1,000,000	
1924/5	8,000,000	
1925/6	12,000,000	
1926/7	24,000,000	
1930/1	24,000,000	
1936/7	21,200,000	

reaffirmed 'son role qui est de défendre les intérêts des actionnaires, même contre le gérant'.[17] Until the years immediately following the First World War, there was no impediment to the maintenance of the Christofle, Champetier de Ribes, and Bouilhet families at the head of the firm. Their position was due, to a large extent, to the outstanding earning capacity of the enterprise, with high returns to shareholders (Table 4.1). The latter never discussed the strategy, even supporting in most cases the *gérants'* strategic options. In the same way, they subscribed to the required increases of capital as well as to new loan issues, the loans being even largely over-subscribed (see Table 4.3).

After 1918 Christofle's situation changed completely. Profits plummeted, and regular increases of capital were required (Table 4.3). With dividends in decline, the shareholders were more and more reluctant to supply the firm with additional funds. Debts rose to such an extent that self-financing was no longer an option, and bankers were therefore able to dominate policy. From that time onwards the family badly needed extra

mismanagement as a whole.' Assemblée générale, 1848: Rapport du Conseil de surveillance, Christofle archives.

[17] 'Their function is to serve the interests of shareholders, even against the *gérant*': Assemblée générale extraordinaire No. 26, 18 Oct. and 19 Nov. 1858, Procès-verbal, Christofle archives.

Table 4.4. *Ownership of Christofle capital, 1845–1940*

Year	Capital owned by Christofle family (%)	Capital owned by Thalmann Bank (%)
1845	50	—
1847	9	—
1853	6	—
1893	22	—
1930	n/a	50
1940	47	—

funds in order to maintain its control over the firm. The period 1918–30 clearly revealed the weaknesses of a family firm. Because there were too many heirs, no common position could be adopted. Consequently, some members of the family were ejected and bankers assumed control because the firm, deep in crisis, needed a large amount of cash to cope with the situation (Table 4.4).

From 1930 to 1940

A triple revolution took place during this period. It all began in 1926 when the firm was floated on the stock market. In fact this was the only way to obtain renewed financial support from shareholders who hesitated more and more to subscribe to and invest in the multiple increases of capital. On 15 December 1930 the firm was converted into a limited company. This legal form was very difficult to adopt and the decision was enforced by the Thalmann Bank as a condition of its support. In order to make the change the Bouilhet family was compelled to separate from the Champetier de Ribes family, which represented a high financial cost. Furthermore it had to put an end to its traditional relations with the families of long-time shareholders, for example the Dubufe family.

This new development, i.e. a bank taking a large majority stake in the company, was a complete shock. The long-standing shareholders lost their position, and from this time one majority shareholder assumed responsibility for the firm's management. All this took place when the enterprise, for the first time in its history, was unable to pay dividends. Cause and effect were obvious.

This exceptional situation finally came to an end in 1940. The Thalmann Bank went bankrupt and sold back its shares to Tony Bouilhet, who then became the majority shareholder of Christofle. A new era began for the firm, one which scarcely conforms to the Chandler model.[18]

[18] A. D. Chandler, Jr., *The Visible Hand* (Cambridge, Mass., 1977; French edn. Paris, 1988).

Table 4.5. *Christofle's profit and loss account: turnover
and profits, 1985–93* (francs)

Year	Turnover	Profits
1985	562,700,000	18,878
1986	526,700,000	−6,080,000
1987	530,900,000	5,451,000
1988	597,698,000	21,179
1989	649,000,000	15,800,000
1990	662,000,000	69,714,000[a]
1991	650,000,000	−6,800,000
1992	621,820,000	−39,500,000
1993	530,000,000	−60,000,000

[a] 9,848,000 frs. omitting the proceeds of a property
transaction.

From 1940

After the Second World War Christofle's position was much more
straightforward because the founders' heirs retained the majority of the
capital. For the first time since its foundation, the enterprise conformed to
the narrowest definition of a family firm. The Bouilhet family and their
related partners, holding most of the capital, also controlled and managed
the firm. The presence of important shareholders was not significant.
At best, a limited collaboration with certain shareholders was made
within a defined commercial and industrial strategy. This was the case
in 1990, for example, when the Taittinger group obtained a 10 per cent
stake. Nevertheless, the financial situation has deteriorated since 1989,
the financial year closing with deficits of about 40 million francs in 1992
and 60 million francs in 1993 (Table 4.5). The firm accumulated considerable debts (over 200 million francs). Unable to recapitalize the
enterprise, the Bouilhet family allowed the firm to plunge into this
crisis because they put undue stress on the maintenance of its familial
character. The Taittinger group, eager to take advantage of the situation,
was allowed neither to increase its stake in the company nor to develop
commercial and industrial alliances. At the end of 1993, bankers and
financiers put pressure on the family to resign. The firm changed hands.
The Borlettis had once saved Christofle in 1930. In 1993 a new generation
did the same thing, when Maurizio Borletti became chairman and
invested a considerable amount of capital, with the help of Hermès
(Figure 4.2).

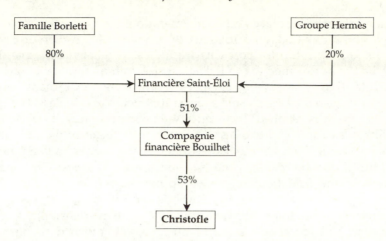

Fig. 4.2. *Christofle's capital structure, 1993*

3. THE MANAGEMENT STRUCTURE

Under Charles Christofle's direction

When he founded Christofle Charles was its only effective manager, making all the decisions. The rapid growth of the firm, the opening of markets abroad, sometimes in distant countries, and the building in 1854 of the Karlsruhe factory made it necessary for him to devise a more elaborate organizational structure. Charles implicitly recognized this when the shareholders complained of unsatisfactory financial results in the early 1850s. He then explained that the many actions he had had to bring for counterfeiting occupied much of the time he should have spent on running the firm and controlling all aspects of business. For example, a dishonest bookkeeper was alleged to have embezzled some money without his noticing it. The shareholders were rather reluctant to let Charles manage the firm alone so they made him pay dearly for it. The bookkeeper's embezzlement was consequently deducted from his wages. At this time the firm did not have a formal management structure.

However, two men occupied important—if not precisely defined—functions. To a certain extent they could be called Charles Christofle's co-managers. We know something about one of them, Jules Gouré. He certainly performed managerial duties while appearing to be a senior partner as well. He appears to have served as acting manager in Charles's absence. But the latter most importantly maintained his control and insisted on making all decisions, even when he was kept away from the firm. When Charles attended London's Great Exhibition of 1851 there was a daily correspondence with his co-manager. Gouré informed Charles about manufacturing and commercial operations, giving, for example, full details about day-to-day instructions to commercial travellers in France and abroad. By return of post Charles indicated what managerial decisions had to be executed to run the enterprise. In the same way, when the Karlsruhe factory was about to open, Gouré went to Germany to find retailers prepared to sign a sole agency contract. Nevertheless, the management in Paris retained the authority to sign contracts. In 1853 Henri Bouilhet was appointed to assist his uncle at the head of the firm. Until Charles's death Henri kept to his restricted role as a chemical engineer in the firm, a domain in which he excelled, unlike Charles, who had no expertise in this field. Bouilhet made improvements to the manufacturing processes and supervised, under Charles's control, the initial production in Karlsruhe. Christofle's laboratory was also his responsibility and, in particular, he supervised Gaston Planté, the distinguished chemist and inventor of the lead accumulator, who began his career with the firm.

Thus, it is clear that there was no real division of authority during the first decade. This was even more the case after 1854, when Charles Christofle was authorized to act as sole manager of both the Paris and Karlsruhe factories. The shareholders decided to increase his wages to 10,000 francs per annum in view of the additional responsibility involved.[19] However, the difficulties in communicating between Paris and Karlsruhe compelled the *gérant* to yield to the facts. In 1860 Christofle recruited an Austrian silversmith, Karl Forst, as director of the Karlsruhe factory. In this way an informal hierarchial organization began to emerge.

Under Charles Christofle's successors

After Charles Christofle's death in 1863 his successors continued to follow his policies and in 1866 a subsidiary company opened in Vienna. Its director was placed under Karl Forst's direct supervision, which broke with the long-standing cultural values of the firm. Paris no longer directly controlled both factories. This new organization lasted until 1916, when the Karlsruhe factory closed down.

More than a decade passed before it became necessary to devise a new structure for the firm with a board of directors. This coincided with the starting up of a second factory at Saint-Denis and the purchasing of a third one in Paris. The new organization was the result not merely of the growth of the firm but also of the dispersion of the industrial plants. Neither the annual turnover nor even the number of employees increased significantly (cf. Table 4.6). The different products of the several factories encouraged the creation of a hierarchical organization. Consider, for example, the position in 1890, when an organizational chart might be

---

[19] This simple fact also indicates the shareholders' confidence in Charles Christofle.

Table 4.6. *Christofle's turnover, 1846–1990* (francs)

Year	Annual turnover
1846	1,569,053
1850	2,524,060
1855	5,026,097
1860	6,295,027
1865	7,788,882
1870	3,345,015
1875/6	9,396,248
1880/1	9,299,391
1885/6	8,341,065
1890/1	11,009,795
1895/6	9,705,201
1900/1	9,426,442
1905/6	10,329,415
1910/11	11,254,360
1915/16	4,878,474
1920/1	23,308,949
1925/6	52,216,000
1930/1	38,673,936
1935/6	23,767,000
1938/9	41,789,258
1945	27,666,323
1951	1,717,242,000
1955	1,360,649,000
1960[a]	17,620,247
1965	32,361,926
1970[b]	83,200,000
1975	172,400,000
1980	378,800,000
1985	562,700,000
1990	662,000,000

[a] Nouveaux francs.
[b] Consolidated.

drawn as in Fig. 4.3. Karl Forst had full management control of the German-Austrian undertaking. Paris only supervised decisions after their execution. The Saint-Denis factory exercised two distinct activities. One concerned nickel metallurgy. The other involved the manufacture of nickel silver flatware. One managing director and two co-directors were recruited at Saint-Denis. The Paris undertaking, which was exclusively a silversmith's factory, was also managed by a director who appeared to exercise a supervision over Saint-Denis as well. The Cheron company,

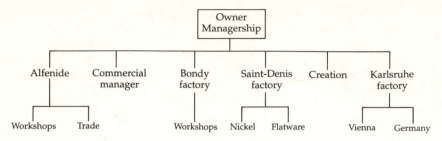

Fig. 4.3. *Christofle's simplified organization chart, c.1890*

purchased in 1877, also needed a director, whose responsibilities were increased with his appointment as commercial and technical manager of the Alfenide company after 1888. From 1900 onwards he assumed additional managerial functions, with responsibility for the Gallia production, which was then a newly launched trade mark of Christofle.

These outside managers were essentially recruited from the same circle. Henri Bouilhet and his cousin Fernand Champetier de Ribes, who were engineers from the École centrale de Paris, preferred to appoint graduates from this school. This was certainly the case with the directors of the Saint-Denis factory and of the Alfenide company. At the end of the 1890s a new managerial function, that of commercial manager, was created. One may infer that this followed the firm's good trading results. Nevertheless, one should not assume that Christofle's *gérants* experienced a diminishing authority during these decades. While there is little information about the relationship between them and their managers, there can be little doubt that all operational decisions affecting the firm remained their responsibility, given their close involvement in its several activities.

The inter-war years

At the end of the 1920s, Christofle faced difficulties which forced the family to allow a bank to buy into the firm's capital. The banker demanded that his own partners be entrusted with key managerial positions in the firm. This reorganization was all the more easily introduced, since the enterprise had been rationalized around only one factory—that at Saint-Denis. A new organizational structure was adopted, which emanated directly from the shareholders—the Thalmann Bank in this particular case. It took the form of an Executive Committee (Comité de direction) which met every week and *de facto* ran the firm. All other members, except Tony Bouilhet, were representatives of the Thalmann Bank.

This situation lasted until the Second World War. Then the Bouilhet family, in the person of Tony Bouilhet, reasserted the family ownership and management of Christofle.

Today

It was not until after 1945 that a modern type of managerial structure was put in place. Nevertheless, this remains limited. In fact, during the 1980s the company was managed by three Bouilhet brothers. Albert entered the firm in 1954, and was chairman from the end of the 1960s. Henri was director for new products and communication from the mid-1960s. Marc joined in the early 1980s as marketing director and, up to 1992, was intended to be the next head of Christofle. A directorate of five, recruited exclusively from the family, supported them. A radical change to the management structure took place in 1993. The new chairman, Maurizio Borletti, has appointed an independent management team, and the family has been excluded. The general manager is the first to have been appointed, having been recruited from the luxury industry. His remit is to introduce further radical changes.

4. CONCLUSION

This study prompts us to ask two questions. The economic development of Christofle was interrupted at the beginning of the twentieth century. Was the familial character of the firm responsible for this situation, thus acting as a brake on its growth? Is the sphere of activities of the firm, i.e. the luxury industry, correlated with the persistence of its familial character? This industry has specificities, such as not being very capital-intensive or highly technological, but requiring instead a very high level of skill. Can this be put forward as an explanation for the strong familial structure prevailing in luxury firms? The changes experienced by this industrial sector raise the question of the ability of family firms to maintain the prominent role which has been theirs for decades.

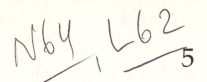

5

Standard Motors 1945–55 and the Post-war Malaise of British Management

NICK TIRATSOO

1. INTRODUCTION

In 1945 many informed commentators expected great things of Standard Motors. Indeed, the company was often rated the most progressive of the 'big six' car manufacturers, with an innovative and dynamic managing director in John Black, a modern plant at its Coventry headquarters, and a highly promising production strategy. Within ten years, however, all this early optimism had evaporated. Standard was now known to be in trouble, a situation that eventually led to its take-over by Leyland.[1] How had defeat been snatched so quickly from the jaws of victory?

According to the historian Paul Thompson, Standard's problems (like those of other Coventry firms) originated on the shop-floor.[2] In the post-war period, Thompson argues, managers and workers throughout the Midlands city colluded in maintaining a factory culture which was highly antipathetic to technical innovation. Local trade unions were especially culpable here, he insists, because they continued to reinforce the neo-Luddite views of their members, rather than adopt the more enlightened, modernizing strategies allegedly being pursued by equivalent organizations in countries such as Italy. The consequences at Standard and elsewhere in Coventry were inevitable. As Thompson graphically puts it, those employed in the local car factories 'helped to dig the pit for their own burial'.[3]

This analysis is open to criticism on matters of detail, not least because

The research upon which this chapter is based was completed while its author was attached to the Business History Unit at the London School of Economics. I am grateful to the director of the Unit—Dr Terry Gourvish—for his hospitality, encouragement, and advice. I am also indebted to Jim Obelkevich, Jim Tomlinson, and various participants at the 1992 BHU Anglo-French Conference for stimulating observations on some of the points raised.

[1] Standard's search for partners during the 1950s and its eventual take-over by Leyland are well described in G. Turner, *The Leyland Papers* (rev. edn., London, 1973), 26–43.

[2] P. Thompson, 'Playing at Being Skilled Men: Factory Culture and Pride in Work Skills among Coventry Car Workers', *Social History*, 13 (Jan. 1988), 45–69.

[3] Ibid. 67.

its author chooses to base his judgements solely on interviews with local workers, and ignores a rich diversity of written evidence (including the very full Standard archive).[4] Nevertheless, the central point advanced cannot be ignored, simply because it reappears in so many of the other local and national studies relating to the 1940s and 1950s. Standard itself has been written about from a number of quite different perspectives, yet most of these accounts are at least consistent with Thompson's broad conclusions.[5] Moreover, many general surveys of Britain's post-war economic performance emphasize the widespread and damaging incidence of labour inflexibility and restrictionism.[6] It is, perhaps, tempting to see Standard's demise as the perfect illustration of a more general national failure to grapple with one particular kind of institutional blockage.

However, though such an interpretation may appear rather seductive, it is highly misleading and needs to be firmly rejected, as this chapter will show. Standard's difficulties did not originate on the shop-floor, but for the most part stemmed from boardroom decisions. Furthermore, the weaknesses evident at the company could also be observed elsewhere, sometimes with similar consequences. The problem here, it will be argued, was not idiosyncratic ill judgement, but rather part of a wider malaise that had developed amongst British industrial leaders, a malaise that concerned the very notion of what management meant. In what follows, attention is first focused on the Standard company itself and then on the overall context. A final section examines how some contemporary reformers attempted to deal with the whole question of management inadequacy, and asks why their efforts mostly failed—an inquiry that inevitably raises, as will become apparent, matters of politics.

2. THE STANDARD COMPANY

Towards the end of the Second World War, John Black decided that export markets would rapidly increase with the peace and that Standard should have a production strategy to match.[7] The need, he felt, was for high-

---

[4] Thompson's reliance on interviews (and, more particularly, on interviews with workers alone) leads him to concentrate almost exclusively on labour process questions, as if these were the only ones of relevance in a business at this time. His unwillingness to use written sources is all the more surprising given the richness of the Standard Motor Archive at the Modern Records Centre, University of Warwick (MSS 226).

[5] See *inter alia* W. Lewchuk, *American Technology and the British Motor Vehicle Industry* (Cambridge, 1987), esp. 195–202; S. Melman, *Decision Making and Productivity* (Oxford, 1958); and S. Tolliday, 'High Tide and after: Coventry's Engineering Workers and Shopfloor Bargaining, 1945–80', in B. Lancaster and T. Mason (eds.), *Life and Labour in a Twentieth Century City: The Experience of Coventry* (Coventry, n.d.), esp. 208–15.

[6] For this literature, see T. Nichols, *The British Worker Question* (London, 1986).

[7] The following description of Standard's production strategy summarizes points made in my 'The Motor Car Industry', in H. Mercer *et al.*, *Labour Governments and Private Industry* (Edinburgh, 1992), 162–85.

volume output of one model aimed specifically at the overseas trade. This
led him to secure the lease of the giant and very modern Banner Lane
'shadow factory' which Standard had operated during the war, and begin
development work on the export car. At this point, Black was introduced
to Harry Ferguson, an Ulsterman who had invented a revolutionary tractor system, whereby attached tools were controlled from the cab via
hydraulic transmission. Ferguson's machine had been made in the USA
by Ford, but he was now in dispute with the American manufacturer and
needed to find a new producer. The upshot was a deal between Standard
and Ferguson, with the former agreeing to assemble tractors which the
latter would market. Specifically, Black decided to concentrate car production at Canley (the company's original factory) and re-equip Banner
Lane for tractors. The aim, it was agreed, should be a daily output of 1,000
units, 500 cars and 500 tractors.

Black recognized that his strategy was something of a gamble, but he
also noted the many outside observers who judged it one worth taking.
The *Financial Times*'s laudatory conclusion was fairly typical: 'the entry of
the Standard Motor Company into the tractor field represents big business.'[8] Nevertheless, by the early 1950s, it was becoming clear that the
managing director had not, after all, been able to realize his ambitions.
Standard was, superficially, a reasonably prosperous company—indeed
net profits had increased from £283,463 in 1945/6 to £886,259 in 1953/4—
but the surface impression masked a number of deeper problems. Thus,
car production at Standard had continued to generate only minimal returns—a mere 2.9 per cent of overall profits in the very bad year of 1954,
for example.[9] Furthermore, the tractor business was also disappointing in
these terms. As *The Economist* later concluded, the Ferguson product provided a 'bread and butter staple', but the butter was 'spread thin'.[10] All of
this meant that Standard's overall margins per unit produced remained
comparatively very low: returns for 1954 showed Black's company earning £6. 2s. per vehicle against comparative figures of £37. 7s. for Ford and
£62. 10s. for Vauxhall.[11] In this situation, it was clear that Standard would
not be able to match the massive investment programmes that its competitors were increasingly adopting in order to maintain market share.[12] Ru-
mours abounded about mergers, with Rover, Rootes, and eventually
Leyland named as possible predators. What had gone wrong?

[8] *Financial Times*, 8 Oct. 1945.
[9] Standard Motor Company Archive, Modern Records Centre, University of Warwick,
MSS 226/ST/3/RT/1/43, p. 11, table headed 'Turnover and Profits'. The full figures for 1954
were as follows: passenger cars (home): turnover £11.46m., profits nil; passenger cars (ex-
ported): turnover £11.91m., profits £65,000 (2.9% of overall profits of £2.27m. on an overall
turnover, including tractors, spares, service, etc., of £52.03m.).
[10] *The Economist*, 17 Jan. 1959.
[11] MSS 226/ST/3/RT/1/9, table headed 'Comparative Unit Margins. 5th May, 1955'.
[12] For these programmes, see e.g. *Statist*, 23 Oct. 1954, which quotes Ford announcing a
five-year £65 million expansion plan.

A number of authorities have argued, to repeat, that the company's difficulties originated on the shop-floor, yet there is, in reality, little evidence to support this assertion. Black had a relatively liberal attitude towards labour, introducing the 'gang system' and paying high wages, which has led some to present a picture of growing shop steward power and inflated labour costs. However, a close examination of Black's strategy shows that the balance of advantage from his innovations certainly lay with the company, a point he himself frequently underlined.[13] Offering good earnings meant that Standard could employ who it wanted, whenever it wanted them—a not inconsiderable advantage in an industry where demand fluctuated, and in a city where labour was extremely scarce. Moreover, there were also beneficial effects on the general industrial relations climate at the company. Disputes and strikes damaged some of Standard's competitors in Coventry at this time, but were unknown at either Canley or Banner Lane until 1956, a significant achievement given that the company instituted several bouts of short-time working, redundancies, and important restructurings of working methods during the intervening years. Finally, there is little doubt that Black gained what was, after all, the main objective of his strategy, namely higher productivity. Under the 'gang system' groups of workers were divided into teams, set production targets, and then left largely alone to achieve them, being paid according to how well they performed. In such a situation, there was an obvious incentive to work harder and more efficiently, and this is exactly what seems to have happened. A *Financial Times* reporter who visited the company in 1948 was certainly impressed, concluding that: 'Productivity at the tractor factory has been steadily increasing, and throughout the Standard organisation is higher than it has ever been.'[14]

In fact, the problems that emerged for the company in the early 1950s had much more to do with poor commercial performance than anything else. The key point about Standard's main motor vehicle product (the Vanguard), for example, is that it was never produced at anything like capacity levels. This meant restricted economies of scale and a high sales price, factors which reinforced each other in a self-perpetuating vicious circle. Why was the company unable to escape from this trap? In part, restricted output reflected difficulties over obtaining raw materials and components, a situation that plagued many manufacturing companies at this time. On the other hand, there can be no doubt that the Vanguard sold less well than it might have done because of various design weaknesses. Black had planned the car around an engine he could also use in the Ferguson tractor, and little thought was given during the subsequent production run to the specific features of the markets that Standard wanted to sell in. Vanguards shipped to Belgium, therefore, were quickly

---

[13] See e.g. C. Chisholm, 'Sir John Black', *Business* (Jan. 1948), 59.
[14] *Financial Times*, 20 Dec. 1948.

found to have inadequate suspension for that country's cobbled roads, while those driven in South Africa became notorious for their lack of dustproofing. By the early 1950s, as a consequence, it was becoming clear that many overseas customers had become distinctly disenchanted with Standard products.[15]

The problems experienced with the Ferguson tractor had somewhat different origins. Standard found, first, that the cost of developing the machine was very much greater than had been anticipated, largely because of inadequacies in the technical drawings and specifications supplied by Ferguson himself. Black's bigger difficulty, however, was about price. At the time of the original deal, Black had been very impressed with Ferguson's enthusiasm about their future prospects and this had led him to quote the Ulsterman a figure which included very little profit for Standard, in the hope that as production increased, and costs fell, margins would improve. Yet this scenario did not develop as expected, since tractor sales continued to be below predicted figures. Moreover, Ferguson proved unwilling to renegotiate basic terms: he made most of his profit, apparently, on implements, and was prepared to use the tractor as something of a loss-leader in his vendetta with Ford. The great things expected for Standard from the tractor deal, therefore, never really materialized.

Obviously, some of Standard's troubles in these areas were due to bad luck and the difficulties in the wider economic environment. However, the company's predicament also reflected poor decision-making, particularly on the part of Black himself. Before looking at these errors in detail, it is necessary to explain how the company functioned at executive level during these years. The formal situation was that Standard, like every other public concern, had a board which was supposed to decide on major policy questions. Nevertheless, actual power in the company was very much concentrated on only one of its leading figures, the managing director. Black was one of Standard's major shareholders,[16] but his authority rested more on force of character and charisma than anything else. He had, anyway, as an admiring journalist explained, 'personal and centralised control', which was reminiscent of 'the almost patriarchal . . . old family business, rather on Ford than Forsyte lines'.[17] Typically, few board meetings were held with all the members present: as many as forty-two of the fifty-seven that occurred in the crucial months of policy formation between September 1945 and December 1946 involved only Black and the chairman.[18] Of course, this situation was not without its advantages for

---

[15] See e.g. M. Adeney, *The Motor Makers* (London, 1989), 207.

[16] In 1954 Black (singly, with his wife, or with others) was the second biggest of Standard's major stock-holders, owning over £67,000 worth of shares. This was probably about 1% of the company's total paid-up capital. See MSS 226/ST/3/RV/1/1, Letter, Registrar, Barclay's Bank, to K. Aspland, 29 Mar. 1954.   [17] Chisholm, 'Sir John Black', 58.

[18] Calculated from attendance notes in the Standard board minutes, MSS 226/ST/1/ 1/9–10.

the company, especially since it allowed speed of reaction. On the other hand, there were clearly few safeguards or checks and balances in operation, and much depended on the managing director making correct decisions at the first time of asking. Unfortunately for Standard, it gradually became evident that Black was in several ways ill-suited to cope with the kind of responsibility placed on him.

Black saw his role at Standard in terms of providing leadership and he believed that this meant, above all, being decisive. 'There comes a time', he told the periodical *Business*, 'when *a* decision is better than *the* decision.'[19] From these precepts, Black had evolved a management style that was both dynamic and authoritarian: his word, once articulated, had to be followed.[20] However, the managing director was by nature an extremely temperamental man and so the fiat of one day, laid down with considerable zeal, could easily be overturned the next.[21] Moreover, Black's forcefulness was hardly helpful when it came to considering some of the complex technical problems that were at the heart of vehicle production. Black had trained as a patents lawyer, served in the Tank Corps during the First World War, and been involved as an executive in car production since 1929, but he had no engineering or design qualifications.[22] He placed great faith in his own practical knowledge of the industry and was loath to accept advice from specialists, especially if it clashed with his own instincts. Consequently, important decisions could be made on the spur of the moment without consideration of detail, very much to Standard's disadvantage.

The Vanguard story, of course, illustrates this point. A more blatant example still occurred over the Mayflower car. At the end of the 1940s Black came to the conclusion that Standard should produce a smaller accompaniment to the Vanguard, aimed especially at the American market. He therefore ordered that such a vehicle should be built and christened it, amid much public relations pomp, the Mayflower. The car was shipped to America, but it soon became clear that Black's predictions about its success there were not going to be fulfilled. The Mayflower reflected the managing director's whims but, being conceived without any market research data, kindled little interest amongst American consumers. The result was that the car apparently 'sold by the half dozen' in its targeted market and ended up costing Standard a considerable amount of money.[23]

---

[19] Chisholm, 'Sir John Black', 59.

[20] Black was not afraid of criticizing any of the Standard executives, no matter how senior: see J. Wood, *Wheels of Misfortune* (London, 1988), 120.

[21] 'Black was not only a dictator, but an unpredictable one as well': Turner, *Leyland Papers*, 28.

[22] Chisholm, 'Sir John Black', 59, and MRC MSS 226/ST/3/JB/2/4/1 (profile of John Black).

[23] R. Langworth and G. Robson, *Triumph Cars: The Complete 75-Year History* (London, 1979), 146–56.

Black's weaknesses were also apparent in his dealings with Ferguson. He had originally agreed to produce tractors over La Grouse d'Écosse and Mumm Cordon Rouge 1928 at Claridges in September 1945.[24] Ferguson was a persuasive potential partner, apparently having friends in high places, and endlessly referring to the great significance of his invention (he coined the slogan 'Agricultural Revolution or Communism'[25]). A measure of his persuasiveness was the fact that Black quickly agreed to tool-up Banner Lane for production at 500 units per day, though this ambitious target figure was suggested by Ferguson with only minimal justification.[26] However, Black soon recognized that the Ulsterman was less trustworthy than he seemed. Ferguson was caught lying to Civil Servants and journalists about the likely price of the Standard-made tractor. Furthermore, when the drawings for the machine's engine finally arrived at Banner Lane, they turned out to be only 'a rough sketch which was not an engineering provision', again exposing Ferguson's assurances.[27] Nevertheless, all of this did not prevent Black from concluding a formal ten-year agreement with Ferguson in August 1946, nor moreover from initialling a contract which a leading lawyer subsequently judged 'vague, uncertain and incomplete'.[28]

Over the following years the Black–Ferguson relationship continued to follow a stormy and argument-ridden pattern, with each man intent on outmanœuvring the other. Sometimes Black would feel that the tractor deal might be Standard's salvation—he even considered turning the company wholly over to tractors in mid-1947[29]—yet there were other phases when Ferguson became almost too much of an irritant.[30] The final act in this saga came in 1953.[31] Without any warning, Ferguson suddenly sold out to Massey-Harris. This appeared to put Standard in a strong position. Massey-Harris had bought Ferguson without realizing that it was only a marketing organization, and now approached Standard to renegotiate the manufacturing contract. Black was instructed by his board to play for time: there were only two years of the original deal struck with Ferguson to run, and Massey-Harris would be hard pressed to find alternative facilities for production, so that Standard might well be able to pressure their new partner into very advantageous terms. However, Black once again ignored the advice of his colleagues and signed an agreement with

[24] Wood, *Wheels of Misfortune*, 118–19, and MSS 226/ST/3/F/1/12 (Claridges' Menu).
[25] See material in MSS 226/ST/3/F/1 and 2.
[26] See Public Records Office, London, SUPP 14/866, Letter, F. C. Limbrey to W. S. Williams, 31 Jan. 1949.
[27] MSS 226/ST/3/F/3/4/2, Memo, 'The Agreement between the Standard . . . Co. and Harry Ferguson Ltd.', 18 May 1946, p. 1.
[28] MSS 226/ST/3/F/12/1, J. Gazdar, 'Counsel's Opinion' [n.d. but 1953].
[29] MSS 226/ST/1/1/10, Special Meeting, 1 May 1947.
[30] See e.g. material in MSS 226/ST/3/F/3.
[31] The following account is based upon MSS 226/ST/3/F/8/4, 'Draft', 2 Feb. 1959, pp. 1–2, and MSS 226/ST/3/F/8/6/1, 'Notes', 13 Feb. 1959, pp. 2–3.

the Canadian company which included a clause reducing the price of tractors supplied to them by £20 per unit, a concession worth £1.25 million a year. Black was repeating his earlier gamble on a fast increase in output, but this never came. Furthermore, Massey-Harris did not pass on the price reduction to their clients, which meant that, as a Standard internal document later concluded, 'in two years Massey-Harris had bought Ferguson for nothing'.[32] Goaded by these events, the rest of the Standard board finally lost patience with Black and in a carefully planned coup had him replaced.[33]

What all of this shows is that Standard's difficulties had very little to do with attitudes and actions on the shop-floor, but rather stemmed from mistakes and miscalculations that were made in the boardroom. Black's overall commercial and production strategies were clearly sensible ones given the character of post-war markets, and were recognized as such by contemporaries.[34] Nevertheless, they were betrayed in execution, as has been shown, and this eventually led to the managing director's downfall. The problem in the end boiled down to the fact that Black's management style and range of competences remained inadequate, especially given the complexities of the business he was involved in. No amount of forceful leadership could make customers like poorly designed products. Nor could bluster alone match the scheming of the wily Ferguson.

Of course, it is tempting to conclude from this that the whole episode should be seen in entirely personal terms—that the company's crisis was a unique event, simply caused by the defects of one particular ego. However, widening the focus reveals that such an assessment would be mistaken. Black's attitudes and weaknesses in relation to management were more typical than might be imagined and cannot, therefore, be ascribed simply to his personal character traits. Moreover, there is evidence, too, that the consequences which stemmed from this particular approach could be as damaging elsewhere as they became at Standard. Some companies were certainly in very good health during the post-war years, but others were beginning to display symptoms of the pathology that has been outlined above. Each of these points can be amplified by looking at the contemporary business and management press.

3. THE WIDER CONTEXT

There is no doubt that British managers of the 1940s and 1950s generally felt uneasy about providing abstract definitions of their vocation. *The Economist* noted in 1949: 'Management, as a whole, is still not as clear about, or as interested in, the nature of its own functions as is the case, for

---

[32] MSS 226/ST/3/F/8/4 'Draft', p. 2.   [33] Turner, *Leyland Papers*, 28–9.
[34] See e.g. *Investors Chronicle*, 13 Nov. 1948.

instance, in the United States.'[35] Nevertheless, despite this lack of reflection and systematization, most knew quite well what the nature of executive responsibility meant. The key characteristic of management, it was believed, must be the provision of leadership in the enterprise. Managers, in this conception, were akin to the classic generals of antiquity, leading their armies into battle. They would need a range of skills, certainly, but there was no doubt which was the most significant. As a relatively liberal and well-informed company chairman explained:

Techniques are of great importance in industrial management but . . . when all is said and done, they are only tools—essential as such, but nevertheless only instruments and means to an end. Management itself is something more than its tools. It is the successful use of all these techniques. And this involves other qualities besides an appreciation of the nature of the tools. It is now fashionable to speak of these other qualities as 'leadership'.[36]

Typically, therefore, when the journal *Future* asked in 1951 what attributes a 'random selection of business managers' were looking for in their successors, most chose answers which reflected their belief in the importance of the leader role:

From a choice of three in order out of a list of nine, 'character' came out a good first with 76 (not out of 100, of course, but just over 300), with 'leadership' (66) second, followed by 'technical knowledge' (63), 'ability to get on with others' (51), 'length of service with firm' (20), 'educational background' (20), and 'age' (13).[37]

Quite logically, given the strength of feeling on this point, there was also much concern during these years about influences that might blunt management's ability to perform its essential calling. One anxiety related to the possibility of being over-educated for the job. Good management, many believed, was a matter of flair or perhaps experience, and it could not be learnt by conventional study. There was frequent reference in some quarters to the saw that 'a manager is born not made', whilst elsewhere stress was placed on the beneficial effects of 'the school of hard knocks'.[38] On the other hand, few were prepared to defend management education. Another part of the *Future* survey already mentioned accurately summarized prevailing preferences:

A strong bias was noticeable . . . in favour of practical rather than bookish training . . . Champions of wider academic training for business and new commercial degrees . . . would be surprised by some of these comments. The value of 'psychological' selection tests was pretty conclusively rejected—only 14 per cent in favour . . . Similarly, outside training bodies, such as the Henley Staff College in

---

[35] *The Economist*, 14 May 1949.
[36] *Manchester Guardian Review of Industry* (Jan. 1951), 33.
[37] Anon., 'Managers of Tomorrow', *Future*, 6 (Aug.–Sept. 1951), 53.
[38] See e.g. Anon., *A History of the Institute of Industrial Administration 1919–51* (London, 1954), 150.

this country . . . were not much better favoured. Forty-seven per cent were against them, with 29 per cent 'don't knows'.[39]

In these circumstances, advocates of formal education not unnaturally often appeared highly defensive. A young manager who was asked by one journal to describe his eighteen months at the Harvard Business School in 1949–50 could thus begin his piece with the blunt recognition that '[most] British industrialists would say I have wasted my time'.[40]

A second area of concern related to the whole question of consultation. Managers believed that, in the exercise of power, it was always necessary to be decisive. Lord Nuffield summed up his management credo in a way that would have found much agreement amongst other executives: 'Y'know . . . when I have to sit around a board table and listen to what the majority decides, I'm finished. My best decisions are made in one minute.'[41] Accordingly, it was imperative to ensure that the chain of command stayed clear, and did not become entangled in unnecessary deliberations. With this in mind, therefore, most managers remained at least suspicious of reformers who argued that trade unions should be brought into policy formulation. As a director of Dunlop somewhat airily declared, 'the modern tendency of those who had never managed any-thing to insist upon what was called "a share in management"' could only be seen as an 'irritating development':

Management was a job which had to be learned, and it was not so rapidly acquired as the ability to lay bricks . . . Management was not a right to be demanded, but a distinction to be learned and a responsibility to be borne.[42]

At the same time, many agreed that technical experts, too, should be kept firmly in their rightful place. The correct prescription was outlined by the 1950 Federation of British Industries (FBI) president, who argued that 'the specialist should be on tap but not on top'.[43] The consequences of any other arrangement were quite evident elsewhere in Europe, a point the experienced industrialist and politician Oliver Lyttelton made to the *Director* in late 1950:

I have had, in my life, considerable contact with German industry, and I think they had one underlying fault. They had a tendency to put technicians at the head of great businesses. The Germans are hard working and their technical people are highly equipped, but neither workers nor technicians are equipped to be the head of businesses and many of their weaknesses arose from this fault.[44]

From this evidence, it seems fair to conclude that Black's attitudes to

[39] Anon., 'Managers of Tomorrow', 53.
[40] M. George, 'Can Business "Know How" be Taught at University?', *Business* (Dec. 1950), 41.
[41] Anon., 'Morris Motors Ltd.', *Fortune*, 34 (July 1946), 93.
[42] Quoted in *Industry*, 15 (July 1947), 13.   [43] Quoted in *Business* (Jan. 1951), 33.
[44] O. Lyttelton, 'Pitfalls in Company Organisation', *Director*, 2 (Dec. 1950), 38.

management were widely shared. A similar point can be made about his day-to-day competences and weaknesses. Black was, as has been shown, an intensely practical manager, who had little time for theorizing about decisions. This led him largely to ignore questions like design, for example. Many other managers in Britain at this time displayed similar orientations, as informed commentators continued to point out.

4. A PATTERN OF WEAKNESS

The trouble, according to the critics, started even before the manufacturing process began. Few companies, especially in export markets, used any kind of market research to gauge the contours of demand.[45] Instead, most depended in relation to this issue (as so many others) on the 'feel' of the leading executive. Ford was the first British car company to introduce product planning in 1953, having up to that date utilized a rather more intuitive approach:

The managing director would simply call in his key men—the engineer, the production boss and so on—and tell them 'I want a new car in two years' time, about the size of the Morris Minor. We'll want 400 a day, the weight should be perhaps 1,600 pounds, the engine displacement 800 to 1,000 c.c., acceleration from 0 to 60 in 26 seconds and a touring fuel consumption of 40 plus. Now I want some styling and engineering ideas from you. Let's meet again in a month's time.'[46]

Such methods were certainly very common in much of British industry long into the 1950s.

On top of this, it was argued that there were some major flaws in the way many firms organized production itself. Most managers prided themselves on being able to do any job in their particular line of manufacture. On the other hand, few did much thinking about the more abstract aspects of the processes they controlled. British industrialists were notorious for their lack of numeracy: they had, according to several witnesses, 'a horror of statistics'.[47] Moreover, they often remained obsessed with the intricacies of producing, and were loath to consider how activity on the factory floor fitted in with other aspects of the business. As a result, one sympathetic observer noted in 1945, 'many branches of management technique' were at 'a very early stage of development', and this included 'the general use of statistical methods in industry, quality control, capacity utilisation, stock control, progressing and many other functions sometimes lumped together under the general term "production control"'.[48] Furthermore, there were a series of common blind spots when it came to

---

[45] Editorial comment, *BETRO Review*, 3 (Mar. 1949), 280.
[46] G. Turner, *Cars* (London, 1965), 19.
[47] O. W. Roskill, 'Business and Businessmen, Part One', *Scope* (Sept. 1945), 56.
[48] O. W. Roskill, 'Business and Businessmen, Part Three', *Scope* (Nov. 1945), 69.

thinking about the product itself. *Future* pointed to one such lacuna in an article of 1949:

Prejudices in industry die hard. One which has been a particularly long time in fading away has been the idea that the finish of an article can be dealt with as an afterthought. A finish, runs the argument, is at best a pleasent, final flourish which you put on an article to make it attractive to the buyer. At worst, it is something put over the top to hide blemishes. The idea that a finish has an important part to play is only now beginning to receive wider acceptance.[49]

Finally, to the critics at least, the weaknesses of the established conventions regarding management thinking were equally observable in relation to the whole question of selling. The common focus on the intracacies of production, allied to the distrust of professional as opposed to practical expertise, meant that few British industrialists took much interest in what went on at the point of sale. Many were ignorant about the price consumers paid for their products, especially if the market was overseas.[50] Moreover, few seemed to care about how goods were presented: British lines were usually 'offered for sale rather than sold'.[51] The predominant attitude amongst those exporting reminded one authority of a restaurateur he had known, who displayed a sign reading 'Be courteous to the waiters, customers are easier to get than staff.'[52] The British Export Trade Research Organization (BETRO), a body formed by some big companies and supported with government money,[53] was a constant campaigner on this issue, but by 1949 had to recognize that much still remained to be done in encouraging more enlightened attitudes:

It needs to be asked . . . how far British exporters are adapting their methods to local conditions . . . It would be satisfactory, as a start, to be able to report that manufacturers were putting at least as much effort into their selling in foreign markets as they are in the home market. Unfortunately, there are very few markets and very few products of which this statement is true. It is certainly not true of the United States and Canada. If British manufacturers paid no greater attention to the requirements of the home market than they give to the requirements of the American market, they would soon be out of business even in this country.[54]

Given these weaknesses in management attitude and aptitude, it was inevitable that other companies would experience the kind of difficulties that were becoming apparent at Standard in the post-war years. After 1945, the Government pressed British industry to export at all costs, using quotas and raw material rationing to enforce its will. In broad terms, the result was an overwhelming success story, with many companies

---

[49] Anon., 'Finishing the Product', *Future*, 4 (Aug. 1949), 67.
[50] Editorial comment, *BETRO Review*, 3 (Feb. 1949), 248.
[51] Editorial comment, *BETRO Review*, 4 (Sept. 1949), 79.
[52] Anon., 'The Technique of Market Research Part Five', *BETRO Review*, 1 (Oct. 1946), 109.
[53] On BETRO, see H. Wilson, 'Know your Markets', *BETRO Review*, 3 (Aug. 1948), 78.
[54] Editorial comment, *BETRO Review*, 4 (Sept. 1949), 79.

reconquering overseas markets and making considerable amounts of money as they did so. However, it was increasingly evident that, in many sectors, British dominance had not been very securely established. The country's goods were accepted by foreign consumers while they had few other choices, but there was little enthusiasm about buying British. Indeed many such customers continued to complain about the shoddy quality or the backward design of what they were being offered.

5. THE CRITICS' CASE

Criticism of British export products began to be heard as early as 1946, with *Business* condemning the 'multitude' of manufacturers who were 'cashing in on a sellers' market abroad at any price' and thereby doing the country's name 'untold' damage.[55] Thereafter, items such as the following—on 'The Egyptian Market: Limitations and Prospects'—became ever more common in the specialist press:

It is unfortunate that British exporters are now rapidly getting a name for default-ing on delivery, and although the quality of goods in general remains high, they are often considered antiquated in design and pattern.[56]

In fact, the issue became something of a cliché in some business papers, commented on with alarming frequency. Friends of Britain, such as the American Chamber of Commerce in London, pleaded for the country's manufacturers to change their ways. What was needed was some recognition of the consumer, wherever he or she might be, and some thought about how products could be tailored to local needs. In one episode, the managing director of Time-Life International was brought to London in order to inform British businessmen about why they were in danger of losing American markets. His observations included the following:

Another problem is the apparent difficulty of adapting yourselves to our national habits of merchandising and selling. To us, in our economy of highly competitive plenty, the planning and technique of selling are as important as the planning and technique of manufacture. So just as we grant you your precision in manufacture, please grant us our precision in selling and meet us, at least, half-way when we set deadlines for delivery, designs, specifications, etc.[57]

However, much advice of this kind seems simply to have been ignored, on the grounds that as long as British goods were selling, everything must be satisfactory. Certainly, BETRO continued to maintain a highly critical and pessimistic attitude about British exports, concluding in 1950, for example, that the situation had become almost irreversibly bad:

[55] Editorial comment, *Business* (Sept. 1946), 35–6.
[56] Anon., 'The Egyptian Market . . .', *BETRO Review*, 2 (July 1947), 40.
[57] Anon., 'How Can I Sell to Oshkosh, Wis?', *Anglo-American News*, 15 (June 1948), 236–7.

There is a disturbing flow of comment from customers and British residents abroad that the much-lauded British quality is a thing of the past. Performance, durability and finish—particularly finish—are all involved. It has reached the point where those who attempt to justify British prices in terms of British quality are now likely to encounter the horse-laugh.[58]

Clearly, what was true of the Standard Vanguard was also true of many other British products, with the same consequences for the firms that produced them. The rot was most evident in the export trade, though it would, of course, in time spread to the home market as well.

The conclusions that emerge from the preceding survey are, therefore, very different from those proposed by authorities like Thompson. As has been shown, the problem with much of British industry in the immediate post-war years was not labour intransigence but management malaise. Too few of those at the top in business really knew their jobs. Too many believed that the provision of 'leadership' was the universal panacea. Looked at in a different way, the country was being pulled down the slope of industrial decline by its managers, not propelled there by obstructive workers.

6. THE CHALLENGE TO REFORM

However, there is one further question that requires attention if the events described are to be made fully comprehensible. It is clear that many in the business community were fairly complacent after 1945. Nevertheless, as has been indicated, there were also critics of this complacency, who continued to be vocal on the subject of management malpractice. The dissidents do not appear to have had much impact—a point that is also evident from the preceding discussion—and it is obviously necessary to ask what explains their failure. Before confronting this issue directly, more detail needs to be provided on the substance of the critics' case and the activities that flowed from it. In practice, this means focusing on the Labour governments of 1945–51. Others (like BETRO) were prominent in the campaign to change attitudes, but it was the Attlee administrations that were most coherent and active on the subject of management reform.

Labour came to power in 1945 with a strong conviction that Britain's industry needed modernizing.[59] Many of the new Ministers had gained first-hand experience of business backwardness during the war, and it was generally agreed that over the following years private enterprise could not be left to repeat its past mistakes. A continuation of existing

---

[58] Editorial comment, *BETRO Review*, 4 (Mar. 1950), 211.

[59] Labour's commitment to industrial modernization at this time is explored more fully in N. Tiratsoo and J. Tomlinson, *Industrial Efficiency and State Intervention: Labour 1939–51* (London, 1993).

inadequacies would threaten the country's very survival. Anyway, welfare reform, even more the creation of the socialist commonwealth, could not occur in times of material scarcity. As Morrison explained in mid-1945, 'without a policy which went to the roots of economic and industrial affairs, to talk about food, houses, work and social security would be meaningless'; it was impossible to get 'a quart of Socialist prosperity out of a miserable pint capitalist pot'.[60]

In policy terms, such an analysis indicated the need for action on a number of fronts. Considerable effort would need to be expended in creating a positive macro-economic environment. However, success at this level would not, of itself, be enough. For much, obviously, depended on the attitudes of entrepreneurs: they might respond to general promptings, but past experience suggested that other, more conservative, reactions were equally likely. There was a strong requirement, therefore, for micro reform. Old patterns of management thought and practice must be discouraged, to be replaced with modern habits and techniques. Specifically, this meant discouraging long-established 'father to son' management dynasties and replacing them with a new, highly trained, and technically proficient cohort of executives. As Cripps argued, amateurism must become a thing of the past: 'Management should now be a profession; there is really no more right for an unqualified person to manage a factory than for an unqualified doctor to perform an operation.'[61] The outcome of these perceptions was a programme carefully fashioned to ameliorate management standards. Some of the constituent policies were concerned with spreading existing 'best practice', and involved, for example, getting tripartite working parties to draw up comprehensive reports on a range of specific industries. Other measures aimed at fostering wider consultation in the factories, in order to develop a new spirit of co-operation and creative endeavour. Finally, there was an important direct assault on the perceived nub of the problem, using the newly established British Institute of Management (BIM).

The idea for a centre promoting good management had originally been floated in Dalton's Board of Trade during the war. Civil Servants and politicans drafted into industry control at this time were frequently shocked by the business standards they encountered, and from this arose a feeling that reform was necessary. Some suggested using an existing management organization as the nucleus of a new, evangelizing agency, but closer investigation revealed that such an option was not viable. The British management movement had staggered on during the inter-war period and was still functioning. However, it remained deeply divided and, anyway, completely irrelevant to most in executive positions—only an 'infinitely small' proportion of the country's managers were involved.[62]

[60] *Daily Herald*, 23 May 1945.   [61] *Manchester Guardian*, 6 Nov. 1944.
[62] Editorial comment, *Industry Illustrated*, 11 (Aug. 1943), 11.

The need, therefore, was for an entirely new organization, created and funded by the State, and this was finally realized after Labour came to power with the launching of the BIM in 1948. Henceforward, Britain was to have an 'organizer and spearhead' of progressive management practice, operating on the basis of Cripps's maxim that 'the man who is really successful is the one who has studied and worked hard at the job'.[63]

Labour's programme was obviously innovative and for a time Ministers felt quite confident about its prospects. Some informed observers were certainly very impressed at the administration's will to succeed, with *Industry Illustrated* concluding: '[there] can be no question of the present Government's serious determination to make British Industry the most efficient . . . possible.'[64] Nevertheless, as the years passed, it was more and more evident that the policies were not working as planned. Each had produced a degree of change, but all were disappointing when judged against their original objectives. The Government had not, at any rate, been able to transform British industry. What explains this relative failure?

No doubt some of Labour's difficulties were self-inflicted, because specific measures were either poorly planned, badly executed, or insufficiently harmonized with other government aims. Moreover, the general conditions prevalent in industry between 1945 and 1951 were hardly propitious for the kind of change Labour wanted. Industrialists had been told to concentrate on output at all costs during the war and received similar instructions throughout the subsequent export drive, which inevitably encouraged a neglect of non-manufacturing questions.[65] The shortages of the post-war period worked in a similar direction. Some executives claimed they spent all their energy chasing up materials and had no time to consider questions like design.[66] On top of this, the rise of labour during the war clearly heightened management anxieties and encouraged the existing predilection for authoritarianism within the firm. 'Leadership' in some cases filled the place once occupied by the 'stick of unemployment'. Finally, the sellers' market itself could easily promote complacency about new methods. As the BETRO journal bluntly remarked in 1949: 'very few firms are yet facing bankruptcy because they cannot pitch their salesmanship high enough.'[67]

Each of these factors inevitably made reform difficult. However, Labour also had to face more direct opposition to its programme of measures. A number of authorities, including Blank, Finer, and Streat, have argued that business for the most part co-operated with the governments of 1945–

---

[63] Anon., 'British Institute of Management', *Industry*, 16 (Apr. 1948), 17.
[64] Editorial comment, *Industry Illustrated*, 13 (Dec. 1945), 11.
[65] F. C. Hooper, 'The Problem of Selling Overseas', *Industry*, 16 (May 1948), 15–16.
[66] Anon., 'The Technique of Market Research Part Five', 109.
[67] Editorial comment, *BETRO Review*, 4 (Sept. 1949), 79.

51, but, as Mercer has recently pointed out, this interpretation is at least questionable, having been undermined by the release of new archive material.[68] Certainly, in terms of the issues being considered here, a more realistic assessment would be that business was very hostile to Labour objectives and actively tried to neutralize them, as the following brief discussion will demonstrate.

Many in the business community approached the 1945 General Election recognizing that major issues about the future were at stake. The *Financial Times* underlined the importance of the contest: 'The choice is between nationalisation, with multifarious controls and regimentation, and individualism and enterprise, with broad guidance from above.'[69] Thus, when Labour won, the dominant reactions in business circles were ones of shock and fear. The Stock Market, it is true, accepted the result with equability, but in boardrooms the mood was very different. The *Financial Times* noted the 'apprehension' which 'afflicted a wide area of private enterprise' in the weeks following the contest, while the journal *Business*, in an edition of early 1946, referred to a 'wave of anxiety' that was 'passing over British industry'.[70] The issue was clear. Labour, the business community believed, might say any number of different things about its plans, but there could be no doubt that the Government's final objective remained full-scale ownership and control of manufacturing. As a leading figure in the Federation of British Industries later remembered, the 'concept of a mixed economy that has since become reality was not at that time within the imagination of industrial people; they thought there would turn out to be no halfway house between complete socialism and complete private enterprise'.[71]

During the following years, there were times when such fear and animus seemed to have subsided. An article published by *Business* in mid-1946 spoke of the 'platonic friendship' that had developed between industry and Government. A year later, City financiers were confident enough privately to patronize Labour Ministers:

The rather odd ideas of Sir Stafford Cripps were dismissed as the peculiar notions of an intellectual Wykehamist. Even Dr. Dalton has not, in spite of his public speeches, completely dissipated the good will due to one who is both competent and an old Etonian.[72]

Nevertheless, dislike of Labour was never far below the surface in these circles, and, as the 1950 General Election approached, once again became

---

[68] H. Mercer, 'The Labour Governments of 1945–51 and Private Industry', in N. Tiratsoo (ed.), *The Attlee Years* (London, 1991), 71–89.

[69] *Financial Times*, 6 June 1945.

[70] Ibid. 14 Aug. 1945; C. Chisholm, 'What Business Wants in 1946', *Business*, (Jan. 1946), 33.

[71] N. Kipping, *Summing up* (London, 1972), 16.

[72] T. Creevey, 'Business at Westminster', *Business* (Aug. 1946), 59; A. Maude, 'Eastwards from Temple Bar', *Future*, 3 (1947), 80.

highly visible. Private enterprise felt it had been constantly maligned, as an editorial in one relatively liberal business journal explained:

For years a spate of inspired propaganda has been flowing unchecked amongst the people, fed by soap-box oratory and bar-parlour or barrack-room prejudice no less than the printed word, and all designed, directly or indirectly, to denigrate organised business. Its language is emotional generalisation, and it is fond of glamorous and half-understood words like 'junta', 'cartel' and 'tycoon'. 'Profit' is the eighth deadly sin.[73]

Moreover, the argument ran, however Labour's actual record since 1945 was assessed, in future it would without doubt become far more extreme. The party remained irreversibly anti-business, the *Director* believed, and was now committed to 'some drastic measures'.[74] Given such feelings, the eventual result of the election produced a great satisfaction in many boardrooms. As *Scope* reported, there was 'intense relief . . . in the business world' over Labour's near defeat. One year later, similar emotions greeted the final demise of a government which, the *Director* judged, had ruled with 'near totalitarian despotism'.[75]

Business, it can be concluded, did not like Labour between 1945 and 1951. However, it is important to stress that for many this was not just a question of attitude but also of action. One facet of the new-found commitment was a growth in business interest groups. During the early years of the war, there were probably 130,000 to 140,000 separate industrial units in Britain, most of which were completely unorganized. Indeed, it was estimated that only 10,000 had joined any of the trade or 'peak' associations.[76] By contrast, reports made after 1945 presented a very different picture. Business organizations themselves had become better run, with higher-quality staff and a greater knowledge of Whitehall ways.[77] More importantly, individuals were showing a much greater propensity to combine collectively. FBI membership doubled between 1942 and 1950, which meant 6,226 firms and 278 trade associations were enrolled at the later date. Meanwhile, other umbrella organizations, like the National Union of Manufacturers, also prospered. The trend even galvanized institutions that had been previously moribund, so that, after the Institute of Directors was relaunched in 1948, its membership grew in three years from 'a handful' to around 5,000.[78] Furthermore, it is clear that many were prepared to go beyond mere organizing, and there was a definite move

[73] Editorial comment, *Future*, 5 (Feb. 1950), 2.
[74] Anon., 'If the Socialists Win . . .', *Director*, 1 (Feb. 1950), 52 and 54.
[75] Anon., 'Directors and the New Parliament', *Director*, 1 (Mar. 1950), 51.
[76] Anon., 'No Common Aim', *Scope* (Sept. 1942), 24.
[77] See e.g. Anon., 'The F.B.I. Pt. 1', *Scope* (Sept. 1949), 48–55 and 77–8; and Anon., 'The F.B.I. Pt. 2', *Scope* (Oct. 1949), 49–50.
[78] Anon., 'No Common Aim', 24; *The 34th Annual Report of the F.B.I.* (London, 1950), 1; Anon., 'The F.B.I. Pt. 1', 52; Anon., 'What Does the Institute of Directors Do?', *Director*, 2 (Aug. 1951) [n.p.].

towards more active forms of intervention. Money poured in to support
Economic League and Aims of Industry propaganda campaigns on behalf
of private enterprise.[79] At the same time, attempts were made wherever
possible to undermine government policies through the use of procedure,
obstruction, or innuendo. To illustrate how these campaigns worked,
reference need only be made to the saga that enveloped the BIM.

The Government's announcement that it was to form the BIM met with
a great deal of enthusiasm in management movement circles. *Industry
Illustrated* commented: 'The plan . . . has a positive air about it . . . is sponsored by a very determined member of the Government and above all . . .
has substantial Treasury backing.'[80] Elsewhere in business, however, attitudes remained very much less positive. Many felt that the BIM would be
the thin end of a socialist wedge: a management institute might or might
not be a good idea in theory, but if the State was involved, private enterprise would be inevitably threatened. In this situation, organizations
such as the Industrial Management Research Association (IMRA)[81] began
lobbying to minimize the BIM's status and impact.

Pressure was exerted in a number of different ways. Businessmen were
advised not to help in the organization's creation, for example, so that the
Government had great difficulty in finding either a chief executive for the
BIM (the eventual appointee was an assistant secretary at the Board of
Trade and gentleman farmer) or members to serve on its ruling council.[82]
Subsequently, a whispering campaign, which extended to North America,
was responsible for the resignation of the BIM's deputy director, who was
accused of having written for 'Communist Papers'.[83] Alongside all of this
was a more public campaign of denigration. Thus, letters to the press from
allegedly informed insiders frequently implied that the BIM was cor-
ruptly run. One correspondent to the *Director* in 1950 wrote of an 'extrava-
gant new bureaucracy' which was 'unloved and unwanted', and asked
questions about the organization's accounts. 'The public' was very concerned, he continued, because the BIM had become 'far too closely linked
with the worse phases of Socialist policy'. A little later, the *Sunday Express*
reported that industrialists were receiving two-page typewritten letters

[79] For which see e.g. Anon., '12, Carteret Street', *Scope* (May 1948), 76–82.

[80] Editorial comment, *Industry Illustrated*, 14 (Apr. 1946), 11.

[81] IMRA (previously Management Research Group No. 1) was a loose aggregation of firms
that met together regularly to discuss matters of mutual interest. IMRA members included
Babcock and Wilcox, Boots, Bristol Aeroplane, Courtaulds, Dunlop, Imperial Tobacco, Lever
Bros., Pilkington Bros., Rowntree, Standard Telephone, Tootal Broadhurst Lee, and United
Steel.

[82] *Tribune*, 23 Jan. 1948; editorial comment, *Industry*, 15 (June 1947), 12; Management
Research Group Papers, LSE, Box 15, Note of 6 Aug. 1947; and Anon., 'The Director of the
British Institute of Management', *Industry*, 15 (Aug. 1947), 15 and 20.

[83] Piercy Papers, LSE, 15/13 pt. i, copy of letter to Russel, 1 June 1949; and Management
Research Group Papers, LSE, Box 15, 517, 'Notes by the Secretary for the E.C. on 24/11/
1949', p. 8.

attacking the BIM on a similar theme ('Here indeed is another groundnuts scheme').[84] Elsewhere, the criticism was that the organization was being run by 'quacks'.[85]

Of course, not every attack aimed at the BIM had its desired impact, but there can be no doubt that major damage was inflicted. The chief executive recognized that 'serious resistance based on suspicion and prejudice' had defeated key measures designed to build up influence.[86] The truth of this evaluation could be seen in the BIM's financial situation at the beginning of the 1950s. The Government had initially agreed to finance the BIM for five years, arguing that industry should show its support for the new organization by eventually providing full funding. Yet, as *The Economist*, amongst others, pointed out, such an outcome had not occurred: in the early 1950s the BIM still needed extensive Treasury support, with business subscriptions only accounting for around half of annual expenditure.[87]

7. CONCLUSION

Taken together, the observations offered over the previous pages may, therefore, be summarized as follows. It is apparent that some British firms did very well in the post-war years and reacted positively to the new market environments. However, others, like Standard, were less successful (whatever the superficial signs). Their difficulties stemmed from a number of factors, no doubt, but it is possible to distinguish a common and very damaging set of deficiencies in commercial strategy. The myopia here stemmed from flaws in the company decision-making process. Most British industrialists—in public and private concerns—continued to believe in a highly autocratic style of management. Moreover, the pervasive ethos amongst business leaders valued practical skills, especially those connected with 'making', over abstract reflection. In these circumstances, the use of specialists in such subjects as marketing remained rare. The '"fools paradise" of a sellers' market', as the president of the Board of Trade, Harold Wilson, called it, reinforced short-sightedness.[88]

Critics were aware of the pattern of failings, but found it very difficult to correct them because of another particular feature of the post-war world—the highly politicized nature of the business community. Business in Britain had not been bowed by the war (as in France, Germany, and Japan). On the contrary it emerged in 1945 with an enhanced sense of its

---

[84] *Sunday Express*, 26 Oct. 1952.

[85] A. Godfrey Croft, 'A Plea for Creative Management', *Industry*, 17 (Apr. 1949), 170–3.

[86] Piercey Papers, LSE, 15/3 Pt. ii C (50) 34 25/10/1950, Memo by director, 'Financial Policy', 13.

[87] *The Economist*, 18 Oct. 1952.   [88] Wilson, 'Know your Markets', 78.

own importance, a set of well-defined (if usually negative) political objectives, and various institutions able to ensure that these were enforced.[89] This meant that reforms, so long as they came from a Labour government, would almost always be rejected.

The real origins of the post-1945 'British disease' were, to conclude, very different from those proposed by writers who are critical of labour. The country had, certainly, been dealt a great blow by its involvement in the war. However, its recovery was impeded, and deliberately so. The problem was not intransigence on the shop-floor but rather ill-equipped industrial leadership. The twin features of management that have been identified in this chapter—its style in the firm and its attitude to politics—proved to be a particularly damaging combination.

[89] See also, on this point, L. Johnman, 'The Labour Party and Industrial Policy, 1940–5', in Tiratsoo (ed.), *The Attlee Years*, 29–53.

PART II

EDUCATION AND TRAINING

6

French Influences on Technical and Managerial Education in England, 1870–1940

MICHAEL SANDERSON

> French views on Technical Education may be said to demand
> attention . . . we may well look to France for some light on a subject to
> which the state, in conjunction with the best authorities of the country
> has devoted close attention for more than 20 years.
>
> (C. C. Perry, 1898)

As Britain faced economic competition from industrial rivals in the later
nineteenth century so she looked inward to supposed defects of her own
education as a cause of retardation. She also looked outward to other
countries to learn from their educational arrangements. Germany was
seen as the exemplar for technical and scientific education and America
for business. Yet the educational relations with France have been much
less emphasized.[1] Unjustly, it may be argued, since the French experience
has had a pervasive and sometimes decisive influence in the areas of
technical, vocational, and managerial education in England.

In some ways this may be surprising since the image of France and
French education was a poor one. At its worst François Crouzet character-
izes the distorted English view of France as 'an economically backward,
poor, dirty country . . . [with] a uniform educational system which
was stifling'.[2] It was criticized as over-centralized, over-bookish, in-
culcating a too docile spirit, and too little concerned with physical and
moral development.[3] Sylvaine Marandon studying the Victorian image of
France likewise found that 'il apparaît très clairement qu'en ce qui
concerne notre École les stéréotypes sont contre nous.' Yet paradoxically

Part of the material in this chapter derives from wider research on technical school education
supported by funds from the ESRC (R000231860) which I gratefully acknowledge.

[1] W. H. G. Armytage, *The French Influence on English Education* (London, 1968) is an
exception.

[2] François Crouzet, 'Problems of Communication between Britain and France in the Nineteenth and Twentieth Centuries', in *Britain Ascendant: Comparative Studies in Franco-British
Economic History* (Cambridge, 1990), 481.

[3] P. G. Hamerton, *French and English: A Comparison* (London, 1889).

English visits and inquiries into French education were 'très largement favorables'.[4]

It was quite reasonable for Englishmen to look to France. France had a long tradition of excellence in scientific and technical education from the *grandes écoles*, the École des ponts et chaussées (1715) and the École des mines (1783), the École polytechnique (1794) and the École centrale des arts et manufactures (1828–9).[5] This was well appreciated in Britain. Charles Kindleberger observes that 'French technical and scientific education had always been of a high standard' whereas England was 'slow in responding to the widely recognised need for more technological education'.[6] Second, even the casual observer could admire French excellence as a pioneer of 'new' technological industries especially from the 1890s. France was the leading European producer and world exporter of motor cars, the world's leading producer of aeroplanes and exporter of films before 1914. The nation that produced the Renault taxis that plied the London streets, the Pathé films in her cinemas, radium, the Blériot flight, and Eiffel's great iron tower had to be taken seriously and the four International Expositions from 1867 to 1900 emphasized the glories of technology to her European neighbours.

Thirdly and more subtly we are now aware that the American tradition of post-1945 historiography denigrating France's slow growth and economic backwardness is greatly exaggerated. O'Brien and Keyder have shown that contrary to expectation labour productivity in French industry was above British levels for most of the nineteenth century until the 1890s.[7] And even in the period before the First World War, 1895–1913, when French productivity was lower, it was still growing at a faster rate (14 per cent) than the British (3 per cent). French industrial goods embodied a higher degree of labour skill than most British industry. O'Brien does not draw any connection between labour productivity and educational levels. But it was not unreasonable for the observant Englishman to admire the products and the labour and respect France's education also.

1. THE PARIS EXHIBITIONS

The major event which initiated French influence on English technical education was the Paris Exhibition of 1867. Whereas England had won most of the prizes at the Great Exhibition of 1851 she won only ten of the ninety classes at Paris, and the Paris displays suggested the great ad-

[4] Sylvaine Marandon, *L'Image de la France dans L'Angleterre Victorienne* (Paris, 1967), 435.
[5] Rondo Cameron, *France and the Economic Development of Europe 1800–1914* (Princeton, NJ, 1961), ch. 3.
[6] Charles P. Kindleberger, *Economic Growth in France and Britain 1851–1950* (Cambridge, Mass., 1964), 152–3, 159.
[7] Patrick O'Brien and Caglar Keyder, *Economic Growth in Britain and France 1780–1914* (London, 1978), 148–51, 163.

vances in Continental industry compared with British in recent years. Education was seen as the chief reason for this; indeed their historian has suggested that 'education was the fetish' of these exhibitions.[8] Lyon Playfair, who had been a juror at the 1851, 1862, and 1867 Exhibitions, noted on his return that 'the one cause upon which there was most unanimity of conviction is that France [and others] possess good systems of industrial education for the masters and managers of factories and workshops and that England possesses none'.[9] It was fair to reply that many British industries had not exhibited in 1867, that Playfair was only a professor of chemistry not a manufacturer or craftsman, and that it was absurd to suggest that France was yet the equal of Britain as an industrial nation. Yet much attention was also paid to the reports of committees of artisans sent to Paris—the real experts.[10] Their critical evaluation found Britain still superior to France in many industries but praised the design of French furniture and cabinet-making, ironwork and silver, and most dangerously found the French superior in fine textiles—ribbons, silk, lace, the lighter woollens, and dyeing. Most tellingly, 'in the admission of the general deficiency of the technical knowledge of our best workmen they [i.e. the visiting artisans] nearly all agree'.[11]

The shock of the Paris Exhibition set in train the series of governmental inquiries into technical education from the 1860s to the 1880s. In the first Bernhard Samuelson interviewed seven witnesses who had visited the Paris Exhibition or otherwise worked in France.[12] Fleeming Jenkin, the engineer, who knew France well, admired the *grandes écoles*, Polytechnique, Mines, Centrale, and the education of workmen. James Kitson so favoured the École des arts et métiers that he employed a manager from there. He also had a high regard for the education and quality of managers at Schneider's works at Le Creusot. Although some witnesses thought Playfair's views exaggerated there was a general agreement among six of the seven that France was superior to England in certain areas of managerial and workmen's education. The Devonshire Commission in the 1870s also paid attention to France and their view likewise was favourable.[13] The Conservatoire des arts et métiers was admired as a museum of applied industrial science which we lacked. The

[8] Paul Greenhalgh, *Ephemeral Vistas: The Expositions universelles: Great Exhibitions and Worlds Fairs 1851–1939* (Manchester, 1988), 18.

[9] Eric Ashby, *Technology and the Academics* (London, 1958). App. pp. 111–13 reprints Lyon Playfair's letter of 7 June 1867.

[10] *Reports of Artisans . . . to Visit the Paris Universal Exhibition 1867* (Royal Society of Arts, London, 1867); William Hawes, 'On the Reports of the Artisans . . . 1867', *Journal of the Society of Arts*, 16 (1867–8), 24 Jan. 1868; *Edinburgh Review*, 127/260 (Apr. 1868), art. iv, and 127/264 (Apr. 1869), art. iii.

[11] Hawes, 'On the Reports', 175.

[12] 1867–8, xv: *Report from the Select Committee on Scientific Instruction* (Samuelson), 'Minutes of Evidence', F. Jenkin, A. J. Mundella, J. Kitson, J. Platt, W. C. Aitken, C. Hibbs, H. Watson.

[13] 1872, xxv: *Royal Commission on Scientific Instruction and the Advancement of Science* (Duke of Devonshire), qq. 1063–5, 1615, 1706, 2401; 1874, xxi: app. iii, Norman Lockyer, 'Report on the Aid Given by the State to Science in France'.

grandes écoles met the usual approval and at a lower level the emphasis on careful drawing in French schools was seen as a useful basis for the technical education of workmen. The signals transmitted by the Devonshire Committee based on its French evidence were the desirability of more government support for science and strong higher education institutions devoted to science for industry, largely lacking in England at that time.

In 1878 another Exhibition was held in Paris and once again the Society of Arts sent artisans to report.[14] They were less concerned with education than they had been in 1867 but in the fullest passage J. W. Phillips praised the Boulevard Villette School for engineering apprentices in Paris. He regretted that there was nothing comparable in England. While he accepted that we relied on practical work in the factory for instruction yet he deplored that English workmen lacked the theoretical knowledge of their best French counterparts. This he saw as a factor in France's rapid catching up and one which would have adverse effects on England's trade. Other artisans discussing pottery, wood-carving, optical instruments, cabinet-making, and printing likewise made favourable comments about French education.

The governmental response to the 1878 Exhibition was Bernhard Samuelson's Royal Commission. This was deeply involved with France. He interviewed nineteen witnesses about France, toured French colleges widely, actually had a session sitting in Paris in 1881, and the First Report of the Commission was entirely about France. With the exception of the jaundiced testimony of Henry Chapman, a civil engineer who detested French engineering colleges as insufficiently practical, the witnesses were impressed with the usual things. They emphasized the superiority of French design especially for high-class goods, the higher technical education of foremen, and they were suitably reverential about the *grandes écoles*. They came to a sensible conclusion that French industry had not overtaken England but that such progress had been made with French technical schools that England had to remain watchful for 'the success which has attended the foundation of extensive manufacturing establishments . . . could not have been achieved . . . had it not been for the system of high technical instruction in these schools'.[15]

In the nearly twenty years between the Paris Exhibition of 1867 and the Samuelson Commission in 1884 English policy-makers had acquired a vast amount of data about French education and had learnt to admire quite a lot of it. This was enhanced in the early 1890s with the development of programmes for English students sent to French training

---

[14] *The Society of Arts: Artisan Reports on the Paris Universal Exhibition of 1878* (London, 1879), 268–76 and 32, 221, 426, 478, 500–3, 524.
[15] 1884, xxix: *Royal Commission on Technical Instruction* (Samuelson), 508.

colleges from 1893 and vacational language courses from 1894.[16] As a popularizer of France to the English reflected at the time, 'never in the history of the two countries did the two nations see so much of each other'.[17] So how did this affect education?

2. THE DEVELOPMENT OF TECHNICAL SCHOOLS

The implication of the reports on the 1867 Paris Exhibition was that England ought to develop technical schools or colleges in manufacturing towns. An immediate impact was on the city of Leeds. George Henry and Arthur Nussey, Leeds textile manufacturers, visited the Paris Exhibition to report on the textile displays and alerted their countrymen to the threat posed by French fashion fabrics.[18] They proposed and established a technical institution for weaving and designing to bring technical education to the masters and workmen of a conservative but backsliding industry. This, together with another College of Science, was a root of the subsequent University of Leeds.[19] Looking further forward W. H. G. Armytage sees a connection between reforms in the French universities in the 1890s and the creation of independent civic universities in England in the 1900s. In 1896 Louis Liard's reforms created a reformed University of Paris and fourteen provincial universities, many of which developed technological specialisms related to local industries.[20] In many ways they paralleled developments in England. The Liard reforms were well publicized in England, referred to in the debates about the creation of a modern teaching University of London, and mirrored in the granting of autonomous chartered status to six provincial civic universities in England between 1900 and 1909.[21]

Yet the French formation of entrepreneurs and technical professionals did not depend on universities. Fritz Ringer has shown that between 1830 and 1930 75.2 per cent of the French business technical élite had experienced some form of higher education but of those 80.6 per cent had attended the *grandes écoles* and only 18 per cent universities.[22] This was a

---

[16] 1897, xxv: *English Students at Foreign Training Colleges*; 1897, xxv: *Holiday Courses in France and Germany*.

[17] M. Betham-Edwards, *Anglo-French Reminiscences 1875–1899* (London, 1900), 303–4.

[18] G. H. Nussey and A. Nussey, *A Technical Institute for Leeds and District* (Leeds, 1867).

[19] P. H. J. H. Gosden and A. J. Taylor, *Studies in the History of a University 1874–1974* (Leeds, 1975), 83.

[20] 1898, xxiv: Louis Liard, *Les Universités françaises*, and its translation by J. W. Longsdon were published by the Board of Education. H. W. Paul, 'Apollo Courts the Vulcans: The Applied Science Institutes in Nineteenth Century French Science Faculties', in R. Fox and G. Weisz, *The Organization of Science and Technology in France 1808–1914* (Cambridge, 1980). See also G. Weisz, *The Emergence of Modern Universities in France 1863–1914* (Princeton, NJ, 1983).

[21] Armytage, *French Influence on English Education*, 68.

[22] Calculations by Fritz K. Ringer cited in Charles Kindleberger, 'Technical Education and the French Entrepreneur', in E. C. Carter, R. Foster, and J. N. Moody, *Enterprise and*

lesson we did not choose to learn: the concept of a stream of higher education superior to the universities producing a genuine élite for technology and industry. Robert Locke argues that we did well not to learn it. He points out that the Central School emphasized 'encyclopedic' knowledge, producing the all-round flexible industrial administrator (like Oxford and Cambridge) rather than the practical engineer with experience in actually constructing things. The Polytechnic too he criticizes as concentrating too much on civil and mechanical engineering to the neglect of the growth industries of chemical and electrical engineering.[23] Above all the level of mathematics was excessively high to be of use to practical engineers or businessmen (reminiscent of Cambridge). The post-1896 universities and their technology faculties had to offset the defects of and supplement the *grandes écoles* as our civic universities had to do the same for Oxford and Cambridge.

One major French influence was on the development of the technical school. A root of this was an institution with a French name but quite different purposes, namely Quintin Hogg's Polytechnic. The École polytechnique had been founded in Paris in 1794 as an élite engineering and military *grande école*. An English polytechnic had been opened in Regent Street in 1837 but had been run as a mixture of instruction and amusement before going bankrupt. It was this that Hogg bought in 1881. He had already been running a Youths' Christian Institute in Long Acre and transferred his premises to Regent Street. But the name long preceded Hogg and its pre-Hogg purpose bore no relation to its French namesake. Ethel Hogg noted that 'once settled into the Polytechnic, the great aim of its founder was to make it worthy of its name'.[24] Hogg developed more technical education at the Polytechnic but hardly of the high élite level of the Polytechnique. But the Polytechnic did develop technical and trade schools for teenagers and in this it received a boost from another part of the French system. Hogg himself does not seem to have been to France before 1881 but he did visit the Paris Exhibition of 1889 and indeed the Polytechnic arranged for over 3,000 students to do so.

The French had a very good system of technical schools for teenagers. There were the *écoles primaires supérieures* which had grown up in the mid-nineteenth century, been revived in the 1870s, and grown rapidly under the Ministry of Public Instruction to 450 by 1914. These were for 12–15-year-olds in applied science and workshop practice. Also the Ministry of Commerce ran seventy *écoles pratiques de commerce et d'industrie*, which dated from 1880, as apprentice schools. At a higher level were the six *écoles d'arts et métiers*, though lower than the École centrale and the Polytechnique. C. R. Day has claimed, 'certainly from the 1880s to 1914 the

Entrepreneurs in Nineteenth- and Twentieth-Century France (Baltimore, 1976), 32–3.

[23] Robert R. Locke, *The End of the Practical Man: Entrepreneurship and Higher Education in Germany, France and Great Britain 1880–1940* (Greenwich, Conn., 1984), 42–5, 48.

[24] Ethel Hogg, *Quintin Hogg: A Biography* (London, 1904), 144.

quality of French intermediate technical schools steadily improved; the schools were modernised and well equipped . . . and most of the technical schools, especially those of the Ministry of Commerce, were closely linked to industry'.[25]

This was admired in England and English observers saw a connection between France's excellence in engineering and her technical schools. Alfred Marshall observed, 'the engineering profession has been held in special honour in France; there is perhaps no other country in which the ablest lads are so generally inclined towards it'.[26] W. F. Stanley, whose tool and scientific instrument firm ran its own technical school, deplored that Britain was falling behind better-educated nations in scientific manufactures and in particular that 'two thousand taxi cabs have been made for London alone within two years by the French who have pushed practical education much further than we have'.[27]

Another observer described his first-hand experience of Parisian schools.[28]

The great industrial schools for boys and girls in Paris are models of thoroughness and efficiency. They are always full, and there is the greatest anxiety on the part of the children in the elementary schools to obtain one of the scholarships which provide for the three years course usually given. I have visited several of these schools at Paris, and in each of them I was told by the principal that the demand for the pupils is so great that before the course ends there are invariably requests from employers for many more children than the school can possibly supply. In the *école professionelle pour jeunes filles* in the Rue Championnet, I heard a lesson given, quite informally, to a large class of girls about fourteen or fifteen years of age, upon the distinguishing features of Norman architecture. I was shown afterwards how each girl had a kind of portfolio in which she kept notes and sketches of different designs from each of the periods of architectural art, which she used for embroidery or some other practical purpose. The intense thoroughness which characterises the work done in all the schools, the meticulous care taken over the smallest details, the keenness with which the children themselves work are signs that augur well for the future. In the École Boulle, the boys make their own machines, and the teachers are in many cases old boys themselves with the keenest interest in the success of the school. There is a really businesslike atmosphere about these schools, for the pupils execute orders for work coming from outside; they know the cost of the raw materials, and the price which their work will bring. In this country we are a terribly long way behind in the provision of opportunities such as those afforded by the schools to which I have referred.

The most influential vehicle through which British policy-makers learnt

[25] C. R. Day, 'Education for the Industrial World: Technical and Modern Instruction in France under the Third Republic 1870–1914', in Fox and Weisz, *Organization of Science and Technology*.

[26] Alfred Marshall, *Industry and Trade* (London, 1919; repr. 1927), 117.

[27] W. F. Stanley, 'Technical Trade Schools', in R. Inwards, *William Ford Stanley: His Life and Work* (London, 1911), app. i, p. 54.

[28] F. C. C. Egerton, *The Future of Education* (London, 1914), 145–7.

of French technical school education was through Robert Morant's study for the Board of Education's Special Inquiries.[29] 'One of the most crying needs of the present day', he claimed, was the need to continue 'beyond the elementary stage and in a *practical* direction, the education of the cleverest children of the working classes'. This France did with the state system of *écoles primaires supérieures*. Their aim was to provide 'hand and eye training and workshop practice as will engender habits of manual industry, increase dexterity and develop taste', or even more vocationally 'a thorough technical training in one of the industries of the district corresponding to a regular practical apprenticeship'. They were entered by examination but were free and provided a maintenance scholarship. They also acted as juvenile labour exchanges and most boys went into manual craft work. What Morant most admired was that the schools were 'an earnest effort at a social reform which recognises that the backbone of the nation is its class of manual workers, both in the fields and in the workshop'. Morant's study was reinforced in the next year by an excellent report on French technical education by C. C. Perry of New College, Oxford. He laid particular stress on the *écoles pratiques de commerce ou d'industrie* as filling the void left by the decline of apprenticeship. He also wrote passionately of the need to learn from the French and the need to make English education more practical and work-oriented.[30]

Two things were remarkable about the studies of Morant and Perry. First, Morant is often accused of being an academic élitist hostile to technical education or the working class, but this fervent belief in the national efficiency of technical training for skilled manual work was another dimension of his outlook. His French experience confirmed and enhanced this. Secondly, both reports carried through into English policy in an unusually direct way. It was in 1905 under Morant's permanent secretaryship of the Board of Education that the first regulations creating the junior technical schools were promulgated, the English equivalent in many ways of the *écoles primaires supérieures* which he admired. And it was still under Morant's tenure that the 1910 Education Act created facilities for vocational guidance in schools.

Another way of developing skill in the young worker in face of the decline of apprenticeship was the continuation school. This provided part-time education for young people in work, supplemented their work training, and extended their school education. France already had an active system with its *cours d'adultes* from 1884; then in 1887 the minimum age was reduced to 13, making them more for adolescents than their name implied. By 1905 there were 47,600 of these classes plus another 5,000 organized by the Bourses du travail and syndicats, drawing

---

[29] 1897, xxv: R. L. Morant, *The French System of Higher Primary Schools.*
[30] 1898, xxxii: C. C. Perry, *Report on French Technical Education.*

about a million pupils.[31] Strongly publicized in Michael Sadler's famous study, the French *cours d'adultes* contributed to that awareness in favour of continuation education which found expression in H. A. L. Fisher's Education Act of 1918. In the next year the French *loi Astier* of 1919 made it compulsory for all young people up to the age of 18 to attend technical classes.

These various forms of technical schools were generally admired and regarded by one English observer as 'productive of unmixed good, both to individuals and the nation'.[32] That they were effective may be indicated by another common observation of English inquirers of the time. This was that French skilled artisans' wages were notably lower than English, one estimate being that 'a French workman is paid from nine and half to ten per cent less than the English artisan'.[33] Yet certain features of the French economy make this surprising. It was a society of notoriously low population growth certainly not producing a glut of labour to drive down wage rates. Nor was it an economy experiencing a massive and rapid shift of labour from countryside to town as England was at this time. Secondly, O'Brien assures us that it was a high-productivity labour force, higher than England. Third, one would have expected it to be a labour force commanding higher wages to offset the high cost of living, including food, caused by French high protective tariffs again in contrast to Britain. Some force was driving down French skilled labour rates in spite of these forces moving in the opposite direction. It may be argued that this ready availability of technical schools was delivering a skilled labour force to the French economy cheaper than would otherwise have been the case, and cheaper than a less well-educated England enjoyed. Two pieces of circumstantial evidence also suggest this. First, the cheap attractiveness in England of products like the Renault taxis and French watches. Second, the consistent fear of and hostility to technical schools in England on the part of the English trade union movement. Perhaps they had only to look across the Channel.

3. THE EDUCATION OF BUSINESSMEN

The major French influence on English managerial education was through the London School of Economics. This began in 1895 as part of a wider concern about the education of businessmen.[34] In this the Americans were

---

[31] Georges Cahen, 'Continuation Classes and Social Education in France', in M. E. Sadler, *Continuation Schools in England and Elsewhere* (Manchester, 1907), ch. xxi. Edith Waterfall, *The Day Continuation School* (London, 1923), 22–3.

[32] *Reports of Artisans* (1867), Robert Coningsby, Special Report, 433.

[33] Ibid., Richard Whiteing, Special Report, 467–8.

[34] F. Hayek, 'The London School of Economics 1895–1945', *Economica* (Feb. 1946); Janet Beveridge, *An Epic of Clare Market: Birth and Early Days of the London School of Economics*

usually seen as the paragons, yet in the case of LSE the influence was clearly French. The immediate impulse was Viscount Bryce's 1892 testimony to the Royal Commission on the University of London. He described and praised the École libre des sciences politiques in Paris and called for a similar institution in the University of London, something between a Faculty of Law and of Economics and History.[35] The Commission was convinced, recommended London students to visit the École libre as postgraduates, and recognized the 'imperative and urgent need [for] this kind of education' in the University of London.[36]

The other shaping force was of course Sidney and Beatrice Webb and the £10,000 from Henry Hutchinson of which Sidney was a trustee. Sidney too admitted the French influence. He recalled: 'my wife and I resolved to ... start a centre of economic teaching and research in London on the lines of Paris.'[37] What Webb admired in Paris was not only the École des sciences politiques but the École des hautes études commerciales, and LSE was to fill both functions.[38] The Webbs, up to 1895, did not seem to have had much first-hand experience of France, though they had travelled elsewhere. Curiously, however, in October 1894, on the eve of the founding of LSE, Mlle Gaudier, a French investigator of women's work and education, stayed with the Webbs for three weeks, and it is inconceivable that they did not discuss Anglo-French educational matters.[39]

Webb's knowledge and enthusiasm for French commercial education was soon enhanced by the well-publicized International Congress on Technical Education in 1897. There Jacques Siegfried described France's higher commercial education and its eleven *écoles supérieures de commerce*, which he regarded as the best in the world. Siegfried also urged the London Chamber of Commerce to get involved in commercial education, a suggestion not lost on them or LSE.[40] When Webb spoke, a few days later, he was warm in his praise of France, the provincial *écoles supérieures de commerce*, 'turning out the most highly cultivated businessman', and the Paris École des hautes études commerciales.[41]

(London, 1960), 16, 49; Sir Sydney Caine, *The History of the Foundation of the London School of Economics and Political Science* (London, 1963), 37–8.

[35] 1894, xxxiv: *Minutes of Evidence Taken by the Royal Commission ... Draft Charter for the Proposed Gresham University of London* (Lord Cowper), Rt. Hon. J. Bryce, 8 Dec. 1892, qq. 16811–17; app. paper ii, École libre des sciences politiques Prospectus, 1892–3.

[36] 1893–4, xxxi (Cowper), pp. xlv and xlvi.

[37] Beveridge, *An Epic of Clare Market*, 49, citing a letter of 3 Jan. 1903.

[38] Sidney Webb, *London Education* (London, 1903), 124–5.

[39] Norman Mackenzie (ed.), *The Letters of Sidney and Beatrice Webb*, ii: *Partnership 1892–1912* (Cambridge, 1978), 26: Beatrice Webb to Mary Playne, ? Oct. 1894.

[40] *Journal of the Society of Arts*, 45 (1896–7), International Congress on Technical Education, Jacques Siegfried, 'Rapport sur l'enseignement supérieur en France', 30 July 1897.

[41] Ibid., Sidney Webb, 'The provision of Higher Commercial Education in London', 6 Aug. 1897.

Accordingly LSE was intended as a mixture of the political and commercial *grandes écoles* of Paris. Sir Sydney Caine suggests that the vaunted École des sciences politiques influence was exaggerated and its curriculum, 'formal, deeply impregnated with legal study', did not carry over.[42] LSE in practice became more of a commercial business school. But there was another French influence on LSE easily overlooked. The LSE taught medieval and early modern economic history in support of economic studies. For this they provided the best training in Britain in palaeography and diplomacy. As the director claimed, their activities undoubtedly formed the nucleus of an École des chartes.[43]

Webb had admitted that his knowledge of France was largely based on reading rather than experience. In particular he had read studies and reports by E. J. James, Eugène Léautey, and the Paris Chamber of Commerce. These items had been bought by Michael Sadler for the library in the Board of Education. It was all adding to the rapidly increasing educational intelligence in Britain about France. Sadler himself reinforced this with yet another study of French commercial education praising the 'admirable provision' of the École des hautes études commerciales.[44] This considerable publicity given to the French experience of the advanced commercial education of businessmen both helped to move LSE in this direction and underlay the proliferation of economics and business courses and degrees created in British universities in the 1890s and 1900s.

If LSE was one London institution trying in effect to be a Parisian *grande école* another was the Academy of Dramatic Art, the later RADA. The Paris Conservatoire was a training school for actors much admired in London and some bilingual English actors had studied there before 1914.[45] Herbert Beerbohm Tree, the leading actor-manager, opened his Academy in His Majesty's Theatre in 1904 and moved it to its present premises in Gower Street in 1905. There was debate whether Tree's Academy could really measure up as a London version of the Paris Conservatoire without state funding.[46] But Parisians took a generous view. Jules Claretie, the administrator of the Comédie-Française, congratulated Tree on his Academy as the English analogy of the Conservatoire.[47] This was premature praise but recognized what Tree was trying to do and what exemplar he was following.

[42] Caine, *Foundation of the London School of Economics*, 38.

[43] 1898, xxiv: W. A. S. Hewins, *The London School of Economics and Political Science*, 87.

[44] 1898, xxv: M. E. Sadler, *Higher Commercial Education in . . . Paris*.

[45] Michael Sanderson, *From Irving to Olivier: A Social History of the Acting Profession in England 1880–1983* (London, 1984), ch. 2.

[46] Richard Whiteing, 'How they Train Actors in Paris', *Nineteenth Century* (June 1904).

[47] H. Beerbohm Tree, 'The Academy of Dramatic Art', *Review of Reviews*, 29 (Jan.–June 1904), 509–10.

4. THE INTER-WAR YEARS

In the inter-war years English educationists took a close interest in developments in technical school development in Europe in general and France in particular. The First World War had blighted the often uncritical admiration for German education and, if anything, increased our regard for our French ally. It was well appreciated that our own trade and technical schools had owed much in their origins to French *écoles d'apprentissage* and *écoles des métiers*.[48] By the early 1930s there were over 27,000 young people aged 13–16 in various forms of technical schools in France.[49] The greater development of this form in France (and Germany) than in England was attributed to two factors. One was the slower and later transition from handicrafts to large-scale industry in France compared with Britain, the other the earlier acceptance in France of publicly funded and controlled education.[50]

Some Board officials wanted to see a more thriving sector of technical schools in England. Prominent among these was Arthur Abbott, the Chief Inspector of Technical Education, who had first-hand experience of Continental developments. He had attended the International Congress on Technical Education at Charleroi in 1925 and visited several technical schools in France and Belgium, finding the French *écoles professionelles du jour* a close match with the English junior technical school.[51] He had already acquired a high regard for such practical schools and an awareness of the greater industrial and less educational bias of such training compared with English schools.

Abbott reflected on recent developments in the relation of technical education to industrial employment and the contrast between England and France. Since 1902 more boys in England with secondary education were going into industry, and this blocked the traditional advancement of ex-elementary school leavers, who found themselves trapped at worker or foreman level. Abbott looked to technical schools for working-class children as the solution and looked to France with its *écoles d'apprentissage* and *écoles professionelles* as preferable to the English reliance on the night school. Abbott considered: 'it is not unlikely in my opinion that we in England shall be compelled to follow the example of other European countries and establish Trade Schools in considerable numbers.'[52]

Abbott accordingly proposed an extended trip around Europe to study

---

[48] *Report . . . on Secondary Education with Special Reference to Grammar Schools and Technical High Schools* (Sir Will Spens) (London, 1938), 82.

[49] Public Records Office, ED 121/247, figures on French technical education supplied to A. Abbott, 7 July 1932.

[50] *Memorandum on the Place of the Junior Technical School in the Educational System*, Board of Education Pamphlet No. 83 (London, 1930), 8.

[51] ED 121/54, International Congress on Technical Education, Charleroi, 1925.

[52] ED 121/247, A. Abbott, 'The Future Development of Technical Education', 9 May 1931.

trade schools. He was accompanied by J. E. Dalton, a staff inspector in technical education who, like Abbott, was competent in French and German. The trip received high-level co-operation from the Department of Overseas Trade and the Foreign Office, with ambassadors alerted and commercial counsellors asked to give assistance. They set off on 14 January 1932.

On 23 January Abbott reported to London from the Hôtel Moderne, Lille. They had made contact with M. Labbé, the Director-General of Technical Education, and had a good day at the École d'arts et métiers, which they found a 'first rate institution'. They were careful to establish links with businessmen over lunch at the Chamber of Commerce and at the Café de Paris, which 'lasted a very long time'. M. Gaillard of the Chamber of Commerce wanted to see some London trade schools—no doubt hoping for a reciprocal lunch. Gaillard gave Abbott a film about the *écoles de métiers*. They then staggered off to an École des vendeuses, where they were plied with port and liqueur chocolates, and thence on to a School of Joinery (more cakes and champagne). Abbott admitted having to help Dalton cross the street afterwards but reassured his London office, 'we work like beavers'.[53]

The outcome was actually the thoughtful and influential Board pamphlet on trade schools on the Continent which Abbott and Dalton published on their return.[54] A number of features about France interested them. They noted that French technical schools provided more workshop practice than in England, probably because many were established to train workers in artistic trades in Paris. Workshop work took up at least a half and sometimes more of the pupils' total time; such trade schools were 'in effect a part of the industrial rather than of the educational system'. Less emphasis was placed in France on part-time education for young workers than in England, though the French were moving more in this direction. The issue for Abbott was whether Britain should adopt the French system. He thought not. Britain did well to retain its emphasis on junior technical schools followed by part-time post-employment instruction, yet, as the French were adopting more of the latter, so 'we too should modify ours, but by a reverse process; that is by a considerable extension of full time pre-employment instruction to supplement our main system of part time training'. The French and Continental visits, while creating no desire to substitute one system for the other, undoubtedly reinforced the Board's technical division in its belief in the value of the JTS and the need to continue expanding them. In particular Abbott's French experience strongly confirmed his view that entry to JTSs should be no younger than 13, a contentious issue in the 1930s. Indeed, in rejecting an application to reduce the entry age to 11 he cited French practice, which also retained 13

[53] ED 121/247, A. Abbott to S. H. Wood, 23 Jan. 1932.
[54] *Trade Schools on the Continent*, Board of Education Pamphlet No. 91 (London, 1932).

for admission to technical schools.[55] This was significantly in the month following Abbott's visit to France.

Abbott kept up his French contacts shortly afterwards at the major conference of the International Bureau of Technical Education in Barcelona in 1934. He led the British delegation along with his successor as Chief Inspector of Technical Education, E. G. Savage. The French sent a massive delegation of 277 members, and spoke far more than any other. Abbott met up again with Edmond Labbé, the president of BIET and honorary Director-General of Technical Education in France. Labbé stressed the vocational role of education, that no trade should be left without instruction. Abbott in reply recognized that in France 'la charge de former les ouvriers est plus importante pour les écoles qu'en Angleterre, où elle est supportée, en règle générale, par les usines elles-mêmes'.[56] Although making this distinction there was much in the French papers that would have confirmed Abbott and Savage in their views that technical schools should be both useful and educative. M. Sautreuil of the École professionelle Diderot put this strongly and M. Jumin described the Parisian *ateliers-écoles* set up by the Paris Chamber of Commerce from 1920, whose unrestricted entry and vocational guidance especially interested Abbott.[57] There were subsequent conferences in Rome in 1936 and Berlin in 1938, as there had been an earlier one in Paris in 1931. Without doubt these too enabled English educationalists to cultivate their French professional friendships and keep up to date their knowledge of the French system with its strong technical emphasis. But none was recorded so fully as the Barcelona meeting.

As well as Board officials a number of local authorities were interested in France and sent delegations to investigate technical education there. Manchester Education Committee did so in 1930[58] and in 1935 Birmingham Education Committee followed them.[59] They were deeply impressed with the École supérieure d'électricité in Paris, financed by the leading electrical firms in France and providing 'the highest grade electrical engineering training in France' for an élite 200 postgraduates. They also praised the École nationale d'arts et métiers, producing mechanical engineers in 'splendidly equipped' workshops with 'admirable facilities'. In the next year the Middlesex Education Committee made a lengthy tour of

[55] ED 12/419, Interview Memorandum, 24 Feb. 1932, A. Abbott.

[56] *Congrès international de l'enseignement technique, Barcelone 17–19 mai 1934* (Paris, 1934), vol. i: Labbé, pp. 130–4; Abbott, pp. 139–41; Sautreuil, pp. 567–71; vol ii: Jumin, pp. 204–10.

[57] ED 10/151, A. Abbot on *ateliers-écoles* in evidence to the Consultative Committee, 26 Jan. 1934.

[58] *City of Manchester Education Committee Report on Higher Technical Education in Europe* (1930). The unique copy in Manchester Central Library no longer exists. Accordingly I have not seen this item.

[59] *City of Birmingham Education Committee Reports on Visits Made by a Deputation to Continental Technical Colleges and Educational Institutions*, 3–17 Apr. 1935, Birmingham City Reference Library, Corporation Documents F/2.

Europe.[60] In Paris they too were impressed by the two *grandes écoles* praised by Birmingham. But they also visited various trade schools including the Atelier-École for Boys of the Chamber of Commerce, which taught a variety of trades, from automobiles to tailoring, cabinet-making to welding, and its counterpart school where girls were instructed in hairdressing, cookery, furriery, and embroidery. They shrewdly called at the École d'alimentation, where the students cooked them 'the best lunch of the tour'. Both reports also found remarkable the 1925 *taxe d'apprentissage* of 0.2 per cent of wage bills, raising 151 million francs from industry for technical education.

Finally, private individuals brought valuable educational intelligence from France in the 1930s. The headmaster of the Day Continuation School run by Tootal Broadhurst Lee at Bolton made an extensive tour in 1938 and sent his report to the Board.[61] He visited many Parisian trade schools, notably the works school of André Citroën and the École pratique d'industrie de Puteaux, a state school which fed students to Citroën and other motor car factories in Paris. Although this form of education was much more trade training than the school the author was running he was enthusiastic and noted, 'this keen demand for practical training is found everywhere on the Continent'. Finally, the best study of Parisian trade schools in the 1930s was by Dorothy Pannett, who was interested in schooling for the needle trades and fashion.[62] Herself a teacher, she found the Parisian *écoles professionelles* much more genuinely professional than London girls' trade schools. The Paris girls worked harder, and the schools were more prestigious, and had closer touch with a wider range of fashion houses and wealthy clients. She confirmed that the JTS stream was worthwhile in both countries but that the English had an academic bias and the French an industrial one.

France in the 1930s had grave defects, notably her slow or negligible recovery from her deflation-induced economic depression and the violent rifting into extremes of Left and Right of her fragile political life. Yet it is remarkable that these many visitors found so much to admire in her education; notably the superb *grande école* training of her technological and managerial élite and the practical vocational education of the non-academic young. It confirmed the continuation and expansion of the English JTS form.

But finally a more subtle French development also influenced those with higher ambitions for the English technical school. From the mid-1930s Sir Will Spens was gathering evidence which culminated in his

<hr/>

[60] *County Council of Middlesex Education Committee Report of a Delegation on their Visit to Continental Technical Institutions* (May 1936), Greater London Record Office and Library, 22.14 MID.

[61] ED 22/218, 'Report on Visits to Certain Continental Technical Schools', 1938.

[62] Dorothy Pannett, 'A Comparison of Girls Junior Technical Schools in London and Paris' (MA thesis, University of London, 1939).

famous report on secondary education in 1938.[63] Spens wanted to upgrade the JTS to a technological equivalent of the grammar school. One of the influences helping to shape this view was French. In 1925–6 due to financial crises it was proposed to close a large number of small French secondary schools, most of which were *collèges* maintained by municipalities. In order to save these institutions higher primary schools or technical schools were housed under the same roof as the *collèges*: 'in a number of cases the lycée has been combined with a technical school.'[64] This led to the creation of about 100 secondary technical schools in France. This piece of evidence to Spens exactly prefigured what Spens himself wanted and proposed a few years later.

5. CONCLUSION

The French influence has been underestimated. This was recognized at the time by Michael Sadler, who observed that, whereas Germany and the USA were enthusiastic in convincing others of the virtues of their education systems, yet 'France somewhat conceals her sense of educational power in her present mood of self criticism.'[65] However, the influence is clear. Along with the German and American it was pervasive before 1914 and instrumental in persuading English opinion of the importance of technical education and governmental involvement in it. More specifically French experience played some part in motivating the civic universities movement, the foundation of Leeds, and the move to chartered independence in the 1900s. The LSE and RADA certainly embodied French ideas. The French solution to the problem of declining apprenticeship expressed itself in the continuation school and most importantly in the excellent system of technical schools for teenagers. The last influenced their establishment in England in the 1900s under Morant and their continued development under the Francophiles Abbott and Savage in the inter-war years.

Yet Britain did not uncritically accept parts of the French system. In particular Britain never accepted the concept of the *grande école* as superior to the university. The English polytechnic movement in particular has been a notable failure, not seeking the high élite ground of the École polytechnique but settling for absorption into the lower level of the English university tradition. Nor did we accept the French enthusiasm for technical schools, still retaining a belief in the importance of workshop

[63] Spens Report (1938).

[64] ED 10/152, 'Notes on Recent Developments in Post Primary Education in France' (n.d. 1934?), in papers of Spens Committee. C. H. Dobinson, *Technical Education for Adolescents* (London, 1951), 61–4 points out some French–Spens parallels.

[65] M. E. Sadler, 'The Ferment of Education on the Continent and America', *Proceedings of the British Academy*, 1 (1903–4), 84.

experience and a scepticism of how much could be done at school. The English preference for the 'workshop in the school' rather than the French 'school in the workshop' held back the development of this strain more usual on the Continent than in England.[66] France has a stronger mercantilist-*dirigiste* tradition which has underlain its approach to technical education and which England lacks. This has restrained us from a fuller acceptance of those French features from which we agree to differ.

France has now a higher national income per head than Britain and leads us in a whole range of technologies from its motor car industry to the TGV, from its air traffic control and telephone communications to the Exocet, from Ariane to its nuclear power stations.[67] We have only to contrast the planned excellence of the rail links from Paris to the Channel Tunnel with the inferior arrangements on the English side. Nor should we overlook the traditional French excellence in those atelier skills for which Paris is renowned, the cuisine and couture worlds of gastronomy and fashion; the jewellery of Cartier, the patisserie of Le Nôtre, the luggage of Vuitton. If the British economy dominated the nineteenth century, the French has been more successful in taking the forward path into the second half of the twentieth. Their education has been an important element in this. We have borrowed some of it but might it not have been to our benefit to accept even more?

---

[66] Michael Sanderson, *The Missing Stratum: Technical School Education in England 1900–1960s* (London, 1994).

[67] 'High-tech à la française', *Horizon*, BBC TV 2, 10 Mar. 1986.

From Inheritors to Managers: The École des Hautes Études Commerciales and Business Firms

MARC MEULEAU

This chapter sets out to study the relationship between a recent newcomer to the field of top management, the commercial manager, and the evolution of administrative methods in large French firms. We shall take as our example the École des hautes études commerciales (HEC) and its graduates. The post of commercial manager first appeared at the end of the nineteenth century with the development of senior management training. The commercial manager concentrated on everything other than production and research,[1] being as it were the counterpart of engineers in matters of commerce, finance, and administration; after the First World War he also competed on equal terms with them for promotion to a directorship.

The underlying analysis is based on the assumption that training provides an individual with knowledge which can influence him in a decisive manner, giving him both technical skills and an ability to react more efficiently to given situations. A second assumption is that, given the managerial demands of a large business, selection for top management posts should be based on ability to respond effectively to problems facing the business, rather than on other factors such as family ties, wealth, or the 'old boys' network'. One should not, however, overlook the weight of tradition, the influence of social origins, or the role of the networks of the *grandes écoles'* alumni in the choice of a career and professional achievement. Moreover, HEC was not the only institution training top managers and men coming from other backgrounds, in particular engineers, were equally capable of adapting to the management requirements of large French companies. This chapter thus aims to provide only a broad survey of a relatively little-known area: that of the relationship between commercial and business training, career patterns, and economic development in France.

---

[1] In the 1950s the term 'administrative manager' (*cadre administratif*) was equally used to describe those who were responsible for management outside the so-called field of production or to describe those who did not have a training as engineers.

An exhaustive study of the careers of HEC graduates is obviously impossible. Although the primary sources are not lacking,[2] studies of the School and its graduates are as yet few in number[3] and the history of business administration in France remains an unresearched area.[4] The École des hautes études commerciales has produced in a century more than 20,000 graduates. This survey is based on a sample, chosen at random, of 500 HEC students, which has been computer-processed with the help of the School's Information Service. Later verification ensured that the results were representative. However, while such data are of great help in establishing the average career profile of the HEC graduate, they are ineffective in measuring the factors affecting professional advancement in business, except in a very general way. An attempt to understand why certain HEC graduates succeeded in reaching the top management of certain large French companies cannot be made by considering only statistical criteria. To measure the real part played by family support, special aptitude, eventual integration into the Civil Service, or business experience, requires a thorough analysis for which existing data are not sufficient. This can be better approached by following the careers of a number of sufficiently representative individuals, whose successes, as well as failures, provide good examples.

1. FROM THE BEGINNING TO THE FIRST WORLD WAR
(1881–1914)

The École des Hautes Études Commerciales: an innovative venture

Teaching began at the School on 4 November 1881, with sixty-two enrolled students.[5] The creation of this institution demonstrated the dyna-

---

[2] The School's archives, of course, are particularly detailed about the internal administration, students, and teachers; the archives of the Chamber of Commerce and Industry of Paris illustrate the business world's perceptions of the School. We have also used numerous documents produced by the Old Boys' Association, in particular the *Bulletin de l'Association des anciens élèves de l'École des hautes études commerciales* and the Yearbooks (*Annuaires de l'Association . . .*), and lastly the various writings of the HEC graduates.

[3] To our knowledge, four studies have appeared up to now: P. Garczinski, *Les Origines de la création de l'École des hautes études commerciales (1881–1913)* (Paris, 1974); H. More, 'L'Invention du cadre commercial (1881–1914)', *Sociologie du travail*, 4 (1982); P. Maffre, 'Histoire de l'enseignement commercial supérieur au XIXème siècle (1800–1914)', (thèse de troisième cycle, Paris, 1983); Marc Meuleau, *Histoire d'une grande école (1881–1981)* (Paris, 1981).

[4] See M. Lévy-Leboyer, 'The Large Corporation in Modern France', in A. D. Chandler and H. Daems (eds.), *Managerial Hierarchies* (Cambridge, Mass., 1980). Company monographs can also cast some light on this vast subject. See in particular P. Fridenson, *Histoire des usines Renault (1898–1939)* (Paris, 1972); A. Baudant, *Pont-à-Mousson (1918–39)* (Paris, 1980); C. Omnès, *De l'atelier au groupe industriel: Vallourec, 1882–1978* (Paris, 1980); J.-F. Picard, A. Beltran, and M. Bungener, *Histoires de l'EDF* (Paris, 1985); J.-P. Daviet, *Un destin international: la Compagnie de Saint-Gobain de 1830 à 1939* (Paris, 1988).

[5] Archives of the Chamber of Commerce and Industry of Paris, section 'Fondation de l'École des hautes études commerciales'.

mism of a certain type of Parisian management which, situated at the geographical centre of the industrialized part of the country, was aware of the country's economic evolution. Science and technology had become necessary in the steel, chemical, and electrical industries; department stores were created, totally revolutionizing traditional commercial structures; and large savings banks began to tap the modest savings of the whole country.[6] These gradual changes were accompanied by new ideas about the conduct of business. Jacques Siegfried, one of the most farsighted figures in the field and an innovator in the teaching of higher business studies, made the following declaration at the international congress in Bordeaux in 1886, which debated technical, industrial, and commercial teaching:

Formerly the technical aspect occupied the attention of manufacturers almost entirely, for industrial processes were imperfect and the least progress, the least saving in the price of the product were sufficient to ensure success and profit. Formerly also, industry was the property of a small number of privileged nations, who dictated their conditions to the buyers. Today, the progress of science has substantially diminished the price of manufactured goods. The gap between the value of the raw material and that of the manufactured products leaves only a small margin for industrial profits.[7] Furthermore, all countries have embarked enthusiastically on production using the most sophisticated techniques. Competition has become more fierce. To sum up, industry is becoming more and more dependent on commerce.[8]

The importance of commercial activity was better appreciated. Selling became indispensable in an economy where crisis lowered demand, but productive capacity kept increasing, thanks to the development of new techniques, and to the creation of large firms. Thus, for the founders of the School, commerce became a science, which had to be taught. Practice was no longer sufficient: it was necessary to master complex patterns, and this was only possible through theoretical knowledge, a good general cultural background, and an ability to theorize, acquired by training.

The founders of the School devised an ambitious syllabus. They wished to teach 'practical knowledge' and 'modern sciences': a combination of pragmatic knowledge (accountancy, languages, production) with theoretical courses more appropriate for forming judgement than giving ideas which would be of direct use (the history of commerce, political economy, and, above all, law) and taught by distinguished teachers (Lyon-Caen and Rataud, professors at the University, or the MP Raoul Duval).[9] Thus

---

[6] F. Braudel and E. Labrousse (eds.), *Histoire économique et sociale de la France*, vols. iii/1 and iii/2 (Paris, 1976).

[7] This tendency to a decline in the rate of profit has been confirmed by historical studies, notably the work of J. Bouvier, F. Furet, and M. Gillet, *Le Mouvement du profit en France au XIXème siècle* (Paris, 1965).

[8] J. Siegfried, International Congress, Bordeaux, 1886.

[9] Archives of the Chamber of Commerce and Industry of Paris, 'Correspondance

equipped, the HEC hoped to appeal to that segment of the French population (put at *c*.40 per cent) which, through its commercial and industrial activity, was primarily interested in the training that this institution had to offer.[10]

New careers?

From the date of the first graduation in 1883 to 1913, the HEC produced on average 100 graduates a year. On leaving the School, they were employed in different areas, including *haute couture* (Lucien Lelong, HEC 1908),[11] mechanical engineering (Jules Guth, HEC 1884, president of the Société alsacienne de constructions mécaniques), the steel industry (Guy de Wendel, HEC 1900), international commerce (Georges Schwob d'Héricourt, HEC 1884), diplomacy (Henry Bourgeois, HEC 1886), and even the management of large country estates by the landed gentry.[12] However, HEC graduates tended to specialize in industry and in particular the service sector (commerce, banking, transport, public service, teaching, etc.). In 1900, as in 1912, 75 per cent of graduates were working in services and 25 per cent in manufacturing, whereas the two sectors employed respectively 28 and 30 per cent of the French working population in 1912. Within the service industry, commerce and banking alone shared half the graduates of the turn of the century, an enormous proportion, explained by the prestige of HEC graduates and the growth of commercial and banking activities. According to L. A. Vincent and INSEE publications,[13] turnover in commerce increased by 29 per cent between 1896 and 1913, and bank assets increased fivefold between 1880 and 1913. Graduates working for industry preferred to join large corporations, for example in metallurgy or the steel industry (the same phenomenon can be observed in transport, particularly in the major railway companies). They were also attracted to new activities arising from the 'second industrial revolution', i.e. the chemical, mechanical, and electrical industries, and were inclined to neglect old small firms. Hence in 1900, though 14 per cent of French industrial workers were employed in the textile industry, only 6 per cent of HEC graduates were to be found there; on the other hand, 4 per cent of HEC graduates worked in the chemical industry, which employed 0.5 per cent of French manpower.

The creation of independent departments organized along Fayol's methods, as well as the obligation of staying closely linked to the market,

échangée entre la Chambre et le Ministère de l'agriculture et du commerce, (1878–81)', Meuleau, *Histoire d'une grande école*, 14–21.

[10] Archives of the Chamber of Commerce, section 'Fondation de l'École'.
[11] HEC 1908: the date refers to the year of graduation.
[12] Yearbooks of the Old Boys' Association.
[13] L. A. Vincent, 'Population active, production et productivité dans vingt-et-une branches de l'économie française, 1896–1962', *Études et conjonctures* (Paris, 1965).

meant that executives with marketing, accounting, and financial skills were required. In the steel and heavy engineering industries, for example, out of 14 HEC executives in large concerns in 1910, 7 belonged to marketing departments, only 2 dealt with production, and 5 were managerial advisers (this function often included accounting and financial services). Among them, Victor-Toussaint de Laage de Saint-Germain (HEC 1889) was head of the commercial department of the Compagnie de Fives-Lilles; and Jules Guth (HEC 1884) was head of the Société alsacienne de construction mécanique commercial department and future president of that company. General statistics confirm this trend. In the period 1900–12, 21 per cent of HEC graduates dealt with finance, 7 per cent with accounting, and 19 per cent with marketing, while production, technical research, and factory management employed only 6 per cent of HEC graduates.

A traditional socio-professional environment

One should not, however, exaggerate the role of the School in the creation of a modern type of commercial manager. In fact, a small number of the HEC graduates were still present in traditional businesses during the nineteenth century, as a result of their social background, family ties (family firms, renown of the family name, father's professional connections, marriages), as well as their own business conceptions. The training provided by the HEC did not have much relevance in the progress of their careers, which owed more to the privilege of belonging to the family owning the firm than to the acquisition of new skills. In the case of metallurgy and mechanical engineering, 27 out of 52 HEC graduates, i.e. 52 per cent, belonged to the owning family or had their father managing the firm in which they worked.

On the basis of their father's occupations, as recorded at HEC registration, most students came from the upper middle class. Over the first ten years of the School's life, numerous scholarships were granted to working-class students (32 per cent), but thereafter 80 per cent of the graduates came from the upper middle class. These were mainly industrialists' and traders' sons: in 1900, 46 per cent of the students had a father who managed a firm. Few came from other walks of life. The teaching profession, the military, Civil Servants, and professionals accounted for only 13 to 25 per cent of the School's intake. The HEC's recruitment was strictly circumscribed. Business people who desired the perpetuation of family business were particularly attracted by the possibilities offered by the School: trading, banking, industry, and the colonies. Moreover, the expensive school fees (1,000 francs for the courses plus 1,800 for board per annum) and the high level of general education required from applicants at a time when France had no more than a few thousand young men of university-

Table 7.1. *Factors contributing to the rise of HEC graduates to top managerial positions*

Social origins of HEC graduates (year of graduation)	Academic excellence (%)[a]	Family support (%)[b]	Business competence (%)[c]	No. of cases
Upper class				
Before 1914	60	100	40	5
1918–39	50	100	75	4
1940–52	67	100	100	6
Middle/upper middle class				
Before 1914	25	75	16	12
1918–39	59	63	24	26
1940–52	52	72	24	25

[a] Graduates who came in the first third in their finals or who could boast a degree in higher education (bachelor's degree in law).
[b] A family business, a board-member father or one with influence, a prestigious name, or a judicious marriage.
[c] The success of a firm founded by the HEC graduate himself, or his attaining a senior position in the professional hierarchy, or of course promotion to a key position in or chairmanship of a large corporation.

Source: Sample of HEC graduates.

entrance level per year (6,385 in 1881, 7,733 in 1913–14)[14] limited the potential candidates to a small percentage of the well-to-do. So it is not surprising that, after 1905, 30 per cent of HEC graduates were business managers and, in 1912, 31 per cent were employed by the family firm. It has to be said that, coming from the well-informed business world in general, they took advantage of the experience passed on by family and friends to choose the most dynamic activities (engineering, chemistry) or to join a corporation where their skills would be in demand.

This does not necessarily mean that the success of HEC graduates derived only from their social background. They might have acquired, during their studies at the School, the knowledge that corporations were looking for and which might have been used to achieve an exceptional career without family help. However, it was not so: only 60 per cent of the HEC graduates who came from the upper class achieved good academic results (see Table 7.1), and this percentage was mostly due to the fact that they studied law,[15] which was most favourably looked on by society. This shows what little interest these scions of great dynasties displayed for the

[14] INSEE, *Annuaire retrospectif* (Paris, 1966), 143.
[15] Yearbooks of the Old Boys' Association.

business part of their studies. Sons and heirs could frequently maintain their position thanks to their social relationships, which opened board-room doors without requiring any great demonstration of talent. Guy de Wendel (HEC 1902), for example, a member of the famous ironmasters' dynasty, remained in the shadow of his cousin François de Wendel, and although he played no significant part in the family concern, he held five directorships in addition to a senator's seat (membership of the Upper Chamber).[16]

Statistics are even more striking for the HEC graduates who came from the middle and upper middle classes: 75 per cent maintained their status thanks to family business or family relationships rather than academic performance. Their professional careers were unsurprising. Regarded as the future bosses as soon as they entered the School, they fulfilled their destiny without struggle or genius. For example, Charles Laroche (HEC 1884) was the son of Jean-Ludovic Laroche, director of the Maison Laroche-Joubert (paper manufacture). Charles quickly rose in the enter-prise and by the time of his untimely death in 1898 was managing director of the Baneau factory near Angoulême (he was successively company secretary at Maison Laroche-Joubert et Cie, joint production manager at the Baneau factory, and finally general manager).

It would therefore appear that the HEC failed to influence the socio-professional evolution of its graduates. *Commerciales*, in reality, was a title that played no particular part in the School curriculum. Not a single lesson was given on selling, market studies, or the relationship between production and marketing. The teaching of advertising did not start until 1911, and then only as an option. The curriculum was essentially made up of accountancy (2 hours a day), languages (2 hours a day), and law ($3-4\frac{1}{2}$ hours a week at first, then more). Political economy, the history of trade, economic geography, by means of which students could have been given a grasp of the changes taking place within the realm of economics and management, were abandoned in favour of the teaching of law, the true noble subject and the basis of the recruitment of senior civil servants. Only accountancy and languages answered the purposes of the School, but could not make up for the other shortcomings.

On the eve of the First World War, banking was the one activity in which HEC graduates had been able to assert themselves, thanks to the originality of their training. The big banks, which were rapidly expand-ing,[17] actively supported the School (Crédit lyonnais, Union des banquiers de Paris et de la province, Société générale, and the Banque de France all

---

[16] J.-N. Jeanneney, *François de Wendel en République: l'argent et le pouvoir, 1914–1940* (Paris, 1976).

[17] J. Bouvier, *Le Crédit lyonnais de 1863 à 1882*, 2 vols. (Paris, 1961), *Un siècle de banque française* (Paris, 1973), and in Braudel and Labrousse (eds.), *Histoire économique et sociale de la France*, iv/1. 168–93.

offered scholarships in the first years of the institution). They appreciated the sound training in accountancy, the mastery of foreign languages, and the high cultural level, which was perfectly adapted to financial institutions. This was emphasized by Alexis Rostand, chairman of the Comptoir national d'escompte de Paris in 1911: 'The École des Hautes Études Commerciales and the French secondary commercial schools (*Écoles Commerciales*) give a theoretical education which the businessmen of my generation lacked.'[18] But, generally, trade and industry still relied on the heirs of influential families. The best example of this is Georges Schwob d'Héricourt (HEC 1884), chairman of the Old Boys' Association (Association des anciens élèves de l'École des hautes études commerciales) from 1905 to 1910. Born in Lure (Haute-Saône), a trader's son, he belonged to a dynasty of the textile industry. His activity was closely linked with the colonies and he travelled extensively. He married a daughter of the Gradis family, which specialized in the West Indian sugar and rum trade. A very keen businessman, he made the most of the opportunities offered by his milieu, developing many contacts in the country's governing circles. As a member of all major colonial organizations (he was a member of the Colonial Office and took part in the organization of the Colonial Exhibitions), he was regularly consulted by colonial administrators. He was rewarded by the Grand Croix of the Légion d'honneur, usually considered a political honour.[19]

2. BETWEEN THE TWO WORLD WARS: THE BEGINNING OF AN EVOLUTION

A new economic environment

During the 1920s, French business firms, after a period of rapid growth at the beginning of the century,[20] had to face a double problem: the opening of a new market in mass-produced goods, and new concepts in management methods. In the automobile industry, one of the most prosperous in France at this time, production grew from 4,000 vehicles in 1900 to 45,000 in 1913 and 254,000 in 1929, before falling to 175,000 in 1936. The three big concerns, Citroën, Renault, and Peugeot (the 'Big Three'), rapidly extended their share of the market, which grew from 35 per cent in 1919 to

[18] In *Bulletin de l'Association* (May 1911). The 'Ecoles Commerciales' were in fact the *écoles supérieures de commerce*.

[19] Archives nationales, *Dossiers de la Légion d'honneur*; yearbooks of the Old Boys' Association; Jean Schwob d'Héricourt, *La Maison Gradis de Bordeaux et ses chefs* (Paris, 1975).

[20] M. Lévy-Leboyer, 'La Croissance économique en France au XIXème siècle: résultats préliminaires', *Annales ESC* (1968), 4: 788–804; F. Crouzet, 'Essai de construction d'un indice annuel de la production industrielle française au XIXème siècle', *Annuales ESC* (1970), 1: 56–99.

60 per cent in 1929 and 71 per cent in 1936. Renault employed 4,000 people in 1914, 30,000 in 1929, and 38,000 in 1938.[21]

Enterprises competing in this new market of mass-produced goods were confronted by a completely different state of affairs, in which financial, accounting, marketing, and administrative problems reached an importance hitherto unknown. Jacques Siegfried's prediction of 1886, 'Industry looks like becoming more and more commercial,' was suddenly a reality. Selling was not the only aspect which mattered. Firms had to become sufficiently large to be able to lower unit costs, with marketing departments adapted to market and product and an organization capable of co-ordinating different services. In 1928 Jean Chevalier (HEC 1922), from the metallurgical firm of G. Duvoisin et Cie, making the most of Henri Fayol and Jean Carlioz's teaching, concluded on the rising importance of organization:

Power for an enterprise is not a matter of abundance of money, but rather the way in which it is used. A firm which, in the same timespan, achieves a production similar to that of a firm endowed with twice the capital, is as powerful as this second one.[22]

In the same period, accountancy and marketing services improved their methods. Cost accountancy, which appeared in France before 1914, realized such considerable progress that it definitely pulled the science of accountancy out of its early empiricism. Under American influence, marketing was better understood. H. S. Denisson's work concerning marketing was discussed in the Comité national d'organisation scientifique.[23] Merchandising and market research then appeared, and advertising endeavoured to become a real science with carefully prepared campaigns.

However, company histories, when available, show that management only made real progress in firms which had run into difficulties, thus confirming Ashworth's assertion that 'in times of market expansion, many firms went along with great prosperity while carrying a somewhat irrational administrative structure'.[24] The 1920s were years of growth and did not encourage much change. On the other hand, the Great Depression started to awaken the business world. The glass and chemical company Saint-Gobain, for example, had made bad investments in petroleum activities before 1930 (see Chapter 10). The firm consequently endeavoured to modernize its management and elaborate new decision-making methods without, however, suppressing the owning families' authority

[21] Fridenson, *Usines Renault*; A. Sauvy, *Histoire économique de la France entre les deux guerres* (Paris, 1965–70).
[22] J. Chevalier, *La Technique de l'organisation des entreprises* (Paris, 1928), 5.
[23] *Bulletin du CNOS* (Mar. 1928), 4, 5; (Apr. 1929), 5–14.
[24] W. Ashworth, review of Alfred Chandler's *Strategy and Structure, Business History*, 7/2 (July 1965), 124.

over the board of directors. This compromise was achieved in 1936 by Baron Pierre Hély d'Oissel, himself a member of the traditional owning classes. Between 1928 and 1932, the big department store Au Printemps chose a new structure which respected Henri Fayol's functional concept, but already heralded the 'staff and line' structure through small staffs attached to operational managers.[25]

Commercial concerns and companies producing goods for the mass market modernized their sales departments and designed new sales techniques. The Nouvelles Galeries department store created fixed-price stores with Uniprix; they were rapidly followed in this by Le Printemps (Prisunic, 1931) and by Galeries Lafayette (Monoprix, 1932).[26] Food and drink companies multiplied their advertising campaigns, decided to train their commercial travellers, and undertook market surveys. The automobile industry tried to devise new marketing policies in order to attract prospective buyers whose incomes had been reduced by the Depression, such as trade-ins and instalment sales over two years for the purchase of a new car.[27] Such an evolution required a new sort of man, with good skills and a different business concept. The HEC graduates did not fail to respond to the challenge. But how?

A new teaching

During that same period, the HEC modified its teaching methods. Three sections had already been created in 1905 in the second year of studies so that students could specialize in one economic activity, industry ('Commerce et industrie' section), banking ('Commerce et banque' section), or colonial empire ('Commerce et colonies' section). It was a brave new idea. This was the first time the institution had considered that training had to be related to the specific demands of particular jobs. The process accelerated after the First World War. New courses appeared from 1919: business management ('Gouvernement des entreprises'), devised by Jean Carlioz, Henri Fayol's disciple; commercial policy of major states ('Politique commerciale des principaux États'), philosophy of commerce ('Philosophie du commerce'). The purpose of these lectures was to link the knowledge of law with the hard facts of business life.[28] With these new bases, the influence of the School in the evolution of the HEC graduates' careers was increased.

[25] Daviet, *Saint-Gobain*, Case of the Centre de préparation aux affaires (CPA), no. 1154, 23 Apr. 1937, kindly transmitted by the CPA.

[26] 'Évolution et concurrence dans le commerce de détail', *Hommes et commerce*, 150 (Oct. 1976), 20.

[27] P. Fridenson, 'French Automobile Marketing, 1890–1979', in A. Akochi and K. Shimakawa (eds.), *Development of Mass Marketing: The Automobile and Retailing Industries* (Tokyo, 1981).

[28] Archives of the Chamber of Commerce.

But what was the true value of these changes? In fact, the new courses played only a modest part. In 1924 they contributed to under 5 per cent of the curriculum, behind 18 per cent for legal studies, 17 per cent for accountancy, and 10 per cent for industrial techniques (technology, transports, and chemistry). Moreover, the School still hardly deserved to be called École des hautes études commerciales. Marketing was still not taught, despite its growing relevance to firms' strategy. Advertising was not highly regarded until the exceptional personality of O. J. Guérin showed its true importance. As for commercial technology, it merely consisted of a description of the tools of the trade (machines, written documents, telephone).[29] The real transformation did not lie in the modest changes to the curriculum but in the School's new method of recruitment. The competitive examination created in 1922 attracted many more candidates, because of the increasing fame of the School, and because of economic prosperity. This was a good way of selecting only those boys of a sufficiently high level. Whereas before 1914 the best ratio of candidates to graduates was rarely higher than three to two, between 1919 and 1933 it oscillated from two to one to three to one. Nevertheless, as before, students came in their majority from the industrial and commercial classes (75 to 80 per cent), with a strong proportion of managers' sons (38 to 40 per cent). Although they knew that, in all probability, they would inherit the family business, they really wished to understand the economic process.

As the audience became more demanding, teachers had to deal with relevant contemporary problems. In spite of the same rigid concepts which still limited the courses, students wanted to discuss Fayol's theories and learn about marketing studies and the use of statistics. The graduates of 1924 chose *La Synoptique* as their promotional name, in memory of that challenging concept. Witnesses from these years say that courses at the HEC were teeming with new ideas, without elaborate teaching, for all that was resolutely commercial.[30] This was indeed some progress, though not necessarily for everyone: it was particularly well suited to the more gifted students or those already well informed about the reality of business.

The HEC executives: increasingly indispensable

Between 1919 and 1939, HEC graduates changed and partly broke away from the traditional business world from which they came. The proportion of graduates employed by large concerns, i.e. firms quoted on the Stock Exchange and big nationalized companies, rose from 25 per cent in 1912 to 31 per cent in 1938. This evolution is much more remarkable in

[29] Archives of the Chamber of Commerce, O. J. Guérin, 'Précis intégral de publicité'.
[30] Interviews with M. Jean Bailley (HEC 1927), M. Léon Caillet (HEC 1929), M. Jacques Guéden (HEC 1931), M. Pierre Ledoux (HEC 1935), and M. Charles Vigneras (HEC 1938).

absolute numbers: 660 HEC graduates in 1912, about 2,100 in 1938.[31] The main beneficiary was the industrial sector. In 1912, 30 per cent of the French work-force was employed in industry, with only 24 per cent of HEC graduates active in this sector. In 1939 the trend was reversed: 31 per cent of HEC graduates worked for industry, against 29 per cent of France's working population. As a result, the proportion of HEC graduates engaged in the service industries (Civil Service excepted) partially declined: 64 per cent in 1912, 53 per cent in 1939. HEC graduates managed to diversify their professional activities. Consequently the HEC, which intended to nurture future senior executives of commercial and banking concerns, found itself preparing students for accounting, banking, or marketing functions in all sorts of corporations.

Saint-Gobain is one example of this phenomenon: from 1881 to 1929 the firm never employed a single HEC graduate. In the 1930s, however, Saint-Gobain reformed its management and hired seven of them to take on banking and accounting responsibilities in its new services. Another example is the department store Au Printemps. In the 1920s the directors of the store, which had been in the hands of the Laguionie family since 1905, realized that they had to reform the old structure, which no longer allowed them to control its rapid growth. As the volume of sales increased, the authority of department heads got out of hand, for directors could no longer exercise the daily personal control which had been their prerogative when Le Printemps was a smaller concern. Directors understood that they definitively needed a qualified staff able to help them.[32]

It took four years to set up a new, functional structure. In 1932 the three directors supervised seven managers, each responsible for a precise activity: purchases, sales, advertising, accounting and banking, staff development, and 'studies' (organization). At the same time, the fixed-price stores Prisunic had been created by Le Printemps. They represented a new commercial organization, quite different from the sales management of department stores. While the latter gathered more than 100,000 items essentially chosen in fashion and clothing lines, the fixed-price stores dealt with a much smaller stock (2,000 to 2,500 items), all of it adapted to daily needs, and they relied on rapid stock rotation and massive orders to manufacturers to keep prices as low as possible. It was these two changes which brought HEC graduates to this department store. The first two HEC recruits were Jacques Daum (HEC 1930), from the Daum glass-

[31] Information concerning large companies remains imprecise. Between 1911 and 1936 the number of quoted companies increased from 720 to 1502, while the proportion of wage-earners working for industrial companies employing 500 people or more rose from 12% in 1906 to 20.5% in 1936. See on this subject M. Lévy-Leboyer, 'Le Patronat français a-t-il été malthusien?', *Le Mouvement social*, 3 (1974); Braudel and Labrousse, *Histoire économique et sociale de la France*, iv/1. 770–94; J. Houssiaux, *Le Pouvoir de monopole* (Paris, 1958).

[32] On Le Printemps, see H. Pasdermadjian, *Le Grand Magasin* (Paris, 1949) and the in-house magazine *Printania*.

cutting family, and Jacques Guéden (HEC 1931). Both of them, and the latter particularly, convinced the senior management of the excellence of the HEC. In 1939 Jacques Daum became advertising manager for the whole company. As for Jacques Guéden, he began his career by demonstrating, through rigorous financial research, that the costs of the mail-order service were much too heavy; the directors closed this department. He also took part in the elaboration of budget control and, finally, played his part in the creation of Prisunic. Less than ten years after the first HEC graduate was engaged, the company employed fifteen HEC graduates[33] and Jean Vigneras, the son of one of the original partners, made his entry into the School in 1936.

The HEC graduates gained ground in large corporations, but they rarely succeeded at general management level.[34] A 1946 survey from the Old Boys' Association stated that 250 graduates worked in chemistry, mostly in marketing, accounting, and administrative functions, though only a few had reached general management. During the inter-war years, HEC graduates remained executives. In the hierarchy of large firms they were still kept at an intermediate level despite their growing usefulness. As before 1914, banking was the only exception. HEC graduates were well trained thanks to the 'Commerce et banque' optional course. In 1946 350 of them were in banking institutions, some with a seat on the main board. Among them were the chairman of the Crédit industriel et commercial (Joseph Deschamps, HEC 1893), the vice-chairman of the Banque de Paris et des Pays-Bas (Émile Oudot, HEC 1908), and the managing directors of the Crédit lyonnais (Robert Masson, HEC 1895) and of the Banque nationale du commerce et de l'industrie (Alfred Pose, HEC 1919).[35]

Their success in the banking world was due to two main factors. First, they had a well-adapted technical knowledge of the profession (accountancy, applied mathematics) and the combination of the HEC diploma with another degree (such as doctor of law or *inspecteur des finances*—financial controller in the public administration) was much appreciated in the financial world. Alfred Pose (HEC and doctor of civil law) is the most outstanding example. At the age of 32 he was appointed general manager of the Banque nationale du commerce et de l'industrie (BNCI), an institution built on the ruins of the Banque nationale du crédit (BNC). He radically reorganized its structure, centralizing administrative and ac-

[33] They were all executives and controlled the departments of purchasing (which henceforth became distinct from sales), accounts, or the *bureau des études*, in charge of organization; but in fact they were a seed-bed of young graduates who were given particular missions by the company's top management. (Guéden studied sales problems while a member of the bureau des études.)

[34] In 1939, out of over 100 HEC graduates, 31 worked in large enterprises but only 5 of them became general managers or directors.

[35] Officially, A. Pose was in 1946 no longer BNCI's managing director. Being General Giraud's partisan during the Vichy period, he was prosecuted by the Gaullists. However, he actually kept on managing the bank until 1950.

counting activities, giving local executives more responsibility, stimulating a new business attitude through training of personnel, investigating the availability of regional funds, and canvassing—what the other banks called *l'aggressivité de la BNCI*. Secondly, they were actively supported by HEC managers who already held important positions.[36] Marius Dujardin (HEC 1900), for example, gained Robert Masson's (HEC 1895) support in his reorganization of the Crédit lyonnais stocks and shares department, an enormous division handling over 2 million files. He greatly reduced the staff assigned to those repetitive tasks, thanks to the restructuring of information channels and the mechanization of transactions; he also set a pattern for other large deposit banks.[37] Statistically, however, the overall weight of family support did not decrease much. Going back to Table 7.1, sons from the upper and upper middle classes received as much support as before 1914. The change came from the increased prestige of professionally qualified businessmen in society. This spelt the end for mediocre heirs: before the First World War, upper-class sons who failed were an exception; after 1918, a quarter of them failed to succeed to business positions.

3. FROM 1945 EVOLUTION SPEEDS UP

The birth of real business teaching

The École des hautes études commerciales was late in taking into account the economic changes which took place during 1944–75 (*les trente glorieuses*), especially the spread of the consumer society and increased business concentration.[38] Despite a reform of 1939 extending the course from two to three years, the academic format of 1881 was maintained. Law, technology, accountancy, and languages were the main topics. In 1952 the Old Boys' Association pointed out the dangers of this academic stagnation in a well-documented report. They noticed a growing gap between the subjects taught and the real needs of the French economy.

Developing administration, organization, sales control, and advertising 'techniques' seems essential to us. They will become the HEC graduates' specific assets.

---

[36] In banks where the 'number one' was an HEC graduate, the number of HEC graduates was higher: there were 50 HEC graduates at the BNCI and 39 at the Crédit lyonnais, as against only 19 at the Comptoir national d'escompte de Paris and 10 at the Société générale.

[37] Marius Dujardin, 'Organisation et fonctionnement d'un service de dépôt de titres', 27 Apr. 1944, at Centre d'études supérieures de banques, École libre des sciences politiques.

[38] Among the numerous studies of the French economy since 1945, see in particular J. J. Carré, P. Dubois, and E. Malinvaud, *La Croissance française* (Paris, 1972); J. Fourastié, *Les Trente glorieuses* (Paris, 1979); M. Parodi, *L'Économie et la société française depuis 1945* (Paris, 1981); Braudel and Labrousse (eds.), *Histoire économique et sociale de la France*, vols. iv/2 and iv/3.

Now, more than ever, they will be able to compete with graduates of other schools to reach the upper levels of Management in Business and Industry.[39]

The School decided to introduce changes. Marketing classes appeared in 1953 as well as sales classes, while advertising courses were developed. However, the main reform only started in 1957, when the École des hautes études commerciales became a business school with its own modern teaching methods. Seven subjects were singled out. Five of them were directly related to business/general economics: financial marketing, accounting, and banking; business functions; industrial relations; company marketing; and politics. The remaining two were languages and business law. The inference is obvious: the American business schools were at their zenith and the sixty-three-strong board[40] which proposed the reform was well informed about transatlantic achievements and eager to emulate them. However, the School started slowly and took time to copy the American model. In the 1950s and 1960s a great number of graduates went to the United States to get an MBA.

The growth of the economy took the École des hautes études commerciales to centre stage, and its recruitment experienced a spectacular period of development. The ratio of candidates at the entrance examination to admissions increased, rising from five to one in the 1950s to eleven to one in the late 1970s, even though the candidates were better prepared thanks to one, two, or even three years of special training after the general matriculation certificate (baccalauréat).

The triumph of managers

The quality of students improved in a school which was keen to respond to the needs of industry. After the Second World War, HEC graduates were much better prepared to face a changed business world. By the early 1970s France had modified its image of a country of small firms. Eighteen giant industrial groups controlled 11 per cent of total value-added in manufacturing industry, 15 per cent of net private domestic capital formation, 23 per cent of the export trade, and 11 per cent of the work-force employed in industry. Henceforth, French industry could stand comparison with other Western nations. The twenty leading companies' turnover represented 15.6 per cent of GNP, against 14.5 per cent in the United States, 17 per cent in Japan, 19.4 per cent in Germany, and 27.5 per cent in the United Kingdom.[41] Industrial companies became diversified and adopted a divisional structure: in 1970, 54 per cent of the hundred largest

[39] Archives of the Chamber of Commerce, 'Rapport de l'Association'.
[40] Out of thirty-one HEC graduates and forty-eight businessmen.
[41] R. de. Vannoise, 'Étude économique et financière de 18 groupes industriels français en 1972', Économie et statistiques (Mar. 1977); M. Hannoun, 'L'Appareil de production des groupes industriels en 1972', Économie et statistiques (Mar. 1977).

Table 7.2. *HEC managers in family and non-family firms (large companies, excluding finance), 1956 and 1982*

	Number of HEC graduate managers	Percentage managing a family firm	Percentage managing a firm without a family link
1956	17	65	35
1982	49	10	90

Source: List of leading 500 French firms in *L'Entreprise*, 9 Apr. 1960, pp. 53ff.; top 1,000 companies in *L'Expansion* for 1982.

industrial firms had a multidivisional structure, as against only 6 per cent in 1950. France had caught up with Germany (50 per cent) and the United Kingdom (57 per cent).[42] The post-war years saw the introduction of numerous American business methods through productivity plans or management consultants. Two functions were emphasized. The first was marketing (in 1972 industry marketed three times as many goods as in 1952).[43] The second was organization based on modern accounting methods and a dynamic policy of human resource management, with the growth of giant corporations (in 1982 Renault had 217,269 workers, and Saint-Gobain-Pont-à-Mousson had 163,000 in 1980).[44]

After 1945 HEC graduates invaded the commercial function. In 1939, 20 per cent of those employed by a firm were working in the marketing department. The proportion had increased to 28 per cent in 1954. The 'marketing era' had started. However, HEC graduates quickly realized the importance of accounting and financial offices and in 1973 23 per cent had found their way there. Recently a new interest has also developed in the personnel function, with 3 per cent of HEC graduates in 1973 and 1980. HEC graduates were quick to adapt to the new requirements of the economy. This adaptability proved very successful. Between 1950 and 1980, HEC graduates finally succeeded in reaching large firms' top management without any family connections, in all sections of the French economy (see Table 7.2). In 1956 two-thirds of HEC graduates reaching the top hierarchy level were still business heirs. Among them were Pierre Vieljeux (HEC 1912), chairman of the company Delmas-Vieljeux (shipping); François Peugeot (HEC 1925), director of Peugeot et Cie (tool kits); Georges Rousselot (HEC 1918), managing director of the Compagnie centrale Rousselot (chemical engineering); and Charles Canlorbe (HEC

[42] Lévy-Leboyer, 'The Large Corporation in Modern France'; G. Dyas and H. Thanheiser, *The Emerging European Enterprise* (London, 1976).

[43] Parodi, *L'Économie et la société française*, 46–50.

[44] 'Le Palmarès des 100 premières entreprises françaises en 1982'. in *L'Expansion*, 227 (Nov. 1983); Roger Martin, *Patron de droit divin* (Paris, 1984), 454.

1904), general manager of the Société des nouvelles galeries (department store).

In 1982 the proportion of scions of business dynasties among HEC graduates who had reached a top managerial position had fallen to 14 per cent. The recruitment of large company managers was henceforth no longer based on asset ownership. Uncommon skills became a more determining factor. Bernard Hanon (HEC 1955), for example, caught Régie Renault's attention with his use of computers and strategic planning studies.[45] In 1969 Francis Gautier (HEC 1944) left the head office of Colgate-Palmolive's French subsidiary company in order to take charge of the BSN group's diversification towards food-manufacturing. Antoine Riboud, BSN's chairman and managing director, decided to call on him because of his marketing experience in consumer brands[46]—a skill BSN had not yet developed, as it only manufactured glass at that time. Francis Gautier had been trained at the École des hautes études commerciales as well as at an American business school, and was used to the Colgate-Palmolive marketing system, mostly inspired by the parent-company's management. He pointed out BSN's deficiencies and fully succeeded in filling the gaps, pulling the BSN-Gervais-Danone group up to first rank in the French food industry. His success led him to become vice-chairman in 1976.

Henceforth, HEC graduates entered senior management in all economic sectors. This transition took place between 1950 and 1973. After the Second World War, the number of HEC graduates who were senior executives was 2.5 times higher in the financial world than in manufacturing or services. After the *trente glorieuses*, industry came first, before services and then banking. HEC graduates who joined large firms, mostly as executives, from 1919 to 1939 asserted themselves after the Second World War as generalist managers able to deal with the biggest groups, whatever their activities.

HEC's teaching success?

The great triumphs achieved by HEC graduates after 1945 coincided with the School's modernization, when its teaching definitely moved towards business administration. However, it would be hasty to conclude that graduates' success was due solely to the École des hautes études commerciales. First of all, in 1982 most HEC senior managers had attended the School before the 1957 reform. Most of them received a traditional training combined with the business administration courses brought in between 1949 and 1957 by the Old Boys' Association, and therefore had, on leaving school, only a vague idea of the new industrial management emerging in France. Secondly, HEC graduates who reached

[45] *Les Problèmes de gestion dans l'entreprise* (Colloque de Cannes) (Paris, 1976).
[46] *Revue hommes et commerce* (Mar. 1984), 16.

senior executive level in the largest firms were not simply HEC graduates. Still in 1982, Bernard Hanon (Renault, the 3rd largest French firm by turnover), Didier Pineau-Valencienne (Schneider SA, 9th), and Francis Gautier (BSN-Gervais-Danone, 19th) also held an American MBA, and this additional training is very likely to have played a major role in their careers. On the other hand, the educational grounding that HEC students had received was good enough to enable them to attend profitably any top-level educational institution and to encourage them to deepen their knowledge. Thirdly, despite the diminished role of the family firm, family assistance was still important. Though fewer HEC graduates had relatives in their company (27 per cent in 1970, 22 per cent ten years later), they still came from the wealthy class (between 1950 and 1980, an average of 75 per cent were from an upper- or upper middle-class background)[47] and continued to be well connected and supported. Professional relationships and good marriages took precedence over family reputation or firm's ownership. Although less noticeable, this kind of support had the advantage of bringing information and essential contacts to the prospective manager of a large firm. It might even have been a more efficient kind of social support if we consider that 60 per cent of the HEC graduates who reached a top position after 1945 benefited from family support, against 43 per cent between the two World Wars. Despite the obvious positive contribution of the education received at the École des hautes études commerciales, social factors continued to play a role in the shaping of a successful career.

4. CONCLUSION

The growing reputation of the École des hautes études commerciales and its students reflected the deep alterations in the French economy. In the nineteenth century, small manufacturers who only paid attention to technology were replaced by large companies, the priority of which was sales management, in a society attracted by all kinds of goods. The change has turned out to be to the advantage of the École des hautes études commerciales since it produces 'commercial managers' able to fill positions created by both the consumer society and the development of big corporations. Nowadays, HEC is the most prestigious French business school. It is part of the small group of the country's highest educational institutions, including the École polytechnique, the École nationale d'administration (ENA), the École normale supérieure (ENS), and the École centrale.[48]

[47] Meuleau, *Histoire d'une grande école*, 116–22.
[48] See the periodical rating of business schools published every year in magazines like *L'Expansion, Le Point, L'Express.*

The École des hautes études commerciales had a beneficial influence. Since its foundation, and despite its shortcomings, it has imparted knowledge and elevated the prestige of commercial activities, which used to be looked down on in France. The best proof of HEC's teaching efficiency is that HEC graduates started to work in businesses closely related to their training and gradually reached the upper level of management in corporations they did not own, thanks to their efficiency at the lower levels. Nevertheless, they still needed a minimum of social support to reach the top. Moreover, when choosing HEC graduates for commercial, accounting, financial, or management positions, companies proved that they could break away from the traditional recruitment methods of family and the old boys' networks of the *grandes écoles*. The promotion of Louis Deveaux (HEC 1926) to Shell-française's chairmanship in 1960 (despite the fact that, from the outset, the oil industry was a preserve of graduates of the École polytechnique) was only made possible by the agreement between the Royal Dutch-Shell Group and the managers of Shell-française that the French subsidiary needed an organizer to look after human resources and commercial matters, rather than a technician well placed on the political scene.[49]

The École des hautes études commerciales has become one of the best business schools, offering an education that complies with the new requirements of managers. Does this mean that this status, gained with difficulty, would be challenged if the courses were not continuously adjusted? This situation is unlikely to arise. Although the solidarity of graduates means that young graduates will always find some promising appointments, the vigorous competition within business will always compel the School to adapt.

[49] Interview with Louis Devaux; *Shell-revue* (in-house magazine).

N33

8

Training Electrical Engineers in France, 1880–1939

ANDRÉ GRELON

In the last third of the nineteenth century, new industrial developments took place in close connection with the progress of applied science and new technology. This was for example the case in the steel industry, with the gradual installation of Bessemer converters and major breakthroughs in the study of alloys; and in the chemical industry, with essential discoveries in the field of synthetic dyes and their application to the textile industry. There was also the use of a new form of energy, which promised a great future: electricity. In order to be efficiently used for industrial purposes, the new technologies had to be handled by competent technicians. How were technicians trained in France at that time? There existed two types of establishments: institutions of higher education, which prepared their students for the engineering profession; and technical schools, which trained foremen.

The institution of higher education recruited their students on the basis of a competitive entrance examination, which usually required two to three years of preparation after the end of secondary schooling. The most prestigious of them was the École polytechnique, which provided the basic training for future state engineers. After two years in that school, the *polytechniciens* moved, according to their rank at the final examination, to one of the engineering schools, known as *écoles d'application* (the École des mines and the École des ponts et chaussées being the two most prestigious ones), where they received, over a further three years, a more specialized training, before joining one of the *corps de l'État*. These *écoles d'application* were also attended by students who were not destined to join the Civil Service, but intended to undertake a business career. In addition, there existed other institutions of the same level of higher education, the purpose of which was to train industrial (as opposed to state) engineers. These were the École centrale des arts et manufactures de Paris (commonly known as Centrale), originally a private institution, but which was donated to the French State in the mid-nineteenth century; and the École

The author thanks the Association pour l'histoire de l'électricité en France for its help in researching the subject of this chapter, and for financing its translation by Philip Reavis.

centrale lyonnaise, managed by industrialists. Various disciplines in pure and applied sciences were taught in these establishments which produced 'French-type' engineers, i.e. generalists capable of working in any kind of industry.

As for the technical schools, the leading institutions were the three *écoles d'arts et métiers*, at Châlon-sur Saône (north-east of France), Angers (west), and Aix-en-Provence (south). The young students who joined them (also on the basis of a competitive entrance examination) had not received a full secondary education, but only a solid basic primary instruction in French, history, geography, arithmetic, and geometry. During their three years of training, they worked six hours a day in a workshop and followed, in the same day, another four hours of lectures in theory and industrial design. Because of its wide character, this hard training turned them into foremen and workshop supervisors who were greatly appreciated in all industries; some of them succeeded in becoming engineers. Next to these engineers and generalist technicians, the new applied sciences were to produce a new type of technologist: the specialist. From this point of view, the case of electricity provides a striking example which deserves further analysis, as it throws a vivid light on the evolution taken by the development of technical education in France before the Second World War.

Electricity was scarcely more than an object of curiosity for experimenters in physics during the eighteenth century, and a scientific phenonomen to be studied in laboratories in the first part of the nineteenth century. Then progressively from the 1840s—with the electrical telegraph, the invention of the dynamo, and proof of its reversibility—it became an applied science, an *ad hoc* technology for industry. Inevitably, the 'electrical science', as it was called, and the development of electrical industries (production of energy, distribution of electrical current, manufacture of electromechanical motors and equipment, etc.) led to demand for specialists in the new field: technicians. But where should they be trained? Certainly not in the science colleges scattered through France, which were poorly funded, lacked appropriate scientific programmes—and even lacked students (France's universities were not to be reformed until the end of the century). Consequently, technical institutions such as the engineering schools were given the task.

Existing schools were engaged. But it was soon seen that schools specializing in electrical technology were needed. New institutions were created to meet the demand. These were formed along hierarchical patterns typical of French educational systems. The history of that experience is described hereafter. Three important periods are analysed:

1. From 1880 to the end of the century, teaching programmes in existing schools were changed by trial and error to integrate electricity into the curriculum.

2. Beginning in the mid-1890s, a network of specialized schools for training electrical engineers began to take shape.

3. After the First World War, electrical engineering schools consolidated their activities. New and more specialized schools were established, dedicated to low current (radio-electricity) and hydraulic power for production of electricity (popularly called 'white coal'). In this period of intensified political organization of the labour movement, a law was voted to protect engineers who possessed diplomas awarded by accredited schools.

1. THE BEGINNING OF TRAINING IN INDUSTRIAL ELECTRICITY

In electricity, the formal teaching of technology came long after the development of the industry. The first electric telegraph line was installed in 1844. Compared to the former optical telegraph by Chappe, the new electrical system came as a shock. From that time onward telegraph inspectors would need knowledge of electricity and magnetism. By 1845 telegraph authorities were asking for a school to train former students of the École polytechnique in telegraphy. But, in spite of the obvious need, the Government and legislators refused the request. It was not until 1878 that a decision was taken to establish an 'École supérieure de télégraphie'.[1] However, at the École des ponts et chaussées (School of Bridges and Roads) lectures on telegraphy and electromagnetism were added to the curriculum. The reason for this was that bridge and road engineers played an important part in the development of railways, and the railway companies installed telegraph lines along their tracks. In other schools, whether the Mines (School of Mining), which trained industrial inspectors, or the Centrale (School of Industrial Engineering), electricity was just one of the chapters in the physics course—at the Centrale, Gramme's invention of the first dynamo was accepted for practical studies only long after it had been adopted by industrial establishments.

How were the first electrical engineers trained? In different ways. Studying scientific knowledge and general technology, they read electricity manuals, which were regularly published (for the most part handbooks translated from German), plus increasing numbers of specialized periodicals, and visited industrial sites. On-the-job training in electrical workshops was the most prevalent method of instruction employed. A

---

[1] Andrew Butrica, 'From Inspecteur to Ingénieur: Telegraphy and the Genesis of Electrical Engineering in France, 1845–1881' (Ph.D. thesis, Iowa State University, 1986; a copy of this thesis has been deposited at the École nationale supérieure destélécommunications in Paris); and from the same author 'The Ecole supérieure de télégraphie and the Beginnings of the French Electrical Engineering Education', *IEEE Transactions on Education*, E30/3 (Aug. 1987), 121–8.

few industrial employers organized training courses in their factories to provide theoretical and practical instruction for their staffs.

The first International Electricity Exhibition held in Paris in 1881, at the same time as the first Scientific Congress on Electricity, was symbolic of the importance of industrial electricity in modern society.[2] Although the French Government, represented by the Minister of the Post and Telegraph, was the official organizer of the event, it was financed entirely by French industrial electricity companies acting as veritable pioneers in the effort. The public response was considerable, and the exhibition was a huge commercial success. Soon after, similar exhibitions followed in other industrialized countries.

The importance of the phenomenon was not lost on educators, who finally saw the need for supplying industry with specialists in electricity and electrotechnology. But the response at the level of schools was slow and stingy: modification of curricula came about piecemeal. At the same time, the Government closed down the École de télégraphie (Telegraphy School), which had been established with great difficulty seven years before, and transferred its students and engineering instructors to the École de l'administration des postes (Post Office Administration School). Meanwhile other European countries were mobilizing educational systems to teach electrical engineering. In the Technische Hochschulen, chairs and sections in electricity were established and laboratories were built. At the Polytechnicum in Zurich a new four-year course leading to a diploma in electrical engineering was instituted. Moreover, in Liège, in 1883, the first real institute of electrical engineering was created. Thanks to a grant from an industrial patron, Georges Montefiore-Levi, the school was dedicated entirely to electricity, and placed under the direction of Eric Gérard, a young engineer of the local Mines de Liège (School of Mining) and graduate of the École supérieure de télégraphie de Paris (Telegraphy School). This school, admirably conceived, was a source of inspiration for the French schools which followed thereafter. Many young aspiring electrical wizards who could not find satisfying schools in France travelled to Zurich or Liège to study. The Société des anciens élèves des écoles d'art et métiers (a benevolent association of graduates of Paris's Arts and Crafts School) even offered grants to finance students' studies at these institutions.[3]

One should, however, mention an interesting effort which greatly influenced future development in the field. That was the establishment in 1882 of the École de physique et de chimie industrielles de la ville de Paris

---

[2] See Fabienne Cardot, 'L'Exposition de 1881', in François Caron and Fabienne Cardot (eds.), *Histoire générale de l'électricité en France*, i: *Espoirs et conquêtes, 1881–1918* (Paris, 1991), 18–33.

[3] On the relationship between the training of electrical engineers in Central European countries and French technical education, see André Grelon, 'L'Influence de l'Europe sur l'enseignement français', in Caron and Cardot (eds.), *Histoire de l'électricité*, 277–86.

(Paris School of Industrial Physcis and Chemistry).[4] The idea for such a school came to the industrialist Charles Lauth at the time of the Paris International Exhibition in 1878. Sent by the Ministry of Industry to report on the Exhibition, Lauth was alarmed by the state of France's chemical industry compared with that of European competitors, and he recommended the creation of a national school of chemistry. The Government ignored his plea, however, and Lauth turned to the City of Paris, which agreed to finance the establishemnt of a school of industrial chemistry. After the electricity exhibition, the project was modified to include industrial physics. Finally, the physics programme was almost entirely oriented to the study of electricity and electrical engineering. It was the first time in France that a school of industrial engineering had had a specialized curriculum—traditionally the French engineer was a general practitioner. Another particularity of the school was that it taught students in laboratories, emphasizing experimental science. Consequently the first place was no longer awarded to mathematics, which became an ancillary tool applied to physics and chemistry.[5] This new method departed from classical curricula for engineering students and was soon after adopted by universities. In spite of this, the effort fell short of what was required: the Physics and Chemistry School did not issue more than thirty diplomas a year, of which only a dozen were in physics.

2. SETTING UP A NETWORK OF SCHOOLS

Not until the 1890s was there a real beginning in the organization of specialized education for electrical engineers. The movement continued until the mid-1900s. During the first period of about fifteen years a hierarchical system of electrical schools took shape. At the summit of the pyramid was the École supérieure d'électricité (a graduate school).

The origin of this school lay in the International Electricity Exhibition in 1881. At the end of the show the organizers made a profit of 325,000 francs. Having declared from the beginning that no distribution of the proceeds of the exhibition would be permitted, they faced the problem of determining how the money would be spent. The industrialists who made up this organization and the directors of the technical services of the Post and Telegraph decided to use it to build a laboratory for testing and standardizing electrical equipment. Such a facility, which did not exist, was considered indispensable for the development of industries in the

[4] Terry Shinn, 'Des sciences industrielles aux sciences fondamentales: la mutation de l'École supérieure de physique et de chimie (1882–1970)', *Revue française de sociologie*, 22 (1981), 167–82.

[5] Hippolyte Copaux, *Cinquantième Anniversaire de la fondation de l'École de physique et de chimie industrielles de la ville de Paris* (Paris, 1932).

sector. A decree was published in 1882 establishing a 'Central Electricity Laboratory', but the Ministry charged with responsibility for the project seemed unable to produce results. An industrial association, the Société internationale des électriciens (SIE: International Society of Electricians), established in 1883, was assigned the task.[6] It set up a provisional framework for the service in 1888. The City of Paris approved the project and allotted land for the building. Subscription of funds from members of the SIE helped build the laboratory, which was inaugurated in 1893.

At the time of its foundation, the SIE took up the serious question of training technicians. Its aim was to set up a real school for specialists. It seemed unthinkable to continue sending French electricians to foreign countries for training. The SIE expressed its concern about the matter in an official letter to the Ministry of Post and Telegraph in 1885. But the Ministry seemed as incapable of handling the training problem as it had been of solving the case of the laboratory. Whether it was because of the difficulty of handling a specific problem concerning a disputable proposal within the government, or because the dossier would disappear in some other more important Ministry, or because of the State's inability to make a decision on industrial strategy, the case was left to the privately owned and operated company to settle, as it had in the matter of the laboratory, according to its own evaluation of the problem. Thus on 1 December 1894 a school for twelve trainees was created under the tentative title of École d'application du Laboratoire central. In a short time the school won its independence with a new name: École supérieure d'électricité; and a new director, the physicist Paul Janet, who spent the rest of his life (forty-two years) running the establishment.[7]

It was an ambitious project. The aim was to constitute a corps of highly qualified engineers in the most recently developed domains of electricity. Recruitment was launched among young graduates with diplomas in engineering and science who would find a year of intensive training at the school. Thus, 'Supélec', as the school was called, would serve as a training ground in applied electricity for a certain number of polytechnicians. The one-year programme covered two general courses and technical lectures given by the most eminent specialists, for the theoretical part; and practical work in testing, measuring, and other laboratory work for the construction of instruments, which occupied most of the students' time. The organization of the studies and work was in great part inspired by that put in place a dozen years before by Eric Gérard at Liège. But the willingness to create an élite of electrical engineers was considerably enhanced.

    [6] After the First World War, its name changed to Société française des électriciens and it was later amalgamated with other scientific associations. See Fabienne Cardot, *Cent ans d'histoire des électriciens, des électroniciens et des radioélectriciens* (Paris, 1983).

    [7] André Grelon, 'Le Laboratoire central d'électricité et la fondation de l'École supérieure d'électricité', in Caron and Cardot (eds.), *Histoire de l'électricité*, 286–93.

In the course of time, the entrance examination for candidates without appropriate diplomas was made increasingly difficult.

The effect of the new school was immediate, and important. On one hand, graduates of the highly respected school founded and supported by leading engineers were quickly recruited for management posts in industry. On the other hand, the École supérieure d'électricité began to play an essential training role in the educational system. First, it stimulated other older establishments, such as the École centrale, to upgrade the importance of electrical engineering in their curricula. Second, the new school encouraged the establishment of other schools to prepare candidates for Supélec's entrance examination, and to train technicians in electricity. Many of these schools hired Supélec graduate engineers as professors and directors.

While Supélec profited by the support of the Société internationale des électriciens, many other small schools in Paris, known by the names of Breguet, Charliat, Sudria, and Violet, established between 1900 and 1905, had to make the transition themselves without help from the industry's employers, and without financial resources other than tuition fees paid by their students.[8] These schools were for the most part created by individuals—teachers, engineers, scientific journalists. They recruited their students in the upper primary and secondary schools for three-year courses leading to jobs as technicians in the manufacture of electrical equipment or the distribution of electrical power. Until this time, electrical technicians were adults who converted from other occupations by studying at evening schools sponsored by various patrons: either by the Fédération des chauffeurs-mécaniciens (steam engineers), or the Conservatoire national des arts et métiers (arts and crafts), or various philo-technical associations, each of which offered different types of courses. From this time on, industry would benefit from technicians properly trained in the new field of electricity. The aim of these schools was, as Charles Schneider, director of the École Breguet, put it, to produce electrical engineers as competent as the famous graduates of the schools of the Arts et métiers—the foremen, technicians, and engineers so important to France's industries. But the ambition of these schools was also to see their students qualify for the École supérieure d'électricité. That is why their courses were designed to prepare candidates for Supélec's entrance examination.

One may wonder why Paris's industrialists gave these schools so little help. First, there was a measure of fear of flooding the labour market with more qualified applicants than those needed for available jobs. After all, France's electrical industries were largely dependent on foreign patents

[8] André Grelon, 'Les Origines et le développement des écoles d'électricité Breguet, Charliat, Sudria et Violet avant la seconde guerre mondiale', *Bulletin d'histoire de l'électricité*, 11 (June 1989), 65–88.

and materials, and that would limit growth. But there was another reason based on some employers' doubts about the quality of training in the technical schools, and those employers preferred to train their own apprentices on the job. It was a paradoxical attitude, because all the graduates of the schools were employed, and the schools continued to increase the numbers of their students to cope with growing demand for technicians in the expanding electrical industry. Thus the prophets of a plethora of electrical engineers unable to profit by their diplomas were confounded. Nevertheless, at the same time, many continued to congratulate themselves on the establishment of the École supérieure d'électricité, and to denounce the creation of more training schools for technicians. This was the inherent problem of a nation which had always preferred teaching an élite of brilliant and competent students—though few in numbers—rather than providing practical training for many in industry.

Provincial industrialists, on the other hand, gave their support to regional universities which grew out of a restructuring of France's national system of higher education. After the Revolution, France found itself without universities. Napoleon set up a monopolistic University of France which covered three teaching levels: primary, secondary, and superior. Science faculties were dispersed throughout the country, were cut off from each other, and some were closed down or reopened according to the whims of successive governments. The central mission of the professors in these universities (who were frequently *lycée* teachers) was to prepare students for a science *baccalauréat* degree, in the first grade of university. A small number of students were prepared for university degrees (*licences*). As for doctoral degrees from provincial universities, one could count them on the fingers of one hand. The Faculty of Science of Paris was the veritable institution of higher learning. Provincial faculty professors offered public courses for varied audiences, but these were not for students in the modern sense of the word. Beginning in 1854, under the Second Empire, provincial professors were authorized to offer courses and give lectures in applied sciences, and contacts between the universities and industrialists began to develop. An example of this is found in Lille, where Pasteur was the first dean.

The aftermath of the war of 1870, when France lost two provinces to Prussia, left the nation in a dangerous state of political confusion. Throughout the country a debate raged to measure the results of the catastrophe. Out of the argument grew a conclusion: it was imperative that the nation be provided with a new élite in every domain. With the establishment of the Republic, a national education policy covering all levels was conceived and set up with determination. As for higher education, it gained mainly from the work of two remarkable government administrators, both directors of top-level schools in the Ministry of Public Instruction, Dumon, and later Liard, who reorganized the universities, modelling them in part after German universities. It took twenty years to pass a law (in 1896) establishing sixteen regional universities through grouping the faculties of science, letters, law, and medicine, including pharmacy.

The business community rapidly responded to the new institutions. In particular, faculties of science were asked to supply competent personnel in various fields of applied science. This encouraged the most progressive professors to turn to local municipalities and industrialists for help in setting up specialized schools which offered, not classical education in pure science leading to a university diploma, but a combination of theoretical and practical training applicable to industry. These were mainly institutes for the study of chemistry, because it was in that area that the greatest need was found. The first were in Lyons, then Nancy, and other university towns. Then, at the beginning of the twentieth century, four institutes of technology in electricity were founded at Grenoble, Lille, Nancy, and Toulouse. What kind of graduates did they offer industry? The founders of these schools pointed out that, in the giant factories of the day, and even more so in those to come, specialization would not only affect the working classes. Except for technical directors, engineers would be expected to offer clearly defined specialized skills. The university proposed to educate these new engineers properly in their chosen fields.[9]

Thus the engineers from the new institutes of the faculties of sciences gradually infiltrated the ranks of industry between the graduates of prestigious schools—of which one was now the École supérieure d'électricité—and the graduates of the smaller schools of electricity.

The success of these new institutes was undeniable—even before the war of 1914–18—especially the school in Grenoble, which was directed by Louis Barbillion, an energetic engineering professor who was one of Supélec's first graduates. But satisfaction on one hand led to jealousy on another, and criticism arose within the university and in other *grandes écoles*, the institutions of higher learning. The critics agreed with each other that the role of the university was to teach pure science and not technology. A posteriori, one cannot help but note that the criticism regularly heard in France *vis-à-vis* the supposed lack of interest of universities in industry is not borne out by a study of history.

3. PROGRESS BETWEEN THE WARS

At the beginning of the 1914–18 war, voices in the industrial community and the world of engineers were raised in favour of a profound study of technical training in general, and that of engineers in particular. Had the

---

[9] André Grelon, 'Les Universités et la formation des ingénieurs en France, 1870–1914', *Formation-Emploi*, 27–8 (July–Dec. 1989), 121–43.

existing system become too complex to be efficient? How valid was the hierarchy in the schools? Should not the curricula of the schools be re-examined? All these questions came up in numerous debates.[10] Proposals of new laws were even formulated. But finally tradition won out. The schools of higher learning held on to their perch, and the lower schools were kept in their place.[11]

The École supérieure d'électricité continued to thrive. It was shifted to new quarters in 1927 (thanks to considerable investment from subscribers and from subsidies). The move gave the school means for further development. Two new sections were introduced to teach other specialisms. The former modest pre-1914 training programme in radio-telegraphy was replaced by a course in radio-electricity, leading to a degree in engineering. Another new course, demanded by industry, was offered in the field of electric lighting. The latter was copied from the British programme set up before the war. At the end of this period, however, the school passed through difficult straits, with the death of its founder Paul Janet, and above all conversion of the curriculum from one year to two years of study. In this manner, the school lost a part of its image as a postgraduate facility. This change took place after the Second World War, when the school finally adopted the classic French engineering school structure: a three-year period of study offered upon successful completion of an entrance examination, available only to students who qualified with two years of preparatory education.

In spite of the angry criticism endured during the pre-war period, the universities' electrical engineering schools survived and developed during the 1920s. A single exception was that of the school in Lille, which was destroyed by the German army. It was not replaced, probably because of local competition from a regional engineering school. This was the Institut industriel du nord, which had an electrical engineering section. Other university institutes were opened, both in the field of low-current electricity (the Institut de radioélectricité in Bordeaux and in Lille) and in the field of hydroelectricity, for development of power through 'white coal' (at Grenoble). This is to say that the method of organizing the teaching of scientific technology was functional. But on the whole, the administrative position of the institutes, under the auspices of university faculties, remained ambiguous, neither completely autonomous nor really dependent on mother-schools. They also suffered from a lack of

---

[10] e.g. a long debate, involving the most prestigious French scientists and engineers, took place in 1917 at the Société des ingénieurs civils de France, in order to re-evaluate French higher technical education. Conclusions were drawn in Léon Guillet, *L'Enseignement technique supérieure à l'après-guerre* (Paris, 1918).

[11] On the development of engineering schools between 1918 and 1945, see André Grelon, 'La Formation des ingénieurs électriciens en France entre les deux guerres', in Maurice Lévy-Leboyer and Henri Morsel (eds.), *Histoire générale de l'électricité en France, ii: 1918–1945* (forthcoming).

co-ordination between themselves. Neither the conditions of recruitment (by competition or by examination), nor the length of studies (two or three years), nor the nature of the curricula were similar from one school to another. Once more, one had to wait, this time until the end of the Second World War, for administrators of the national school system to formulate a coherent and identical statute for all of the universities' institutes, which finally in 1947 were reclassified as écoles nationales supérieures d'ingénieurs (national schools of engineering for graduate studies).

As for other schools, those in Paris in particular were finally recognized by the educational authorities. Their administrative and technical councils were reinforced with eminent scholars, famous engineers, and leading industrialists. They strengthened their programmes, opened pedagogical laboratories, and even invited the State's technical education inspectors to survey and endorse the quality of their teachers' performance. But in spite of the efforts of their faculty members, and the support of graduate associations, their students on receiving their diplomas continued to be employed at the bottom of the ladder in companies that could offer but modest career prospects compared with those available to engineers coming out of other schools. The conservative nature of French society, particularly that of the industrial community, seemed to block the breach in the wall against all efforts to shake up the system, grown rigid in its relationship to training and employment.

But, in a more general way, the two decades between the wars were a particularly important period for France's engineers.[12] The bad news was that for the first time, as a social and professional group, engineers were experiencing a grave problem of unemployment. The economic crisis which began in France in 1930 affected nearly all sectors of engineering—chemists and electricians in particular. Young graduates coming out of school, and older engineers, were hardest hit. A twofold problem beset the profession. The first was fear of professional disqualification. A job seeker faced with a lack of work as an engineer was tempted to take anything available. Engineers' unions fought for recognition by employers of equal status for engineers titled by schools and engineers actively engaged by industry. Second, engineers felt endangered by demotion in the workaday world, and they fought for an intermediate and autonomous role for themselves between industrial employers and manual labourers. The Confédération des travailleurs intellectuels, a society of educated workers, was a leader in promoting this cause.

The good news was that legislation to protect the status of diploma-bearing engineers came about finally in July 1934. Thereafter, no one could claim to be an *ingénieur diplômé* unless he came out of an accredited school with a recognized degree (the term 'engineer' by itself remained in

---

[12] André Grelon (ed.), *Les Ingénieurs de la crise: titre et professions entre les deux guerres* (Paris, 1986).

common usage). To establish a list of accredited schools authorized to issue such diplomas a permanent commission was created, in which engineers' associations were represented, along with industrial employers' associations, the remainder of the members being teachers in engineering schools. In this way the profession protected itself with a kind of auto-control system over the admission of newcomers to the fold. Because of this law, industrial collective conventions, signed in 1936, at the height of the organized labour movement, took into account the diploma of engineer, creating at the time a category of *ingénieur débutant* with a minimum salary and a description of his responsibilities. This was something engineers' unions had never before been able to obtain. Thus the title of *ingénieur diplômé* became the sole legal title recognized by France's industrial world. Sixty years after its publication in the government's *Journal officiel*, the law of 10 July 1934 is still in effect, and very important to French engineers. In it they see their only means of distinguishing themselves from the mass of educated personnel in their world of business and industry.[13]

---

[13] For further information see Charles R. Day, *Les Écoles d'arts et métiers: l'enseignement technique en France, XIXème–XXème siècles* (Paris, 1991); Robert Fox and George Weisz (eds.), *The Organization of Science and Technology in France 1808–1914* (Cambridge, 1980); Harry W. Paul, *From Knowledge to Power: The Rise of the Science Empire in France, 1860–1939* (Cambridge, 1985); Terry Shinn, 'The French Science Faculty System, 1808–1914: Institutional Change and Research Potential in Mathematics and the Physical Sciences', *Historical Studies in the Physical Sciences*, tenth annual volume (Baltimore, 1979), 271–332.

9

Engineers in the Boardroom: Britain and France Compared

CHRISTINE SHAW

1. INTRODUCTION

Misguided and prejudiced attitudes to engineering and to engineers in Britain have been seen as forming one of the most serious cankers to weaken and cripple British industry in the twentieth century. Indeed these prejudices have, notoriously, been detected well back into the nineteenth century. 'For the century after about 1850 or 1860', wrote Donald Coleman and Christine Macleod, 'a mountain of apparently damning evidence on the British businessman can be built up. He can be presented as sliding into incompetence, displaying the while an attitude to new techniques which combined ignorance, indifference, hostility, prejudice and complacency in a dosage which ranged from the damaging to the lethal.'[1] One of the central arguments of G. C. Allen's famous and influential essay *The British Disease* was that 'Britain's industrial progress was gravely hindered by the strong prejudice in government and many branches of industry itself against the expert, a prejudice rooted in social and educational tradition, a prejudice which carried into a technological age the practices and attitudes of mind inherited from a pre-scientific time.'[2]

A technical education, however thorough and demanding, even if it includes a first-class university degree in engineering, it is maintained, has brought little recognition and less status in many British manufacturing firms. The path of the technical expert to the boardrooms of major companies has been blocked by a pernicious alliance of scientifically illiterate 'gentlemen' who despise skills they are incapable of appreciating, and socially uneasy 'practical men' who consider a formal technical education to be of little worth in resolving the practical problems of production. 'In its attitudes towards engineers . . . its belief in apprenticeship and evening school as appropriate training for technical personnel . . . the business

---

[1] D. C. Coleman and Christine Macleod, 'Attitudes to New Techniques: British Businessmen, 1800–1950', *Economic History Review*, 2nd ser. 39/4 (1986), 588.

[2] G. C. Allen, *The British Disease: A Short Essay in the Nature and Causes of the Nation's Lagging Wealth* (2nd edn. London, 1979), 50.

community continued to demonstrate the persistence of nineteenth-
century attitudes,' according to Coleman and Macleod.[3]

So hostile was the atmosphere in many firms for graduate engineers
that even those with a genuine enthusiasm for industry could quickly
become disheartened—'frequently the graduate, persuaded by his university that he could have a satisfying future in industrial production, soon
returned totally disillusioned', wrote Geoffrey Sims in an essay on scientists and engineers in a collection entitled *The British Malaise* published in
the early 1980s. 'The most common complaint was that he was tired of
being told that when he too had been doing the job for thirty years . . . it
might be appropriate for him to speak.'[4] Engineering employers in their
attitudes to graduate engineers, maintained Alexander Kennaway (himself a graduate engineer who had worked in industry) in his contribution
to the same volume,

have learned nothing and thought nothing useful over the last one hundred years.
It is a consequence of having industry run by Petit-Bourgeois Man, perhaps a half-
educated, former foreman, who can do no better than to apply poorly-grasped
mechanistic principles to a job he was never educated or trained for. He is fearful
and jealous of the graduate and adopts the standard reaction—the graduate
should know practical things, theory is unnecessary, he needs to be immediately
useful in the plant. . . . There is no point in having engineers registered as competent if they are to continue to work for incompetent directors.[5]

Kennaway maintains passionately that such views are peculiar to
Britain. He and other critics of the values and attitudes which they would
argue have been largely responsible for Britain's economic decline often
seem, explicitly or implicitly, to work on the assumption that such failings
are not to be found abroad, in Britain's main competitors. The critics of
British attitudes to engineering rarely recognize that some of the faults
they see here can also be detected in companies in other countries, other
cultures—that many US corporations, for example, have seemed unable to
make proper use of their graduate engineers.[6] Generally comparisons are
only made to the disfavour of Britain, with Germany in particular being
held up as a model for the education, training, employment, promotion,
and status of engineers.

But France also comes in for its share of praise from some British
commentators. In France, they say, vocational and technical education is
valued at its true worth, and engineers have high status and are welcomed
into the upper echelons of industry—as is proven by the status and

[3] Coleman and Macleod, 'Attitudes to New Techniques', 604.

[4] Geoffrey Sims, 'Scientists and Engineers', in Gordon Roderick and Michael Stephens,
The British Malaise: Industrial Performance, Education and Training in Britain Today (Barcombe,
1982), 85.

[5] Alexander Kennaway, 'Industry, Society and Education: A Multi-national View', in
Roderick and Stephens, *The British Malaise*, 112–13.

[6] Ian Glover and Michael Kelly, *Engineers in Britain: A Sociological Study of the Engineering
Dimension* (London, 1987), 178–9.

careers of the graduates of the *grandes écoles*, particularly the École polytechnique. In contrast to the boardrooms of British firms, boardrooms in France, said Alexander Kennaway, 'are staffed by graduate engineers who have been joined by colleagues from every discipline and in this way have provided a proper team, marrying the requisite business skills and understanding the basis of the business'.[7] Thomas Kempner, the principal and Professor of Management Studies at Henley, in an article written in the early 1980s arguing that British industry was being overshadowed by its competitors because British management lacked adequate professional training (such as was to be found at Henley), inferred a respect for vocational education in France from the prestige of the graduates of the *grandes écoles*.[8]

But have graduate engineers and other technical experts really found it so much easier to rise to the top of the major companies in France than in Britain in the twentieth century? And has their presence in French boardrooms been an indication of the prestige attached to their discipline?

2. THE BRITISH CASE

Direct statistical evidence on patterns of promotion of engineers, especially graduate engineers, to be directors of British companies is surprisingly thin on the ground, given the importance which has been accorded to the issue. Such statistical surveys as there are, however, do indicate that, since the late nineteenth century, Britain has generally had a lower percentage of graduates of all disciplines among the leaders of her large companies than France has had. In both countries, though, there has been a correlation between the proportion of the directors and top managers of a company who have had formal tertiary education, and company size and industrial sector. The larger the firm, or the more complicated the production process, the higher the proportion of graduates at the top levels of the company is likely to be. But even when these factors are taken into consideration, British directors and top managers of major firms have still been less likely to be graduates than their French counterparts.[9]

Studies indicate, however, that British managers and directors who have been graduates have been far more likely to have read science, mathematics, or a technical subject, including engineering, than to have read an arts subject. A survey of graduates in industry in the 1950s conducted by the organization known as Political and Economic Planning

---

[7] Kennaway, 'Industry, Society and Education', 117.

[8] Thomas Kempner, 'Education for Management in Five Countries: Myth and Reality', *Journal of General Management*, 9/2 (1983–4), 6.

[9] These observations are based on comparisons of a number of surveys of various groups of British and French managers and business leaders, which are too complex to set out in detail here. See my forthcoming book on businessmen in Britain, France, Germany, and Italy.

found that only one-ninth of them had taken degrees in the arts.[10] A survey by the journal *Director* in 1966 of about 2,400 members of the Institute of Directors found that, of those holding a degree, 54 per cent had read sciences, 33 per cent the arts.[11] A close correlation between the technical demands of the industry and the proportion of science and technology graduates among directors has been observed. Roger Betts's analysis of the qualifications—academic and professional—of directors of around eighty companies in five industrial sectors in the mid-1960s found that they were related to the technical demands of the industry. Of the directors with qualifications in the radio and television manufacturing companies he surveyed, for example, 55 per cent were engineers; of those in food-manufacturing, only 5 per cent.[12] But another, negative, correlation has also been observed: at the top of the company hierarchies, particularly in large firms, scientists and technologists begin to lose ground, above all to accountants or economists, and also to lawyers. In a group of managers studied by D. G. Clark in the mid-1960s, among the top managers and directors there were fewer scientists and technologists, and more lawyers and economists, than among the group as a whole.[13] A 1965 survey of nearly 6,000 members of the Institute of Directors found that in larger companies (defined as those with a capital of half a million pounds or more) qualifications in accountancy or the arts were more frequent than those in the sciences.[14]

These findings could be read as proof of prejudice in the upper reaches of British manufacturing companies against technical experts, including engineers. But, in the light of surveys of engineers in British industry which have revealed persistent self-doubt about their own competence in financial, personnel, and general administrative tasks, they could also be read as a product of a collective inferiority complex among British industrial engineers. 'Many' for over 400 practising chartered engineers surveyed in the 1970s 'felt inadequate in terms of "communications" and "human relations", in relation to subordinates, superiors and colleagues from other backgrounds'. A project involving interviews with 250 graduate engineers and 200 of their colleagues around 1980 found that 'Both the engineers and their colleagues felt that technical competence was not lacking, but that appreciation of business and especially financial matters were, as were social skills.'[15]

[10] Political and Economic Planning, *Graduates in Industry* (London, 1957), 9.

[11] 'The Director Observed', *Director* (Apr. 1966), 85.

[12] Roger Betts, 'Characteristics of British Company Directors', *Journal of Management Studies*, 4/1 (1967), 75–6.

[13] D. G. Clark, *The Industrial Manager: His Background and Career Pattern* (London, 1966), 53–4.

[14] 'The Anatomy of the Board', *Director* (Jan. 1965), 89.

[15] Both surveys are reported in Glover and Kelly, *Engineers in Britain*, 174–6. Other surveys are summarized there, pp. 176–81.

The British engineering profession, argues R. A. Buchanan in the conclusion to his history of the engineering profession in Britain from the mid-eighteenth century to the First World War, seems to have had an inferiority complex: 'It is uncertain about its scope and its status: it is uneasy about its relations with other professions and with society at large; and it senses that it is losing out in competition with other traditions of engineering formation.'[16] This inferiority complex was not evident among mid-Victorian engineers, but apparently developed from around the 1880s. According to Buchanan, the collapse of the railway bridge over the River Tay in December 1879 was an important turning-point, severely damaging the self-esteem of a profession which had begun to feel it could do no wrong. W. J. Reader, in his essay on the engineer in Victorian society, felt that the evident advantage of German and American competitors in fields like electrical engineering during the last two decades of the nineteenth century played a part.[17] Whatever the contributory causes, the effect was to weaken the resistance among leading professional engineers, wedded to the pragmatic training based on apprenticeship they had received themselves, to the setting up of systematic, theoretically based courses for engineers. But, as Buchanan points out, 'The acknowledged need for more theoretical knowledge by having a university training or its equivalent [was] grafted on to the existing apparatus of apprenticeship and self-education through membership of the professional institutions.'[18] The image of engineering education in Britain long remained that of apprenticeship and 'learning by doing', and membership of a professional institution, rather than holding a particular degree, the certification of a fully qualified engineer. In fact, though, the 'emphasis of engineering education in Britain has been notably less practical and more scientific than in several major competitor countries', according to Ian Glover and Michael Kelly in their study of engineers in Britain published in 1987.[19]

Once recruited into industry, graduate engineers in Britain have shown a distinct preference for working in research and development or design departments rather than those concerned with production. Employers have complained it is difficult to persuade them to move out of specialized technical tasks into other functions in the firm such as sales and marketing.[20] The better the degree an engineer held, the less likely on the whole he was to have thought of a career in management, J. E. Gerstl and S. P. Hutton found in their study of British mechanical engineers pub-

---

[16] R. A. Buchanan, *The Engineers: A History of the Engineering Profession in Britain 1750–1914* (London, 1989), 208.

[17] Ibid. 106; W. J. Reader, ' "At the Head of All the New Professions": The Engineer in Victorian Society', in Neil McKendrick and R. B. Outhwaite (eds.), *Business Life and Public Policy: Essays in Honour of D. C. Coleman* (Cambridge, 1986), 184.

[18] Buchanan, *The Engineers*, 175.   [19] Glover and Kelly, *Engineers in Britain*, 96.

[20] Ibid. 28; Allen, *British Disease*, 56.

lished in the mid-1960s, although a good degree, especially if it was a less specialized degree, was a key to the advancement of engineers into management.[21] That is to say, if the holder of a good degree in engineering was prepared to look beyond his specialized technical interests and take on other roles within a company, he would not find his promotion to a management position blocked by prejudice against his technical qualifications. In fact, it looks as though by wishing to stick to technical posts, and by their lack of confidence in their ability to deal with people or financial matters, many British graduate engineers have excluded themselves from consideration for the general management positions which most often lead to the boardroom. The question should be put—have many British engineers in industry *wanted* to reach the boardroom?

3. THE FRENCH CASE

A collective inferiority complex is the last affliction one would expect to find among the graduates of France's most prestigious engineering schools who have gone into industry. They would seem to have no doubt about their ability, indeed their right, to lead large companies. But their self-confidence has not been derived from their technical training, nor the value accorded to industrial engineers *per se*. Only the graduates of certain institutions enjoy high status, and the specialist element of their education has frequently been criticized by French businessmen for providing a poor preparation for the needs of industry.

It has been the prestige accorded to the graduates of the École polytechnique which has often been taken to symbolize the status of French industrial engineers. For much of its history, however, the École polytechnique frowned upon its graduates entering industry. It was founded in the 1790s as the training school for state engineers, and the service of the State—which has traditionally carried high prestige in France—was considered to be the only fitting employment for its graduates. Supplying engineers for French industry was not a fit task for the professors of the Polytechnique, and other schools were founded to undertake it. The first *écoles des arts et métiers* set up in the provinces by Napoleon were intended to provide a practical, technical training for industry. Significantly, they were originally supposed to cater for the sons of the lower ranks of the army, and their graduates were clearly considered the social inferiors of those from the Polytechnique. In 1829 a group of industrialists set up the École centrale des arts et manufactures to provide training for engineers for industry, but Centrale never attained the status of the Polytechnique and was not recognized as a *grande école*

---

[21] J. E. Gerstl and S. P. Hutton, *Engineers: The Anatomy of a Profession: A Study of Mechanical Engineers in Britain* (London, 1966), 37, 50–1, 57–8, 89.

until the late nineteenth century. In the later nineteenth century a number of other engineering schools were set up, in Paris and the provinces, partly at the prompting of industrialists who complained of the lack of suitably trained engineers, particularly in chemistry and physics. They provided a combination of theoretical and practical training, oriented towards the solution of industrial problems; soon their graduates were making their mark as industrial managers.

These developments displeased the corps of state engineers and the Polytechnique. They feared that the practical orientation of the training such schools provided, and their emphasis on the solution of concrete problems, risked debasing the standing and the authority of engineers. They proposed the schools should be shut, and the Polytechnique left as the sole training establishment for engineers, for industry as well as for the State.[22] Fortunately for French industry, this piece of special pleading was ignored.

As the prospects in state service and the relative value of Civil Service salaries contracted in the years before the First World War, careers in industry came to seem more attractive to *polytechniciens*—though not all industrialists were gratified by their condescension, considering their high-minded, theoretical education had left them ill-equipped for such work. The recovery of prestige by military engineers during the war opened the doors of industrial firms more widely to the graduates of the *grandes écoles*, including the Polytechnique. But while the *polytechniciens* were being welcomed in the upper reaches of the hierarchies of industrial firms, specialists like chemical or electrical engineers had a status and salary akin to workmen.[23] There were simply too many engineers for the posts available, and the decline in their prospects and status led to a renewed emphasis on the distinction between graduates of different schools, and on the hierarchy of prestige of the various institutions.[24]

The stratification of status and divergence in career patterns among engineers in French industry according to the institution they had attended has continued since the Second World War. Graduates of less prestigious schools such as the *écoles des arts et métiers* are to be found throughout industry, but rarely make it to the very top, particularly in French-owned firms, as René Darrigo and Pierre Serre found in their study of the ' "Gadz" Arts' (students of the *écoles des arts et métiers*).[25] Most French employers still prefer to recruit from the Polytechnique or the equally prestigious École nationale d'administration, whose primary purpose is to turn out Civil Servants, rather than from institutions like the

[22] Terry Shinn, 'Des corps de l'État au secteur industriel: genèse de la profession d'ingénieur, 1750–1920', *Revue française de sociologie*, 19 (1978), 67.

[23] *L'Ingénieur dans la société française* (Paris, 1985), 267.

[24] Luc Boltanski, *The Making of a Class: Cadres in French Society* (Cambridge, 1987), 74–8.

[25] René Darrigo and Pierre Serre, ' "Gadz" Arts et société', in *L'Ingénieur*, 192; see also p. 291.

écoles des hautes études commerciales which actually aim to train for business management.[26] A recruitment network based on 'the old school tie' has helped to make certain industries and certain major firms the preserve of one or other *grande école*. One result has been that in the mid-1980s, as Michel Bauer and Bénédicte Bertin-Mourot found, a quarter of the heads of the 200 largest French firms (by turnover) were graduates of the Polytechnique alone.[27]

This is not an indication that the engineering knowledge acquired at the Polytechnique is highly valued in industry. The same criticisms have recurred for several decades—the courses are too theoretical, too concerned with grand concepts, and too little aware of the practical requirements of industry. Not that such criticism much concerns the Polytechnique, which still 'glories in not teaching any *technique*', in the words of Alain and Philippe d'Iribarne in their interesting critique of attitudes in French industry to new technology, for the prestige of the *grandes écoles* is linked to the degree of theoretical abstraction in the courses taught there.[28] Its graduates have been expected to attend yet another institution, an *école d'application*, such as the École des mines, before they are considered employable.[29] It is the generalist with a well-trained mind that the Polytechnique has prided itself on turning out, with the study of mathematics having the symbolic, quasi-moral overtones that used to be attached to the study of the classics in the British educational system.

French employers have found the education of the *polytechniciens* has had other shortcomings, beside a disdain for mere *technique*. They are not noted for their willingness to innovate or to take risks. Very few have gone on to found their own businesses, for they usually prefer the well-defined hierarchies of large firms where they will be on the fast track. The exacting paperchase through the French educational system leaves the ostensible winners, the graduates of the highest-ranking *grandes écoles*, physically and mentally exhausted. For some, the strain has been increased because they have ground on through the years of intensive work against their own real inclinations, with family pressure reinforcing the expectations of schoolteachers that a boy of good family who shows ability at mathematics will automatically try for the engineering *grandes écoles*, particularly if his father attended one of them.[30]

[26] Jean Louis Barsoux and Peter Lawrence, *Management in France* (London, 1990), 40.

[27] Michel Bauer and Bénédicte Bertin-Mourot, *Les 200: comment devient-on un grand patron?* (Paris, 1987), 179.

[28] Alain and Philippe d'Iribarne, 'Nouvelles Technologies et culture française: le mariage du noble et vil', *Revue française de gestion*, 64 (1987), 45.

[29] Jane Marceau, 'Plus ça change plus c'est la même chose: Access to Elite Careers in French Business', in Jolyon Howorth and Philip Cerny (eds.), *Elites in France: Origins, Reproduction and Power* (London, 1981), 115.

[30] Ibid. 109–11.

But the subject of study has been almost immaterial to many employers of graduates of the most prestigious *grandes écoles*. 'Companies are apt to look upon the *grandes écoles* as elaborate sifting systems rather than purveyors of knowledge—and some make no secret of the fact that they are primarily purchasing the *concours* (entrance exam)', say Jean Louis Barsoux and Peter Lawrence in their recent book on management in France. 'Company indifference regarding the transmission of occupationally relevant management skills merely endorses the view of qualifications as "entry tickets".'[31]

A French businessman recruiting a graduate from the Polytechnique, if he is not simply taking on a new member of his own old-boy network, is not recruiting an engineer, he is recruiting a *polytechnicien*—someone with proven intellectual ability and capacity to work hard, but above all someone with social skills and useful connections. 'It is indeed hard to distinguish the use of the "diploma" itself from the persona that possession of it implies and hence from membership of a group with important contacts,' Jane Marceau found in her study of access to élite careers in French business.[32] It is the 'generalists', those with social graces and an authoritative air, who are perceived to make it to the top.

4. CONCLUSION

The boardrooms of large French companies are, in fact, much more socially and educationally exclusive than those of British firms. If a higher proportion of engineers has been admitted to the inner sanctum, it has been a peculiar breed of engineers, one prized not for their specialist knowledge or capacities but for their skills as 'generalists'. Engineers from less prestigious schools, who are hired for their technical skills, have found the road to the boardroom perhaps even more difficult to travel than the 'practical men' in British industry have done. Just as the hierarchy of the *grandes écoles* is based on the degree of abstraction of their teaching, so the prestige of engineers within French industry is linked to their distance from the sordid business of actually making things. 'In engineering, electronics has a higher element of abstraction and therefore of purity and nobility, which places it above electrical engineering with its high currents, and way ahead of mechanical engineering, which requires brute force . . . The greater the physical, as well as intellectual, distance from the shop floor, the higher the prestige of the function.'[33] An engineer proper in French industry principally produces paper—he who touches any other material 'appears to lose caste'.[34]

---

[31] Barsoux and Lawrence, *Management in France*, 40.
[32] Marceau. 'Plus ça change', 119.
[33] Barsoux and Lawrence, *Management in France*, 68–9.
[34] 'A l'air de se déclasser'—*L'Ingénieur*, 241.

Arguments about ill-informed prejudice holding back the advancement of engineers to the top of British manufacturing companies cannot be dismissed, and anecdotal evidence suggests they have an element of truth. Yet if comparatively few graduate engineers have reached British boardrooms—in comparison with some of her major industrial competitors, that is—it has been due at least in part to diffidence and reluctance on the part of engineers themselves to undertake the challenges of moving from their specialized field to general management, not just because ignorant directors fail to consider their advice of any worth. Comparisons with the prominence of engineers at the top levels of French industry need to be made with care. If French boards have been eager to recruit graduates of prestigious engineering schools, it has not been because they prize the knowledge of engineering in itself, and it says little about the prestige of technical education in France.

Much may be wrong with the British use of engineers in industry and recruitment to British boardrooms, but comprehending this is not helped by superficial comparisons with other countries. Above all, it does not help to assume that only in Britain can 'social qualities'—be it social skills in communication, or social advantage from the 'right' family background, or educational advantage from attending the 'right' institution— affect recruitment to the top levels of business management. All too often, denunciations of the social ills which are held to have afflicted British society and affected the health of British industry seem to be based on the assumption that Britain has been the only society in which cultural traditions, snobbery, and social prejudice have affected the way industry has been run. A better understanding, particularly of attitudes to industry in Continental European societies, is needed if we are to break out of such tired assumptions and circular arguments which cloud efforts to comprehend the social context of Britain's economic decline.

PART III

MERGERS AND SURVIVALS

N64 10

An Impossible Merger? The French Chemical Industry in the 1920s

JEAN-PIERRE DAVIET

The purpose of this chapter is to examine an ambitious merger project that would have changed the history of the French chemical industry. In 1926–7 the creation of a national federation, uniting all firms within the industry, under the 'Union chimique française' banner, was considered; it would have been like the Union chimique belge or, a closer comparison, ICI in Great Britain or IG Farben in Germany.[1] The companies which were involved thought the idea had come from bankers, and the Crédit commercial de France, founded in 1894 under the name of Banque suisse et française, was the bank most often cited. This plan started a process of consultation, and the firms which were involved showed an extreme reluctance. Though the initiative eventually failed to reach its original goals, it was none the less useful in many respects, and it contributed to the advancement of a new set of ideas. Analysing this project provides a deeper understanding of the historical development of France's chemical industry, an industry which suffered from many ambiguities, but also displayed in the 1920s an increased awareness of the ties between the banking community and industry. This study also helps to understand the strategic and organizational characteristics of French companies during the first half of the twentieth century.

One of the key issues of the period was the trend towards concentration within French industry; this evolution, though obvious in France, was less pronounced than in other countries.[2] The top 100 French firms accounted for 12 per cent of the nation's industrial output in 1912, and 16 per cent in 1929; in the latter year, in Great Britain, the figure was 26 per cent. Still, not only were the largest companies (more than 500 employees) becoming stronger in France, but so were medium-sized companies (100 to 200 employees). Around 1930, large businesses produced 20 to 25 per cent of

---

[1] The information presented here was obtained through detailed research in the archives of Saint-Gobain and Crédit commercial de France (primarily minutes of board meetings). Cf. J.-P. Daviet, *Une multinationale à la française: Saint-Gobain 1965–1989* (Paris, 1989).

[2] Cf. J.-P. Daviet, 'Some Features of Concentration in France (End of the 19th Century/20th Century)', in Hans Pohl (ed.), *The Concentration Process in the Entrepreneurial Economy since the Late 19th Century* (Stuttgart, 1988).

all industrial output, while the medium-sized category was responsible for 30 to 35 per cent. Small businesses, with 45–55 per cent of the output, had lost some of their pre-war supremacy (formerly 55 to 60 per cent). In 1938 the first six French chemical groups accounted for half the turnover of the entire sector; yet there was no single dominant national producer, representing, for example, 40 per cent of the total.

Another key issue is the industry's growth. While growth rates were high at the time, this did not necessarily suggest a move away from conventional industrial organizations or an evolution towards a 'management-driven' form of capitalism, as exhibited in the United States. An industrial concentration, whether successful or not, does involve some factors that could be considered random, such as general economic circumstances or the personalities of the decision-makers. Yet it also reveals the links that exist between product strategies and the models of business administration, management structures, and corporate cultures. Was this failure to concentrate a fatal blow to the French chemical industry? Would its success have led to improved industrial results?

1. DESTINY FOR THE FRENCH CHEMICAL INDUSTRY

Where did the French chemical industrial sector stand at the time of the merger plan of 1926?

Over the previous half-century it had drastically changed, under the pressure of the phenomenon that may be called the second industrial revolution.[3] The main mineral-based chemical industry, previously relying on sulphuric acid, underwent a renewal and lost some of its unity during the last quarter of the nineteenth century, with the introduction of industrial processes that completely differed from the Leblanc process. These new processes included: the fabrication of ammonia-soda (beginning in France in 1872); the electrolysis of sea-salt solutions (with experimentation on chlorates *circa* 1886–8 and the production of electrolytic chlorine really beginning to develop around 1900, to replace the use of the Deacon process, which had appeared on the French market in 1888); and the synthesis of ammonia (in Germany, 1913). Sulphuric acid retained a prominent position within the economy, albeit oriented towards other market niches (notably fertilizers, superphosphates, and ammonium sulphate, which were produced in very large quantities). As a result, the heavy mineral-based chemical industry become more and more splintered into distinct categories of companies.

The small-sized chemical firms, specializing in extracting substances from natural raw materials, were being slowly supplanted, but did not

[3] Cf. J.-P. Daviet, 'L'Industrie chimique française au tournant de la seconde industrialisation (1860–1939)', *Culture technique*, 23 (1991).

completely disappear. These kinds of activities were being conducted in small-scale plants, with a wide variety of techniques, and worked for end-users in fields as diverse as pharmaceuticals or para-pharmaceuticals, dyeing, perfumery and cosmetics, and sometimes also the food-processing industry. In addition, these mineral-based chemical processes utilized arsenic anhydride, boron, bromine, iodine, and oxides and salts of various metals such as antimony, silver, barium, chrome, copper, tin, magnesium, manganese, lead, zinc, and iron. There was also an old style of organic chemical process based on extractions as opposed to synthesis, using tallow (from which oleic acids and stearic acids could be drawn), blood collected from slaughterhouses (for albumins), animal bones (for glues), wine-making sediments (for tartaric acids), tropical trees (cinchona bark for quinine, brazilwood), tinctorial, aromatic, and medicinal plants (opium, belladonna, cloves, etc.). Nevertheless, an organic chemical industry, developed around chemical synthesis, was emerging; it was divided between large-scale organic chemical-manufacturing (intermediate products, base materials such as benzene, anthracene, naphthalene, and acetic acid, followed shortly thereafter by acetylene—made from calcium carbide—and close derivatives, like sodium phenacetin, phenol, nitrobenzene, maleic anhydride, and anthraquinone) and specialized organic chemical-manufacturing (dyes, pharmaceuticals).

As an example for synthetic dyes, an initial research effort developed in Europe, concentrating on benzene and benzol derivatives (aniline, mauveine, and fuchsine, 1856–60). Then, thanks to Graebe's work, the value of anthracene derivatives was discovered (alizarin, 1868). Finally, on the basis of research undertaken by Baeyer, naphthalene derivatives were studied (indigo, in 1880, with large-scale industrial production during the 1890s by BASF). With respect to pharmaceuticals, benzene derivatives of the arsenobenzol type were being investigated (for the treatment of syphilis), salicylic acid (for aspirin), malonic ester (for barbiturates), resorcinol and salol (for antiseptics), and antipyretics, along with anthracene derivatives (quinoline). Also under examination were the chemical substances from the ethyl series (chlorine and ether), or from the methyl series (chloroform, methylene blue). The first synthetic plastic material to experience some success was bakelite, patented by Baekland in 1907. The massive molecule was formed by associating two less complex molecular bodies, formol and phenol, the latter being derived from benzene. These findings helped to establish the advantages of a synthetic chemistry founded on substances extracted from coal, utilizing the processes of nitration, halogenation, oxidization, and the chemical union of diverse types of molecules. Therein evolved an industry of scientists and laboratory engineers, who manipulated kilograms of material rather than hundreds of tons, through repeated testing and experimentation.

From that point onwards, the chemical industry found itself facing a wide range of imperatives, which were at times contradictory:

- scientific imperatives (the problem of developing an industrial research laboratory was raised as early as 1880);
- mechanization imperatives (the importance of handling heavy loads on the conventional side of the industry);
- equipment imperatives (the need for special-alloy piping, catalysing techniques, and soon thereafter high-pressure apparatus);
- control and measurement imperatives (up to this period, performance was still being judged by the colour of the smoke, or by the odour and tactile senses);
- investment imperatives and those associated with penetrating very diversified markets.

France did not deal with these changes under favourable conditions. The reasons that can be cited are in part intellectual (a lack of qualified chemical research engineers), in part financial (hesitation in allocating resources to industrial research laboratories, while relying solely on university research, which itself was poorly funded), and in part commercial (reluctance to enter the mass consumption market, especially in agriculture and textiles). The base materials of organic chemistry, starting with benzene, were often produced at municipal gas plants as well as at coking plants, the commercial strategy of which was far less dynamic than in Germany. The very excellence of the old organic chemistry of extraction in France may also have been an obstacle to accepting change, whereas Germany had to build new industries from scratch. None the less, a very real advance was taking place within France, where the main mineral-based chemical industry (including fertilizers) was employing some 35,000 people before 1914, while the various other chemical industries had about 85,000 employees altogether. The average growth rate of the industry as a whole, in terms of output, was of the order of 3 per cent per year from 1860.

Rightly or wrongly, some observers of the time felt that the French chemical industry was not concentrated enough, even though several large firms did exist, which are worth mentioning. In 1913 the biggest one was Saint-Gobain, though at the time its activities were split evenly between glassware and chemicals. Its chemical-manufacturing alone accounted for 20 per cent of output within major, conventional mineral-based chemical industries, but only 6 per cent of the entire chemical industrial sector. The company was hindered by a lack of in-house research facilities, by the difficulty of innovating within its existing business organization, by an inability to find uncharted areas for potential growth, by a poor knowledge of the new markets emerging beyond fertilizers, by an over-confidence in its policy of co-operation (the company had participated in nineteen co-operative agreements within the industry by 1890), and by an aloofness from the major banks (self-financing was preferred). A somewhat similar corporate culture was taking shape within the majority of the large, mineral-based chemical companies. Following the death of Frédéric Kuhlmann in 1881, his company pursued a growth strategy which was not fundamentally different from that of Saint-Gobain up to 1914 (when it employed roughly 2,500 workers). Péchiney, which had inherited the original company founded at Salindres in 1855, failed to take advantage of two specific innovations that occurred during the 1880s. The first one was the utilization of electrolysis in the fabrication of chlorates; Henry Gall, head of the laboratory at Salindres and credited with the first applications of electrolysis, was forced to leave the firm when his technique was rejected. The second was the production of aluminium by electricity, thanks to the work of Paul Héroult in collaboration with Louis Merle, son of the founder of the Salindres plant. The new director, Adrien Badin (a graduate of the Mining School of Saint-Étienne), made up for this strategic mistake by setting up an aluminium factory in Saint-Jean de Maurienne in 1906 and by taking control of the Société des forces motrices de l'Arve (production of chlorate and aluminium at Chedde). However, from that time onwards, Péchiney sought to distance itself from pure chemistry, in order to devote more resources to the priority area of aluminium production.

Cellulosic artificial textiles gave rise to a new branch within the chemical industry: the Comptoir des textiles artificiels (CTA), largely controlled by the Gillet family, was created in 1911 and consisted of five companies (Soie artificielle d'Izieux and Soie artificielle de Givet, both of which were in a process of industrial reconversion, Société française de la viscose, Société ardéchoise de la viscose, and Société française des crins artificiels). One other equally uncharted field was electrochemistry. The Société industrielle de produits chimiques de la Motte-Breuil (in the Oise *département*) launched a small-scale production facility for electrolytic chloride in 1898. A key figure in electrochemistry was the Swiss Henry Gall, closely affiliated with the Lonza company; he was appointed to the board of the Société d'électrochimie, which manufactured aluminium and chlorates at Saint-Michel de Maurienne, and calcium carbide at Notre-Dame de Briançon and at Saint-Avre-La-Chambre. He was also chairman of the Société des produits azotés, founded in 1906 with the backing of Geneva banks, in particular the Union financière de Genève, along with the assistance of Bozel (founded in 1898 by the Usine électrique de la Lonza). It is only natural that a figure like Henry Gall would be very closely associated with a new and dynamic bank, the Banque suisse et française, founded in 1894, which went on to become the Crédit commercial de France in 1917. Among the clients of the Banque suisse et française were several of the original chemical companies from the pre-1914 period, such as the French Nobel industrial group (the only French industrial firm to be quoted on the futures market of the Paris Stock Exchange at the beginning of the 1890s), the Société anonyme de matières colorantes et produits chimiques de Saint-Denis, and Poulenc frères.

The Société anonyme des établissements Poulenc frères was created in 1900 (with a capital of 4 million francs) and backed by the Banque privée Lyon-Marseille. Its real origins date back even further, to the time of the pharmacist Étienne Poulenc (1823–78), who in 1858 joined his father-in-law in the company Wittmann et Poulenc jeune (photography-related products, collodions, fixatives, developers). This company ran two plants in 1913, in Ivry and Vitry (the latter having been built in 1907), and manufactured not only medicines, such as bismuth salts, limesalts, and lithium carbonates, but also organic pharmaceutical products (arsenobenzol), perfumes, and more technical products (diaminophenol, for example), as well as laboratory instruments. The company had a staff of 480. It would merge in 1928 with the Société chimique des usines du Rhône (the status of which as a public company dated back to 1895, with an initial capital of 3 million francs), to become Rhône-Poulenc.[4] The Société chimique des usines du Rhône was created from the former family business Gilliard, Monnet et Cartier, which had been located in Saint-Fons ever since 1883, following its creation at La Plaine, a Geneva suburb, in 1868. Its founder, Prosper Monnet (1834–1914), was the former technical director of La Fuchsine. It produced dyeing material and pharmaceutical products.

Backed by the Société générale from 1899, this company experienced a sharp downturn during the first years of the twentieth century and was reorganized under the supervision of bankers in 1905–6. It had a payroll of some 800 employees in 1913, and its turnover reached 7.7 million francs in that year. It turned out that the two partners, who would merge to form Rhône-Poulenc, could both trace their origins back to the same common ground of the 1860s, an era that nurtured the hopes and the contradictions of the nascent French chemical industry. The state of affairs for pharmaceutical products was somewhat contrasted, as French firms had to conclude patent and co-operation agreements with their stronger German colleagues. Yet, for dyeing materials, the situation seemed still more disquieting, as market supremacy went undoubtedly to the Germans, followed by the German-speaking Swiss, with the Bayer plant at Flers, near Lille (actually a packaging factory for imported products), the Farbwerke Meister Lucius und Bruning (Hoechst) establishment at Creil, the BASF plant at Neuville-sur-Saône, the Cassella site at Lyon-Vaise, and the Aktiengesellschaft für Anilin Fabrikation factory at Saint-Fons, not to mention the CIBA (Bâle) works at Saint-Fons in 1900.

The period starting with the First World War was one of transformation

⁴ Cf. P. Cayez, *Rhône-Poulenc, 1895–1975, contribution à l'étude d'un groupe industriel* (Paris, 1988).

in many major fields. World-wide growth in the chemical industry continued at an average long-run (1913–39) rate slightly above what had been experienced in the nineteenth century. However, the chemical industry of 1939 no longer corresponded exactly with the pre-1914 one, because of the suppression of some old types of production, a more precise categorization of the major sectors of activity (within the food-processing industry or oil-refining, for example), and the continuing emergence of new products (textiles, plastics, insecticides). The boundary between the major mineral-based chemical industries and the smaller, specialized chemical firms of yesteryear no longer had much significance, since many firms had decided to split their operations into various types of activities; organic chemistry could, at this point, aim at higher output levels. The chemical industry had also become more scientific and more closely tied to research, whereas, before 1914, only its more technologically advanced components had been research-driven. It began employing a greater number of engineers and technical professionals (perhaps a threefold increase compared with 1913 levels). It relied to a much lesser extent on empirical industrial processes, know-how, and material handling.

The First World War *per se* had upset the relative position of the companies active in the industry. Huge orders were coming in for chlorine, as the government had financed electrolytic chlorine facilities capable of producing 25,000 tons of chlorine per year from eleven plants (the top producer was the Société d'électrochimie at Bozel, followed by Péchiney, and Froges, which went on to merge in 1921). Incentives had also been proposed to spur the production of calcium carbide, in order to supply nitric acid from a cyanamide base; the major producers were the Société des produits azotés, the Société d'électrochimie, Péchiney, and Froges. The Usines du Rhône received some very sizeable orders from government, for phenol in particular (used in the fabrication of melinite), resulting in the opening of a new plant at Roussillon, and for mustard gas. Its employees grew to 2,500 at the end of the war. Poulenc sold very little to the armed forces, but did manufacture substitution goods, for the civilian market, for German chemicals (arsenobenzol, gonococcus vaccines, and various medicines) and had a work-force of 2,000. The Kuhlmann company, deprived of the use of its plants in the northern part of the country, redeployed its resources with the assistance of the banking community and relocated, among other sites, to Port de Bouc, Marseille-L'Estaque, Paimbœuf, and Bordeaux, thereby becoming a national and no longer a purely regional firm. Kuhlmann was recognized as the project director within the Compagnie nationale de matières colorantes, sponsored with start-up funding by the government's Service des poudres in 1916 (these two entities would go on to merge in 1924). This success eventually opened the debate over nitrogenous products, as France was taking over the control of German patents.

From that time onwards, the urgent problem was the creation of a well-

equipped centre of the French chemical industry, shielded from the over-
sight of the three tutelary authorities: scientists, banks, and government. It
was understood that the chemical industry was a strategic industry, and
the major questions posed, besides the one concerning nitrogenous products (the creation in Toulouse of a national office, a public-sector enterprise, in 1924), pertained to cellulose, dyeing materials, plastics, synthetic
fuels, and other new areas requiring large investment efforts. Major
mergers had already taken place between medium-sized companies, in
addition to partnerships that brought some companies into closer relationships (the Usines du Rhône, manufacturer of cellulose acetate since
1912, created a joint subsidiary with the Comptoir des textiles artificiels,
called Rhodiaceta, in 1924).

2. THE MERGER PLAN AND THE BANKING COMMUNITY

The plans for mergers between the leading French chemical firms first
appeared in September 1926, following the restructuring of the public
sector's financial system under the guidance of Raymond Poincaré's
cabinet, which had been formed in July 1926. It is possible that the
stabilization of the financial situation did also play a role in fostering these
plans, because exporting was to become more difficult after the de-
preciation of the French franc had been stopped. Therein lies the reason
behind the urgency for the financial system's reorganization. A handful of
individuals seems to have been associated with the initial debate on the
subject:

- a banker, Benjamin Rossier, managing director of the Crédit commercial de France (CCF);
- two directors from the chemical firm Kuhlmann, namely the chairman of the board of directors, Donat Agache, and the managing
  director, Raymond Berr;
- also, very likely, Henry Gall, head of the Société d'électrochimie,
  which had bought out the Société du Giffre, the Société des carbures
  métalliques, and then, in 1922, the Forges et aciéries électriques Paul
  Girod d'Ugine (commonly this firm was simply called Ugine); and
  finally
- a representative from the Usines du Rhône.

The decisive meeting to conclude the merger agreement was held in
October 1926, in the offices of the CCF, 103 avenue des Champs-Élysées,
in Paris. All the main firms were represented.

The really constructive phase came between the autumn of 1926 and the
spring of 1927, with the creation of a Committee of French Chemical
Industries. This body, which divided into several working groups, gener-

ated a great number of ideas. One of them was to develop a public company, a sort of umbrella holding company, gathering the member chemical firms within the structure of a French Chemical Union. A slightly milder version was to favour a partial grouping of firms with joint-stock participation and joint subsidiaries for some new products. Strategies were also considered within the chemical industry which would be more coherent both with regard to a sector-wide direction and to individual policies for each product (chlorine, nitrogenous products, and synthetic fuels, for example). Raymond Berr, who knew the German chemical industry well, included in this plan the ambition to create a European industrial trade centre for chemistry, to deal with transfers of technology (German patents for dyes and pharmaceuticals) and, in broader terms, to achieve an overall level of co-operation which could act as a counterweight to the United States. He further sought to rationalize the industry, by undertaking to further technical progress, heavy investment, and reduction of prime costs while raising wages. If these goals were reached, the French union would negotiate with the Germans under the best possible conditions. Doctor Bosch was invited to deliver a paper in Paris, and his visit was carefully prepared during an information-gathering mission of French experts in Germany, during the first quarter of 1927.

These interesting suggestions, based on a comparison with the United States and Germany, had concrete results. The main opposition came from Saint-Gobain, which did succeed in coaxing the smaller firms to support its views. The merger plan was distinctly perceived as serving the interests of Kuhlmann, which had become the leading French chemical firm. Its president, Donat Agache, appeared more often at the centre of the stage in the debate than Raymond Berr, because he was more 'fashionable' and, on his mother's side, was the grandson of Frédéric Kuhlmann. Born in 1882, the son of Édouard Agache, he became an appointed member of the board of directors in 1915, then chairman of the board in 1920. Extremely brilliant, very knowledgeable of both England and the United States, Donat Agache was the architect of Kuhlmann's resurrection during the war, much as he was the driving force behind the closer relationships with Penarroya, the Asturienne des mines, the Vieille Montagne, and behind the merger with the Compagnie nationale des matières colorantes in 1924. He became a board member of the BNC, then of the CCF in 1924, and he believed in the necessity of close ties between banking and industry, while Raymond Berr was considered more as a 'technician'.

In the initial merger plan, the role of the banker Benjamin Rossier must be highlighted.[5] He worked diligently to present the plan to other bankers and to win their support. Born in 1865 in Vevey, of Swiss nationality

[5] Cf. J.-P. Daviet et M. Germain, *Crédit commercial de France, une banque dans le siècle* (Paris, 1994).

(although with some French Protestant ancestry), and very well connected
to the banking community in Basle, Benjamin Rossier was certainly not
the most influential banker in the Paris financial world. Yet, he did symbolize the innovative features of banking policy that were emerging from
the end of the nineteenth century.

During the 1920s the CCF held a somewhat ambiguous position. It was
a deposit bank, recognized as one of the six 'major credit establishments'
in Paris, which had formed a sort of club (with total assets of about 50
billion francs in 1929, at a time when France's GDP totalled 345 billion). It
was, however, considered as the 'little brother' of the family, being the
smallest in terms of assets (3.8 billion francs); this position did provide the
possibility of being at times more creative than the other members. At this
point, under the leadership of Benjamin Rossier, three themes appeared
essential in the CCF's overall strategy. First, Benjamin Rossier did not
fully subscribe to the classical distinction between deposit bank and investment bank; he held that a deposit bank, while not exactly an investment bank in disguise, could none the less play a vital role in assisting
businesses to get ahead. Secondly, he developed ties with commercial and
industrial firms which were heavily involved in the most active and
dynamic sectors as well as being committed to technical progress. These
efforts led him to friendly relationships with the directors of many companies, for which he became financial adviser, to a limited extent. Thirdly,
he outlined a new financial approach towards business firms. While the
old school of bankers granted financing on the base of collateral guarantees, the modern banker would promptly proceed with a financial analysis of the state of the business. This approach assumed that the companies
themselves had been equipped with a capacity for financial management
which the bank's assistance would strengthen.

Benjamin Rossier, judging from his interests and his insights, was a
good witness of the second industrial revolution, that stage when science
and technology formed a new set of bonds. He became enthralled with the
development of electricity, in connection with urban development (tramways, street lighting, household appliances). He took a close interest in the
dynamic sectors of industry: aluminium, special steels, tubes, mechanical
engineering, precision chemistry for medicines and synthetic products
(rayons, dyes). He recognized the importance of objects and goods associated with a more technically oriented civilization: the automobile, the
submarine, cinema, radio, telephones, gramophones, and typewriters. He
understood the need for large amounts of capital for 'older' industries,
which were transformed by processes aimed at increasing mechanization;
he also knew about continuous production runs and the techniques for
controlling materials and processing. He was not at all reluctant to act as
an arbitrator. In 1925, Péchiney sought to take control of Ugine through a
hostile take-over bid. Benjamin Rossier was able to reconcile the two

companies by negotiating a co-operative agreement for aluminium (with 80 per cent going to Péchiney and 20 per cent to Ugine, up to a threshold of 200,000 tons for French production per year, and an even split beyond that level).

The role of the banking community in general, and deposit banks in particular, proved to be crucial. The economy was becoming more monetarized. Increasingly, the middle classes began to diversify their investment from land or buildings into securities. Companies were in need of short-term financing and higher-performance financial instruments (letters of credit, export credits, foreign joint ventures). The Paris financial market began to thrive inasmuch as the city became an international trading centre. These phenomena had already emerged before 1914. Even though, immediately after the war, France struggled with the bitter consequences of an expensively won 'victory', these developments did continue to characterize, to a large extent, the 1920s. The banking system accompanied the movement towards modernization and, in so doing, modernized itself, though the business climate offered plenty of constraints.

Each year, the financial market raised the equivalent of 2 to 3 per cent of French GDP. During the first post-war years, this figure was largely accounted for by public-sector borrowing, intended to finance reconstruction. Starting in 1924, a significant portion of what the public subscribed served to finance a large investment effort by the country's major firms. A company like Saint-Gobain increased its capital in 1920, 1925, 1928, and 1930, whereas it had not called on the financial market from 1890 to 1914. The key figures that summarize Saint-Gobain's needs during the 1920s are worth quoting: 2 billion francs was spent within the company, of which 1.3 billion was for investment in glass and chemical works (the rest was in 'reconversion' and raising working capital). The financial market brought in 533 million francs (or 40 per cent of total investment).

Each deposit bank provided services to a number of companies for which it was the 'primary' bank (Péchiney and the Gillet group for the Crédit lyonnais, Usines du Rhône for the Société générale) and that defined its base of favourite clients. None the less, there was no monopoly. Banks also had relationships with other industrial or commercial firms, by accepting a supporting role behind a fellow bank, which would take the lead in serving the client, while requiring the presence and expertise of an investment bank (Paribas for the Thomson company). This type of joint banking for clients led to a division of risks and an interdependence among banks as well. The various companies which used banking services in this fashion were granted short-term loans which were often becoming syndicated if risks appeared to be significant. The bank would study a financing plan as the business deal was progressing, and would guarantee financial equilibrium and to uphold the principles of a well-balanced financial organization. The date and the amount of stock or bond issue would be mutually agreed upon; also, an investment syndicate would be created, and the lead bank would take on the leadership.

Deposit banks had two good reasons to be concerned with long-term capital held by companies. On the one hand, individuals who held bank accounts entrusted the banks with their securities, to be managed as an investment portfolio. Although the exact figure has never been made available, there is a strong presumption that the portfolio of securities managed by deposit banks was of the order of total bank holdings. A great number of individual investors, who were scarcely informed about the details of transactions, had bought their securities on the advice of their bankers. Banks also acted as proxy for their clients and could attend the shareholders' general assemblies in their clients' stead. The banks would provide the financial services associated with the securities, which did mean, among other things, that bank employees would manually detach the quarterly coupons; this provided a significant source of employment. On the other hand, bankers watched carefully over the financial health of the businesses which benefited from their help. At the time, a banker would only approve short-term financing when the borrower held a substantial working capital as a buffer.

A firm had to ascribe to working capital a share of its permanent capital which was clearly higher than its fixed capital investment (for example, 1.5 times as high). This working capital, according to the prevailing views in the 1920s, was supposed to sustain a sort of war chest, or in other words easily negotiable assets, beyond the needs of the normal operating cycle. Permanent capital formed the long-term resources of the company and was composed of shareholders' equity and long-term debt. The proportion of borrowed capital had to be less than half of shareholders' equity. If short-term debt was taken into account, shareholders' equity had to be greater than the combined indebtedness. The deposit banks, guardians of the orthodox doctrine whenever possible, encouraged increasing capital and long-term indebtedness within a regulated set of proportions, as a complement of short-term commitments.

In practical terms, the banker in many cases was not only the master administrator of long- and short-term resources; he was also a confidant, a watchdog, and an analyst. Whenever a business venture started to show unhealthy financial symptoms, it was not at all odd to see a bank participate in a kind of reorganization and a restructuring that, admittedly, was not always well accepted. Such was the case for Nestlé in 1922. Benjamin Rossier had suggested the nomination of Louis Dapples, whose career path had included the Crédit lyonnais and the Banca commerciale italiana, as director. The result was the introduction of a new management style, more rational, more finance-driven, and less familiar. The move was a success; on the other hand, André Citroën did not heed the advice of his bankers, who had been called upon in 1927 to improve his firm's management.

The key sectors of activity where the assistance of banks appeared to be the most beneficial were the following: a part of the coal industry (Anzin, Béthune, Lens, Aniche, Liévin, etc.), the steel industry (Aciéries du nord et de l'est, Wendel, Marine-Homécourt, Senelle-Maubeuge, Knutange, Hagondange), aluminium, heavy mechanical engineering (including the activities of Schneider in shipbuilding), the production and distribution of electricity, electrical apparatus (Alsacienne de constructions mécaniques, CGE, Philips, Thomson), telephone equipment, cinema, chemicals and metallurgical chemistry, oil, the automobile industry, pneumatics, aircraft, the most dynamic and concentrated parts of the textile industry and the food-processing industry (sugar, beer, aperitifs, chocolate, oil), paper-mills, and printing. Trade with the colonies and foreign countries was also much dependent on banks.

Bankers of that time should neither be idealized nor accused of all the period's evils. When industrialists, spurred by government's industrial policy, were driven to innovate, they generally found co-operation from the banking community. That was the case with telephone cables and long-distance connection apparatus, under the stimulus of research done in laboratories dependent upon the Ministry of Postal Services. The equipment for SELT (Société d'études pour les liaisons télégraphiques et téléphoniques) was based on an idea generated by General Electric that was successfully 'Frenchified'. It is worth stressing that the president of the CCF, Adolphe Salles, sat on the executive committee of SELT. In contrast, French telephone exchanges were far from being a success, as foreign-based technologies were clearly dominating the market (especially ITT). The banks were not really responsible for this situation, as they both backed companies that were unsuccessful and financed importers of American equipment. In a nutshell, the necessary critical mass had not been reached in France. As for heavy chemicals, banks underwrote large-scale investment programmes that turned out to be of little profitability. They placed too much confidence in some industrialists, while they had no means of achieving an objective approach. Still, the attitude of the banking community in 1926–7 could be depicted as one of prudence. While banks did stimulate the restructuring of the economic machine, they none the less wanted to be able to back out from over-direct—and so over-risky—ventures. Their objective was to see industry take off on its own to a greater extent, to become a more consolidated, less dependent, and, perhaps, more profitable partner.

3. STRATEGIES, PERFORMANCE, AND ORGANIZATIONAL CAPACITY

Finding out the reasons behind the failure of the 'great merger' of 1926–7, in which a part of the blame lies with Saint-Gobain—a rather traditional company in its policies in the field of chemicals, requires highlighting some of the sharp disagreements, or at least differences of opinion, of the day. The quarrel between 'the old school' and 'the new school' was at the very heart of the development of industrial strategies. The issues raised pertained to the role of banks and of government and, on a broader scale, to the managerial methods in use.

Even though companies like Saint-Gobain did need banks for issuing stocks or bonds, they mistrusted at times the zeal of bankers, whom they suspected of being indiscreet and poorly qualified to evaluate long-term strategies. There was, indeed, a bond between the most traditional industrial firms and the more conventional bankers, based on the mutual respect of a strict division of roles. This approach was seen as compensating, at least in part, for personal relationships which were devoid of any over-technical discussion. As mentioned previously, the contribution of Benjamin Rossier, a Swiss to top it all, was not unanimously appreciated. This point will be further developed within the context of French business management techniques.

The issue of the Government's role also left opinions split. Within Saint-Gobain, Raymond Berr was thought to be cultivating good relationships with the State's technocratic structure, especially within the Ministries of War and Agriculture. Since he would have been the logical choice for general director of a Chemical Union, such relationships were crucial. Actually, at the time, two major lawsuits had already brought some state-run chemical firms into conflict, and a third litigation seemed likely to follow. The potash deposits in Alsace had been discovered in 1906 when the region was still part of the German empire. A quarter of the field was being mined by an Alsatian-owned operator, Kali-Sainte-Thérèse, and the remainder, which was under German control, was sequestered in 1919. In 1921 it was decided that the State would buy the property rights from the previous owners; the deed of sale was not signed until 24 May 1924. The major chemical companies sought to have the mining concessions granted to one or several operators in 1920–4, but this request was defeated in parliament in March 1922. This ruling led to the creation of a public mining operator. Some politicians had even considered awarding the potash commercial company the monopoly to sell binary and compound fertilizers containing potassium (those that contained a small amount of potassium, but also included nitrogenous and phosphorous components): even if the fertilizer had contained only one-third of potassium, it would still have been considered a potassium fertilizer. This point continued to be debated within the Finance Commission of the Senate during the winter of 1926–7.

The second lawsuit, concerning nitrogenous products, was even more serious. In 1919, the French Government acquired the Haber patents, but without possessing the know-how necessary for their application. At the same time, two competing processes were developed: the Italian process Casale and the French process Claude. Very quickly thereafter, and contrary to other industrial firms, Saint-Gobain conducted an analysis that was very pessimistic about the State's ambitions to become a nitrogen producer. While the granting of operating licences to private industry for use of the Haber process could have been considered, Saint-Gobain's directorship felt that the military and senior Civil Servants wanted to maintain too tight a control over the future of the nitrogenous products industry. The resulting strategy called for the creation of a joint subsidiary with Air liquide, which held the Claude patents. This new company, called Société chimique de la grande paroisse, was formed between May and July 1919 and placed Saint-Gobain in a strong position in the negotiations taking place between government and the chemical industry. In case of a deadlock in these negotiations, the company would at least have been able to do without the Haber patents. From a different perspective, Saint-Gobain could have given the impression of working towards a compromise between the two processes, in order to devise an intermediate technical solution. In the synthesis of nitrogen and hydrogen, the Claude process introduced two new features: a high-pressure reaction and a type of catalyser which, for the same weight, could produce 12 times more than the Haber process. Also, it was the first process that sought to use gas from coking ovens as a starting-point, even though the method was not yet entirely perfected in 1919.

A small group of hard-line military leaders gradually focused attention on a state-led solution, and the Toulouse site was chosen, which was seen as 'sheer madness' by Saint-Gobain. However, the company had to wait until 1924 before its views were heard in more moderate political circles. During the negotiations of 1919–20, the Kuhlmann company was seen as the leader of a group which wanted to reach an agreement with the State over a mixed private/public formula; it was retained by the director of the Service des poudres, Patart, as the firm which would assume technical leadership. The same outcome had been decided in the case of the Société nationale des matières colorantes in 1916–17. The third litigation, concerning oil, would not be heard before 1928, but already Saint-Gobain mistrusted the information being circulated by the Office national des combustibles liquides.

The industrial community was deeply divided, and their interests did not appear to be compatible. If some overriding reason had forced them to merge, would something other than an ungovernable monster have been created? Benjamin Rossier, Donat Agache, and Raymond Berr all imagined an extremely broad, diversified French chemical group, capable of obtaining the confidence of bankers and of financing large research projects and technology transfer programmes. It would have been essential for this group to be equipped with effective managerial techniques, in order to develop the ability to make long-range decisions aimed at achieving a profitable level of market competitiveness in the long run.

In the United States, Alfred D. Chandler has placed the chemical industry at the core of the managerial revolution that was taking shape during the 1920s, along with the automobile industry, the electronics industry, and some commercial companies, all characteristic of the second industrial revolution.[6] The need for top management to refocus on the task of allocating long-term resources was strongly felt, providing directors with the time and the information necessary to resolve new strategic problems as they arose. Autonomous divisions were created around major product lines or distinct geographic markets and were given operational decision-making powers. From one point to view, the updated business structure was the result of previous diversification policies; from another angle, this structure incited other firms to diversify. In sociological terms, a reshuffling of former management teams was being observed, because of the rapidly expanding pool of competent management professionals. Does this suggest that the chemical industry would have had some affinity with the new approaches towards capitalist management? The opposing viewpoints, which were heard during the discussions of 1926–7 in France, led to a slight adjustment of this attitude by exposing several distinct strategic models.

The initial debate was about diversification strategies. The chemical industry seemed well suited to diversify, as new products were being introduced into a variety of different markets. However, this diversification masked some of the contrasting forces within the industry and could be either well, or not so well, conducted. Three examples of the most heavily involved firms in the merger plan of 1926–7 will be examined: Kuhlmann, because of its role as leader of a group of firms; Saint-Gobain, by virtue of its opposition to the plan; and Rhône-Poulenc, because, from its creation in 1928, this group was the product of a sort of 'small-scale merger' between the Usines du Rhône and Poulenc frères, immediately following the failure of the 'great merger'.

In 1938, the two groups vying for the top position within the French chemical industry were Kuhlmann and Rhône-Poulenc. Judging from its turnover, the Rhône-Poulenc group had taken the lead (with a figure of 1 billion francs in 1938 against 0.8 billion for Kuhlmann), although its staff was somewhat smaller than that of Kuhlmann, the products of which

⁶ A. D. Chandler, *Strategy and Structure* (2nd edn. Cambridge, Mass., 1989).

were less expensive. Kuhlmann employed 15,000 persons, including its subsidiaries, while Rhône-Poulenc must have had just over 10,000. Total turnover for the French chemical industry amounted to roughly 6 billion francs, if the definition of the chemical industry is restricted more narrowly than it was in 1914. At present, the category of chemical industry activities would only include those utilizing fundamentally chemical molecular combinations. (However, this definition is arbitrary, since metallurgy, glassworks, the ceramic, and the rubber industries, to name only a few, also utilized a physical/chemical treatment of materials.) It was not a matter of chance that these two companies were both tightly linked to the banking community: Rhône-Poulenc to the Société générale and the Crédit commercial de France; Kuhlmann to the Crédit commercial de France, Paribas, and, to a more limited extent, to Rothschild and Mirabaud.

The Rhône-Poulenc group, under the strong leadership of a remarkable entrepreneur, Nicolas Grillet, was able to operate, under favourable conditions, a subsidiary devoted to cellulosic artificial textiles (Rhodiaceta), in partnership with the CTA; to develop tremendously its pharmaceutical production within a completely autonomous division (Special, Prolabo, Theraplix); to play a central role in the plastics industry (initially artificial plastics, with acetate of cellulose, followed by synthetics); and to negotiate skilfully with the Germans in a spirit of mutual respect (despite a clear imbalance that would become strikingly apparent in some one-sided contracts during the Second World War).

Compared to other firms, Rhône-Poulenc did not invest heavily, but rather invested intelligently in promising markets (and was scarcely hurt by the Depression of the 1930s). Its resources were devoted to research at a time when others were investing in heavy machinery. At the same time, it did not overlook assessing market potential for more refined chemical products; it was the firm that best matched the 'Chandler model'.

Kuhlmann had bought out many former small and medium-sized businesses, to a point where it controlled operations at twenty-three plants. In addition, it had created joint subsidiaries with the coal industry (Anzin-Kuhlmann, Courrières-Kuhlmann, Marles-Kuhlmann), both for nitrogenous products and for organic industrial applications (ethylene chemistry, for example). In the mean time, the firm had succeeded in supporting what had become a genuine French industry of dyestuffs, without neglecting either mineral-based chemical products or fertilizers; but it failed in the artificial textiles market. In 1927, thanks to Donat Agache, Kuhlmann founded, through the intermediary of the family-run business Agache de Pérenchies et Dollfus, Mieg et Cie (DMC), the Société des textiles chimiques du nord et de l'est (artificial cellulose textiles). The CCF did give its help, and Albert Rossier (Benjamin Rossier's brother), a director of DMC, was called in to sit on the board of the newly created company. The support provided by the CCF to Textiles chimiques du nord et de l'est was considerable (around 15 million francs in loans in 1929, while awaiting an eventual flotation on the Stock Exchange). In 1937 the CCF board of directors was given a devastating assessment of the financial situation; liabilities totalling 50 million francs had been accumulated, of which 28.7 million represented CCF loans. The bank abandoned the greatest portion of its outstanding debt in exchange for shares estimated at 40 per cent of their face value. This failure proved that diversification into a market which is remote from a firm's basic area of expertise is not always successful, and that the participation of the banking community in no way guarantees the soundness of the investment.

In 1938 Saint-Gobain had a turnover for its chemical activities of 700 million francs, against 600 million for Péchiney and 400 million for Ugine. Two diversification attempts into quite distinct areas had failed: one was in the oil industry, the other in cellulose. The company had spent a sizeable sum of money to create an oil refinery that was put into operation in 1931, but did not pay any dividend before the war, and more importantly did not provide an expansion into the chemical use of ethylene, as was initially expected. In cellulose, dividends were no better; only pulp used for wrapping paper was being produced and not the cellulose intended for artificial textiles. As far as nitrogenous products were concerned, their performance displayed mixed results. Sales of nitrogenous products by Saint-Gobain and its subsidiaries amounted to 13 per cent of total fertilizer sales in France in 1938 compared with a figure of 26 per cent for Saint-Gobain in 1913. This relative decline can be explained by the weak growth in phosphate fertilizers when compared with the phosphorous slag produced in the steel industry (to the detriment of superphosphates); by a sharp increase in the use of potassium fertilizers; and by an unsatisfactory market positioning for nitrogenous fertilizers. Under the auspices of the Grande Paroisse, Saint-Gobain supported a major research effort, without obtaining any return on capital invested. This partial failure was due, to some extent, to excess capacity in the Toulouse plant, which operated at a loss, with many technical mishaps, during its start-up phase; yet it did supply 32 per cent of nitrogenous fertilizers sold on the French market during the 1930s. It was also due to the exclusive use of the Claude process, which represented 28 per cent of the French output of ammonia. An intermediate solution, somewhere between the Claude and the Haber processes, would have been preferable. Saint-Gobain began to focus on the chemical industry once again in 1936, having set up a research laboratory in organic chemistry and having started to make plastic materials.

The failure of Saint-Gobain to diversify, and its recovery in 1936, provided the opportunity for a fresh evaluation of its financial performance.[7]

---

[7] A. D. Chandler, *Scale and Scope* (Cambridge, Mass., 1990).

The company's results depended on many operational and strategic decisions taken by managers, both at the middle and top executive levels. Organizational capability, which takes into account socio-cultural factors, affected the manner in which managerial authority was exercised and in which resources were effectively allocated within an extremely complex and ever-changing environment. Directors had to exploit the cost advantages associated with economies of scale and with diversification, using a strategy of interdependent investment in the three functional areas of production, marketing, and management. It is by no means certain that attitudes in France in 1926 were mature enough for this kind of organizational capacity to have been sufficiently utilized, considering the equipment and the management techniques that were common at the time.

Within a large number of businesses, financial knowledge and analytical instruments, in matters of both investment and results, remained fairly rudimentary. Responsibility was partially delegated to the supremacy of the very 'technically oriented' engineers, who were not familiar with financial realities and the art of management. They tended to concentrate more heavily on the production function than on commercial and financial functions. The dominating values and the criteria for judging action emphasized devotion, loyalty to the company, pride in workmanship, and 'honour' over quantifiable objectives. Shareholders were given very little information and were generally satisfied with receiving regular dividends. These singularities of the French management style, located at the intersection of a technical subsystem (related to materials and technology), an organization subsystem (related to men and their use of power), and a financial subsystem (related to money), did not really give a fighting chance to a giant industrial group. Meanwhile, more modestly sized companies were experiencing undoubted success, thanks to the exceptional personalities of some of their directors, as exemplified by Emmanuel Chadeau, in the case of the Gnôme et Rhône aircraft engines at about the same time. However, this company did make profits three times as small as those of Saint-Gobain, and one single shareholder did own three-quarters of all stock.

4. CONCLUSION

A merger is always a delicate moment in the life of a business, since the firms involved have a tendency to persevere in their former roles, and this creates problems in evaluating assets, in authority, strategy, and, from an overall perspective, in cultural identity. It is a time for introspection. The corporate strategies of the élite holding power within the various chemical companies in 1926–7 revealed different approaches to the understanding of ongoing changes; if common problems did arise inside the industry, the structure of the latter was not necessarily uniform. An individual producer could not rely on any single production model or on mass markets.

Three fundamental reasons, none the less, could have encouraged a merger: first, enlarging research capacities jointly, and jointly negotiating international agreements on patents' rights; secondly, closing smaller plants to the benefit of larger, more rationally designed works, and finally, in-house logistics operations for co-ordinating the fabrication of 'intermediate' products and final products. These factors did not weigh heavily enough. Had the merger succeeded, it certainly would not have resulted in a satisfactory management of strategic resources, considering the condition of managerial methods at the time in France.

N64

11

Mergers and the Transformation of the British Brewing Industry, 1914–80

TERRY GOURVISH

1. INTRODUCTION

While this chapter is empirical in character—it is concerned with the transformation of British brewing's industrial structure after 1914—there is a theoretical observation underpinning the study. It is that because markets are complex and differ from country to country, the causes and extent of increased industrial concentration differ also. In addition, corporate motivations require careful evaluation, since entrepreneurial and/ or managerial responses are ultimately critical to the process.

Increasing concentration has been a characteristic feature of modern brewing industries in the developed world. However, the extent of this concentration, and its timing, have varied from country to country. In the UK, the degree of concentration, measured by output per plant or per company, was more limited than in most European countries, with the exception of Germany and Belgium. British brewing was certainly less concentrated than in France. Thus, while the top five French enterprises enjoyed a market share of 90 per cent in 1990, and the two leading French companies, Boussois Souchon Neuvesel (BSN) and Française de Brasserie, had 75 per cent of the market, the figures for the UK were 70 per cent and 36 per cent (Bass and Allied) respectively. Only in Germany was there a lower level of concentration. Here, the top five companies (in West Germany) enjoyed a mere 28 per cent of the market.[1] This chapter has as its central concern an analysis of the merger and growth activity which led to higher levels of concentration in UK brewing. However, it is important to observe that some of the factors responsible for a global change in the structure of brewing industries had more force in some markets than in

[1] Barclays de Zoete Wedd Research, *UK—Brewing: The MMC Inquiry into the UK Brewing Industry: Are Leaner Times ahead?* (London, Dec. 1988), 3, 23. Data collected by the Monopolies and Mergers Commission indicated that in 1985 Bass and Allied brewed 38% of UK output: T. R. Gourvish and R. G. Wilson, *The British Brewing Industry 1830–1980* (Cambridge, 1994), 588–9. In West Germany, the position was complicated by the existence of conglomerates and interlocking shareholdings, which means that the true concentration level was much higher. In Belgium, the market share of the top five enterprises was very high (95% in 1990), notwithstanding the low average output per brewery.

others. This chapter attempts to explain this, and, in particular, why more small and medium-sized enterprises survived in the UK than, for example, in France.

2. BEER MARKETS IN BRITAIN AND FRANCE

Before analysing British developments, it may be instructive to point out, in the context of this volume, that the British and French markets were very different. Beer production and consumption per capita in the UK have been nearly three times greater than in France since the late 1950s. UK production amounted to 43.4 million hectolitres in 1960, compared with 16.7 million in France, and was 64.8 million hectolitres in 1980, compared with 21.7 million. The British drank 85.1 litres of beer per capita in 1960, compared with only 35.3 litres in France, and 118.3 litres in 1980, compared with 44.3 litres.[2] Beer is clearly a much more important alcoholic drink in Britain than in France. In 1960, it accounted for 74 per cent of the total volume of alcohol consumed, compared with a French figure of only 8 per cent. And although the increasing popularity of table wine in Britain from the 1960s narrowed this differential, the disparity in the two countries was still significant in 1980: 58 per cent in the UK, 14 per cent in France.[3] There are further important market differences, too. Beer has been and still is much more heavily taxed in the UK. For example, the excise duty in 1980 amounted to 22.0p a litre, compared with only 1.1p in France; at the beginning of 1993 the margin was even greater, 55.4p compared with 1.4p.[4] The situation has encouraged opportunistic forays in the Channel ports by UK consumers, aided by British entrepreneurs, to exploit the price differential in the two countries which this produces.[5]

A further disparity lies in the packaging of beer. Draught beer, drawn from the cask or barrel, dominates in the UK, while bottled beer is the most common form of packaging in France. Thus, for example, in the UK 79 per cent of beer sold was draught beer in 1980, compared with only 21 per cent in France. The proportion sold in bottles was 11 per cent in the

---

[2] Data from Brewers' Society (BS), *International Statistical Handbook* (3rd edn. London, 1983), 15, 17, 36, 40, and *Statistical Handbook 1993* (London, 1993), 68.

[3] Brewers Association of Canada, *Alcoholic Beverage Taxation and Control Policies* (8th edn. Ontario, 1993), 130, 428; information from Brewers and Licensed Retailers Association (BLRA). Of course, there are significant regional variations in France. Beer is a much more important alcoholic beverage in northern France and Alsace (where per capita consumption in the 1980s was *c.*50% higher than the average) than it is, for example, in the south.

[4] Data for beer of 5% a.b.v. (1050°) (no deduction is made here for the 6% waste allowance in UK calculations). Information from Mr C. W. Thurman of BLRA.

[5] Note, in particular, the activities of enterprises such as 'EastEnders' and 'Beers aRe Us'. *Daily Telegraph*, 10 Apr. 1993; *Sunday Telegraph*, 13 June 1993; *People*, 7 Mar. 1993; *Off-Licence News*, 8 July 1993 (BLRA press cuttings).

[6] BS, *Statistical Handbook 1993* (1993), 17; information from BLRA.

UK, but 78 per cent in France.[6] Finally, we may observe that the extent of vertical integration is very different in the two markets. In the UK, brewing company ownership of licensed retail outlets had been a dominant feature since the nineteenth century, which was not the case in France. On the other hand, it is clear that the French breweries have employed a 'loan-tie' mechanism, similar to the system common in London in the eighteenth and nineteenth centuries, which complicates a precise comparison of the extent of *effective* vertical integration in the two countries.[7] What is clear, however, is that beer-drinking in 'on-licensed premises'—pubs, clubs, restaurants, cafés, etc.—has been, and remains, much more important in the UK. In 1980 it accounted for about 88 per cent of consumption, compared with only about 40 per cent in France.[8] Thus, any comparative analysis of merger activity in the brewing industry must address the issue of consumer preference, which often acts as a brake on the realization of theoretical production scale economies; and also government regulation, not only in terms of taxation policy but also in relation to the regulatory regimes imposed on the business sector.[9]

3. BREWING CONCENTRATION IN BRITAIN

Returning to the British case, the first point to observe is that a fair measure of both horizontal and vertical integration was established in brewing at a comparatively early stage. Consequently, the general debate about the causes of concentration in the twentieth century, involving a judgement about the relative significance of merger on the one hand and internal growth on the other,[10] has reduced significance in brewing. Here there was a market strategy which, as early as 1880–1900, was based firmly upon the acquisition of existing enterprises and vertical integration. By 1939 beer sales through public houses which were 'tied' to, i.e. owned or leased by, brewing companies accounted for about 60 per cent of the total sold in the market. Mergers and acquisitions were in these circumstances the principal strategy for companies seeking to grow. Internal growth did occur when leading companies developed a unique consumer product. Thus, in Dublin, Guinness built up a substantial trade on the reputation for quality and strength of its distinctive black beer Extra

[7] Gourvish and Wilson, *British Brewing Industry*, 128–36.

[8] Ibid. 457; Communauté de travail des brasseurs du Marché commun (CMBC) and EFTA Brewing Industry Council (EBIC), *Combined Statistics 1986*, 12. Data for 1990: UK: 20%; France: 65%. CMBC and EBIC, *Combined Statistics 1992*, 12.

[9] Cf. Tony Freyer, *Regulating Big Business: Antitrust in Great Britain and America 1880–1990* (Cambridge, 1992).

[10] Cf. Leslie Hannah and John Kay, *Concentration in Modern Industry: Theory, Measurement and the U.K. Experience* (London, 1977); S. J. Prais, *The Evolution of Giant Firms in Britain* (Cambridge, 1976); P. E. Hart and R. Clarke, *Concentration in British Industry* (Cambridge, 1980); P. E. Hart, and L. Hannah and J. A. Kay, 'Symposium on Bias and Concentration', *Journal of Industrial Economics*, 29 (1981), 305–20.

Stout, which was sold in bottles. It became the only major brewer without a tied estate in Britain. In Burton upon Trent from the 1840s, and later in London and Edinburgh, distinctive pale ales were developed, and breweries such as Bass, Worthington, Whitbread, McEwan, and William Younger built up both national and export trades in such beers, which also became popular in bottled form. Whitbread's production of bottled beer, for example, increased from only 10,000 barrels in 1880 to 350,000 in 1910. For much of the nineteenth century these were not vertically integrated concerns. Bass, for example, owned only 27 public houses as late as 1883, while Whitbread owned a mere 36 London pubs in 1875, far fewer than the 127 it held in 1850.[11] However, both these companies went on to invest heavily in pubs, particularly from the 1890s, and their newly acquired tied estates became more important to them in the depressed demand conditions of the inter-war years.[12]

The degree of concentration in the industry is hard to measure precisely before the twentieth century. What is clear is that in London a dozen large companies had emerged by 1830, as Peter Mathias's study indicates; and the history of the next hundred years is one of steady corporate growth, based partly on market growth (up to the mid-1870s), and partly on acquisition and merger. The process certainly gathered pace after the limited company formations of the 1880s, and the 'scramble for property' in the period 1890–1914, which was particularly evident in London. The surviving data, if incomplete on a national basis, certainly point up the extent of the change. Thus, in England and Wales, the production of the 1,700 or so 'common brewers', i.e. commercial and wholesale brewers, increased from 54 per cent of the total in 1831 to 95 per cent in 1900, as the production of licensed victuallers (publican-brewers) and others declined. In London, the eleven leading companies produced about 1,255,000 barrels in 1830, 9.5 per cent of English output. Fifty years later, these companies produced 3,650,000 barrels, 13 per cent of the total. In Burton upon Trent, the average production of the 17 brewing companies in 1851 was a mere 18,000 barrels; by 1900 21 brewers were each producing 167,000 barrels on average, equivalent to 11 per cent of English production.[13] Thus, by 1914, a fair measure of concentration was already evident, as Table 11.1 indicates. At this time eight brewing companies were each producing half a million barrels or more, their combined production being equivalent to about 20 per cent of the total market. Scale does not imply managerial sophistication, however. It is true that some of the large companies, such as Bass and Guinness, had claims to be exceptions to the rule of the personally managed enterprise which Alfred Chandler isolated as typical of the British economy in his *Scale and Scope*. Certainly Chandler saw them as exceptions: they had a measure of professional management

---

[11] Gourvish and Wilson, *British Brewing Industry*, 131, 275, 300.
[12] Ibid. 335–41.   [13] Ibid. 24, 67–9, 79, 89, 91.

Table 11.1. *Concentration among UK wholesale brewers in 1913/14 and 1985/6*

No. of bulk barrels produced[a]	No. of brewers producing	Estimated market share (%)
1913/14		
500,000+	8	20
100,000–499,999	46	—
20,000–99,999	280	—
10,000–19,999	197	—
1,000–9,999	580	—
Under 1,000	2,536	—
Total	3,647	
1985/6		
3,000,000+	6	73
1,000,000–2,999,999	3	—
500,000–999,999	3	—
200,000–499,999	9	—
Under 100,000[c]	47	—
Total	68	

[a] Bulk barrel = 36 gallons or 1.63659 hectolitres of any gravity.
[b] A large proportion of the brewers producing under 1,000 barrels p.a. were licensed victuallers (publican-brewers).
[c] In addition, there were about 95 micro-breweries and 80 publican-brewers.

Source: T. R. Gourvish and R. G. Wilson, *The British Brewing Industry 1830–1980* (Cambridge, 1994), 350, 588–9; Monopolies and Mergers Commission, *The Supply of Beer* (Mar. 1989), PP 1988–9, Cm. 651.

and their networks of agencies and bottling plants demanded a rudimentary managerial hierarchy. However, in many ways they remained what may be termed 'partnership managements'. Yet this was not necessarily detrimental to their ability to increase their market share by exploiting scale economies and making the famous 'three-pronged investment' in scale production, distribution and marketing, and management organization.[14]

Seventy years later, in the mid-1980s, the extent of corporate concentration was clearly much greater. The top six brewing companies, which each produced at least 3 million barrels per annum, controlled 73 per cent of UK output, while a further six companies were also sizeable producers, manufacturing between half a million and 3 million barrels (Table 11.1). In the intervening period, the 1,100 or so brewers producing at least 20

[14] Alfred D. Chandler, Jr., *Scale and Scope: The Dynamics of Industrial Capitalism* (Cambridge, Mass., 1990), 266–7; Gourvish and Wilson, *British Brewing Industry*, 377–8.

Table 11.2. *The emergence of the 'Big Six', 1960–72*

Company	Major mergers
Allied	Tetley Walker/Ansells (1961), Friary Meux (1964)
Bass	Mitchells & Butlers (1961), Bent's (1967), Charrington (1967)
Courage & Barclay	Simonds (1960), Bristol Brewery Georges (1961), John Smith's (1970)
Scottish & Newcastle	Scottish Brewers/Newcastle Breweries (1960)
Watney Mann	Phipps, Walker, Ushers (1960), Steward & Patteson, Bullard (1963), Drybrough (1965), Webster (1972)
Whitbread	Tennant Bros. (1961), Flowers (1962), West Country (1963), Dutton's (1964), Threllfall Chesters, Fremlins (1967), Strong (1968), Brickwoods (1971)

Source: Gourvish and Wilson, *British Brewing Industry*, 461.

barrels a week (1,000 a year) on the eve of the First World War had contracted sharply to under 70 (Table 11.1).[15] When was the decisive period of change? It is sometimes implied, particularly in the more journalistic accounts, that the shift to higher concentration in brewing after 1914 came mainly after 1959, when Charles Clore, the property speculator, launched his unsuccessful take-over bid for one of the largest London companies, Watney Mann. Certainly, the evidence for substantial corporate change from the 1960s is firm. The Clore bid was quickly followed by a series of mergers which established what became known as the 'Big Six': Allied Breweries (1961, from 1978 Allied-Lyons), Bass, Mitchells & Butlers (1961, from 1967 Bass Charrington), Courage Barclay & Simonds (1961, from 1970 Courage, taken over by Imperial Tobacco, 1972), Scottish & Newcastle (1960), Watney Mann (acquired by Grand Metropolitan, 1972), and Whitbread (which acquired nineteen companies in the 1960s). The leading mergers/acquisitions in this process are listed in Table 11.2.[16]

The significance of the 1960s is not challenged here, but we must not ignore the extent of the merger/acquisition activity in the period 1914–58 in diminishing the number of players, if not in contributing so much to larger-scale brewing. The existing measures, none of which is entirely satisfactory or accurate, are summarized in Table 11.3. These indicate that

[15] It should be noted that the 1970s and 1980s saw the reappearance of publican-brewers and very small 'micro'-breweries selling traditional or 'real ale' to the free trade. There were about 175 of such enterprises in the mid-1980s. BS, *Statistical Handbook 1986* (1986), 77.

[16] Guinness, the 7th company, did not participate in the acquisition of British breweries and pubs, but concentrated instead on expansion overseas and the sale of new products (Draught Guinness, Harp Lager) in the outlets of other brewers.

Table 11.3. *Measures of concentration in brewing, 1914–79*

Year	Production share of top ten brewers (%)	Production average per brewer (barrels)	No. of licensed brewers	No. of brewing companies
1914	25	9,540	3,647[a]	941[b]
1939	40	27,880	840	428[b]
1958	n/a	62,920	378	247[b]
1973	84[c]	249,300	162	88[d]
1979	n/a	293,670	145	80[d]

[a] 1,111 = brewers of 1,000 barrels p.a. and over.
[b] Data for 1920, 1940, and 1960.
[c] Estimate.
[d] Excludes micro-breweries and publican-brewers.

Source: BS, *UK Statistical Handbook 1980*, 7, 88; Gourvish and Wilson, *British Brewing Industry*, 349–50.

the greater part of the reduction in the number of brewers in the period 1914–73 was established before 1959 (3,269/3,502 or 94 per cent for brewers, 694/861 or 81 per cent for companies). On the other hand, only 22 per cent of the increase in scale production in the period 1914–73 was established before 1959.

4. THE INTER-WAR YEARS

What were the circumstances in which the increased concentration of 1914–39 took place? Change occurred against a backcloth of difficult trading conditions immediately after the First World War, followed by a substantial fall in demand in the Depression of 1929–33. However, merger and acquisition were not entirely a response to gloom and uncertainty. First, in spite of all the difficulties which the brewing industry faced during the first World War, with Lloyd George's threats of either prohibition or nationalization, and the sharp decline in consumption following production controls, there was a healthy increase in company profitability. Here, as prices rose, unit costs fell, principally because production quality was sacrificed. Distribution on these profits was restrained due to wartime controls (including an excess profits duty from 1916), and after the war several cash-rich companies were able to acquire the properties of competitors who for various reasons (death duties, the lack of suitable successors, gloom about future prospects, high prices, production quotas, etc.) were anxious to sell. Companies which bought clearly had the expan-

sion of market-share as a motive, and this was to be achieved by purchasing breweries with retail outlets (pubs). Later on, circumstances
changed radically. By 1923 beer consumption had stabilized at about 25
million barrels (or 41 million hectolitres) a year, well down on pre-war
levels and 20 per cent lower than in 1919. Excess productive capacity
was common among companies which had expanded earlier. Furthermore, consumption declined by a spectacular 30 per cent in the period
1929–32, with beer prices increasing in relative terms, the consequence of
high taxation, notably in the Labour Goverment's 1930–1 budgets. Rationalization, together with co-operation in marketing, became the prime
motives for further purchases and mergers, and they can be found in
the principal transactions—the merger of the Burton brewers Bass and
Worthington (in name at least) in 1926, of Taylor Walker and Cannon of
London in 1930, and of Ind Coope and Allsopp in 1934. The number of
UK brewers (excluding Eire) fell from 2,464 in 1921 to 840 in 1939; the
number of brewing companies fell from 941 in 1920 to 428 twenty years
later.[17]

5. THE POST-WAR PERIOD

A similar mix of events can be found in the merger and acquisition activity
after the Second World War. Demand again fluctuated, producing varying responses from the brewing companies. A post-war decline in the
demand for beer meant that consumption was only 75 per cent of its 1945
level in the 1950s, a situation encouraged by rationing, austerity controls,
and high taxation. Depressed trading conditions persuaded smaller brewers to sell out, and purchasers to achieve economies via rationalization.
The number of brewers again fell sharply: from 840 in 1938 to only 378 in
1958 (Table 11.3). From this point, however, the situation changed markedly. There was a sustained increase in beer drinking which lasted until
1979. Total consumption in the UK increased by 71 per cent or 2.5 per cent
per annum, 1958–79, from 24.6 million barrels to 42.1 million (40.2 to 68.9
million hectolitres). The increase was a European phenomenon. In France,
there was an increase from 16.3 to 24.4 million hectolitres (a rise of 50 per
cent) over the same period. The increase in beer drinking was particularly
marked in the period 1967–73, when UK consumption grew at a rate of 3.5
per cent per annum.[18]

Why did this increase occur? Population growth may have been a
factor, the UK population increasing by 9 per cent, from 51.7 million in

---

[17] BS, *UK Statistical Handbook 1980* (1980), 88; Customs and Excise Reports.
[18] Gourvish and Wilson, *British Brewing Industry*, 452; Commission of the European Com-
munities, *L'Évolution de la concentration dans l'industrie de la brasserie en France* (Luxembourg,
Oct. 1975), 28; BS, *International Statistical Handbook 1983* (1983), 49–79 *passim*.

1958 to 56.2 million in 1979, and the population aged 15 and over rising by 11 per cent (39.8 to 44.2 million).[19] However, it is important to observe that per capita consumption of beer also rose in the period, by 58 per cent or 2.2 per cent per annum.[20] Here, the search for causal elements must be influenced by the observation that a per capita rise in beer consumption was characteristic of most of the major markets in the developed and developing world. And the UK increase, although greater than that in France and Belgium, was not large in comparison with the impressive increases in Japan, Denmark, Mexico, the USA, and West Germany.[21] The long boom or *trente glorieuses* associated with the period from the end of the Second World War to the oil crisis of 1973 was clearly a common element; so too was the emergence of a comparatively large group of younger drinkers in the 1960s, as the post-war 'bulge' generation reached drinking age. Finally, the West, and countries associated with it, experienced dramatic changes in styles of life associated with the 'communication explosion' and the growth in leisure activities, both based upon the marked increase in living standards.

In the UK case there is strong confirmation of the general hypothesis. Economic growth in the period 1951–73, expressed as real output per worker employed, was historically high. Consumers' expenditure increased by a similar order of magnitude.[22] There is also evidence of a deepening of the beer market, with appeals to the middle class, women, and the young. The 'bulge' generation became drinkers in the period, and the number of 15–24-year-olds in the UK population increased by a third between 1951 and 1981.[23] As we have already indicated, a 'merger mania' accompanied this rise in demand. By 1973 there were only 162 breweries and 88 brewing companies, excluding the new micro-breweries (in France, there was a similar reduction in the number of breweries and companies, where activity was particularly intense in the late 1960s[24]). In the process the 'Big Six' (a 'Big Seven' with Guinness) emerged, which dominated production and sales for thirty years. Together they accounted for 73 per cent of production in 1967, and 80 per cent by 1972.

How is this latter phase in British brewing's development to be ex-

---

[19] However, the population also increased in 1938–58, by 8%.

[20] Calculated from Gourvish and Wilson, *British Brewing Industry*, 630.

[21] The rise in per capita consumption of beer 1960–80 amounted to: UK 39%; France 25%; Belgium 17%; Japan 297%; Denmark 83%; Mexico 70%; USA 61%; and West Germany 54%. CBMC/EBIC, *Combined Statistics 1967–86*.

[22] Growth rates: real output per worker employed: 2.3% p.a., 1951–64; 2.3% p.a., 1964–73; consumers' expenditure in real terms: 2.5% p.a., 1959–79: N. F. R. Crafts, 'Economic Growth', in N. F. R. Crafts and Nicholas Woodward (eds.), *The British Economy since 1945* (Oxford, 1991), 261; Central Statistical Office, *Economic Trends: Annual Supplement 1991*, 35.

[23] From 6.6 to 9.0 million. Gourvish and Wilson, *British Brewing Industry*, 455.

[24] In France the number of brewery plants fell from 225 in 1960 to 144 in 1967 and 90 in 1973; the number of companies fell from 122 in 1966 to 61 in 1973. In 1980 there were 65 plants and 50 companies. BS, *International Statistical Handbook* (1983), 59.

plained? First, we need to isolate general causal stimuli from factors peculiar to British brewing. As is well known, higher concentration and heightened merger activity were characteristic features of most British industries from the late 1950s, and indeed of industries in most developed countries. Once again, then, some explanatory variables can be established which are applicable to the brewing industries of several countries. They include: a buoyant stock market encouraging purchases and mergers facilitated by an exchange of shares instead of cash; the search for economies of scale in production (and in distribution too, although in brewing this did give rise to problems in satisfying consumer demands for a variety of beer types); and the desire to retain and increase market-share, a motive stimulated by the challenge of trading in markets which had become increasingly globalized. There were also elements unique to the UK though not confined to its brewing industry. These include: the regulatory policies of successive governments in relation to monopolies, cartels, and restrictive practices; and the provisions of Companies Acts. Referring to the latter first, the Companies Acts of 1947, 1948, and 1967 certainly appear to have forced the more secretive limited companies to reveal a great deal of additional financial information (for example, on assets and reserves). This must have been invaluable to potential purchasers. The impact of government regulation is a more complex matter, however. While we can say that the actions taken by successive governments to regulate business activity served to encourage merger activity, there was a considerable amount of indecision and inconsistency about the process. While the attack on restrictive practices and cartels, embodied in the legislation of 1956 and 1964, blocked off alternative strategies to formal combination, there was a pragmatic, even permissive, attitude to concentration itself. Thus, while the Monopolies Commission of 1948 widened its remit to embrace mergers in 1965, in the following year the Labour Government established the Industrial Reorganization Corporation, which positively encouraged mergers in industries where the Government believed greater concentration would improve international competitiveness. In this way, it could be argued that government support and government restrictions acted together to stimulate companies to merge.[25] Entrepreneurial responses were also significant. The emergence of property tycoons and take-over specialists, for example Charles Clore of Sears Holdings, who were attracted to companies which were failing to realize the full potential of their assets, fuelled the 'mania', as did the growing divorce of ownership and control in larger companies, which came with the decline of family management.[26]

[25] Cf. James Fairburn, 'The Evolution of Merger Policy in Britain', in James Fairburn and John Kay (eds.), *Mergers and Merger Policy* (Oxford, 1989).

[26] Gourvish and Wilson, *British Brewing Industry*, 450–1; Leslie Hannah, *The Rise of the Corporate Economy* (2nd edn. London 1983), 148–50; Fairburn, 'Evolution of Merger Policy', 193–6.

In brewing, the timing of take-over activity differed from the general pattern, and the mix of causal stimuli varied also. Two distinct periods may be isolated: 1959–61 and 1967–73. The first was by far the most important, and in this respect brewing differed from the rest of the British economy, where activity peaked in the mid-1960s and early 1970s.[27] Hawkins and Pass found that of 98 brewing mergers 35 or 36 per cent occurred in 1959–61; the more comprehensive data assembled by Gourvish and Wood isolated 164 mergers in 1958–72, with 75—46 per cent—occurring in 1959–61.[28] Motivations were different in the two periods. In the first, it was uncertainty, even gloom about market prospects, together with panic about Clore's bid for Watney Mann in 1959 and fears generated by the ambitions of the Canadian entrepreneur E. P. Taylor, that was dominant. It took some time before brewers' prospects changed as a result of regular rises in annual consumption. Conversely, the second wave coincided with buoyant demand for beer, which also attracted leisure/consumer product conglomerates into the industry. First, Grand Metropolitan was involved in a fiercely contested battle with Watney Mann for Truman in 1971. Having won the day, Grand Met. went on to acquire Watney Mann, after a second bitter struggle, in the following year. Also in 1972, Imperial Tobacco bought Courage after the latter had failed to reach agreement to merge with Scottish & Newcastle. The other major merger of the period was that of Bass Mitchells & Butlers and Charrington United in 1967, which made the combined company the largest in the industry.[29] However, in both periods, a major theme was the accusation that the brewing industry was, in the words of *The Economist*, a 'picturesque dinosaur', sitting complacently on large, under-utilized capital assets. Many brewing companies were certainly vulnerable to bids from those who felt they could realize this potential, or rationalize retailing by disposing of surplus public houses for their development value.[30]

The second merger wave was clearly associated with new developments. These included: a broadening of demand for beer and other drinks; the successful development of new, consistent products—keg bitter and lager—and improved packaging—non-returnable bottles and cans—and a spectacular growth in demand for lager (only 1 per cent of the market in 1960, but 29 per cent in 1979, and 51 per cent in 1992). Another important change was the liberalization of the licensing laws in 1961 and 1964, which stimulated a massive increase of 42,000 (33 per cent) in the number of

[27] Data on the number of acquisitions and mergers of companies show particularly high levels in 1964–5, 1968, and 1972–3. Cf. Dept. of Trade and Industry, *Business Monitor MQ7*.
[28] Kevin Hawkins and C. L. Pass, *The Brewing Industry: A Study in Industrial Organisation and Public Policy* (London, 1979), 64–5; Terry Gourvish and Fiona Wood, data in app. x of Gourvish and Wilson, *British Brewing Industry*, 623–9.
[29] In 1978 Allied Breweries merged with J. Lyons & Co. The move followed Allied's failure to reach agreement with Unilever (in 1969) and to acquire Trust House Forte (in 1971). Gourvish and Wilson, *British Brewing Industry*, 472–8.
[30] *The Economist*, 19 Sept. 1964; Gourvish and Wilson, *British Brewing Industry*, 459–60.

liquor retailing outlets 1959–79. A new type of licence was introduced, the 'restricted on-licence', for restaurants, hotels, etc., and there were 20,000 of these by 1979. In addition, in the twenty years to 1979 15,000 new off-licences were created. Here, there was a notable expansion in the take-home market assisted by the shift to supermarket shopping. There were nearly 7,500 superstores and supermarkets by 1979, almost all of them possessing off-licences. They provided new opportunities for purchasing alcoholic drinks for consumers who did not normally go to public houses, and encouraged the growth of the 'free' trade (business conducted in establishments not owned by a specific brewer). The proportion of beer sales associated with the take-home market, which amounted to only 5 per cent in 1960, rose to 12 per cent in 1980 and 22 per cent in 1992. Marketing thus assumed greater importance, advantaging the larger companies. Many of the medium-sized and smaller brewers had reached the limits of what Edith Penrose has called the 'limits to managerial growth.'[31] In other cases the limits of *financial* growth were reached by ambitious but small companies already expanding beyond their means. Note, for example, Flowers of Stratford-upon-Avon, which merged with Whitbread in 1962 after attempting to promote its keg beer on a national scale, and Hammonds United of Bradford, which, led by its shrewd chairman H. L. Bradfer-Lawrence, swallowed up a number of smaller concerns, but was eventually forced to submit to the strategy of E. P. Taylor, and join with him in the Northern Breweries merger of 1960. These and other companies, then, were forced to seek refuge in a sale or merger. The large companies, on the other hand, having built up national brands (bitter beers such as Double Diamond, Worthington 'E', Red Barrel, Whitbread Tankard, and McEwan's Export, and lagers such as Skol, Carling Black Label, and Harp), invested heavily in new large-scale brewing plant, road distribution networks, and large retail chains.[32]

6. CONCLUSION: BRITISH AND FRENCH DIFFERENCES

Why, then, did British concentration levels remain below those in countries such as France? I would suggest that the answer lies in a combination of elements. First, in a comparatively large domestic market, there was clearly room for a variety of what may be termed 'niche' beer brands. The British, while moving to standardized, longer-life beers such as draught lager, did not do so as enthusiastically as consumers in France. Lager has only just over half of the total beer market after thirty years of so-called 'spectacular growth'. Draught, cask-conditioned ale did not, as

---

[31] Edith T. Penrose, *The Theory of the Growth of the Firm* (2nd edn. Oxford, 1980).
[32] For a detailed examination of these trends see Gourvish and Wilson, *British Brewing Industry*, chs. 11–13.

was once forecast, disappear: its market share was 17 per cent in 1984, and still 16 per cent in 1992. Demand was sustained by nostalgia for regional and local beers (also strong in Germany), but its cause was also promoted vigorously by one of the most successful consumer pressure groups of the post-war period—CAMRA: the Campaign for Real Ale. CAMRA's lobbying helped to sustain those independent small brewing companies, such as Wadworth of Devizes and Young's of Wandsworth, which showed a determination to carry on trading despite the challenge of the large national brewers. The trend also helped some of the middle-sized regional companies, such as Greene King of Bury St Edmunds and Boddingtons of Manchester. Second, it is also true that the retention of the tied-house system in the UK—despite numerous inquiries into its potential for monopoly and, more recently, the Government's successful efforts to restrict it with its Beer Orders of 1989—helped to sustain the sales of smaller brewers, especially in more remote locations. The retention of family control, together with the skewing of equity voting rights, in some of the smaller companies was another factor. It can be seen in the actions taken by Young's of Wandsworth and Fuller Smith & Turner of Chiswick in the early 1950s, and the private status of Samuel Smith of Tadcaster. The moves ensured that there was no chance of a predator bid, but did not of course represent a sufficient condition for survival. Turning to market strategies, it is clear that some of the smaller companies prospered because they did not accept the industry's received pathway to survival and growth; that is, they did not follow Alfred Chandler's 'three-pronged investment' in scale production, distribution, and management systems. An alternative market/investment strategy was adopted in which the emphasis was on quality real ales. These companies did not rush into lager, as some smaller companies did to their cost. The emphasis instead was upon minimum production costs, licensing arrangements for the buying-in of beers not manufactured, and an ability to maintain dividend payments to investors. In this way companies such as Eldridge Pope of Dorchester, Hall & Woodhouse of Blandford Forum, and Daniel Thwaites of Blackburn have continued to trade independently. How far they and other brewers of similar size will be able to maintain their independence in the difficult trading conditions of the mid-1990s remains to be seen.

12

Paribas and the Rationalization of the French Electricity Industry, 1900–30

ERIC BUSSIÈRE

For many years it has been asserted that French industry has been reluctant to adopt a high degree of concentration, and has only belatedly
followed—often not before the 1960s—the American or even the
German model. This has proved to be true for a certain number of industries, for example the steel industry, and the chemical industry, where, as
shown by Jean-Pierre Daviet, no merger on the scale of IG Farben in
Germany or ICI in Britain took place, despite some advanced negotiations
in the mid-1920s. The move towards higher concentration was often encouraged by external influences. The State was certainly active in this field
during and after the First World War. However, its ambitions as well as its
capacity for intervention were not as effective as in the 1950s and 1960s.
Did the banks then, as powerful partners of French industry, assume that
role during the inter-war period, and encourage a process of concentration which they undoubtedly favoured?

This question is part of the wider debate about the structure of the
French banking system and the particular role of the *banques d'affaires*
(investment banks). Historians have hesitated for some time between
a minimalist view of their role (they were characterized as having
neglected industrial investment to the benefit of capital exports) and an
opposite, maximalist view, according to which they were at the centre of
large industrial groups which tried to exert a monopolistic power upon
industry. Such interpretations usually had political implications and were
the starting-point of the institutional changes which followed the Second
World War: an attempt to nationalize investment banks in 1946, their
actual nationalization in 1982, plus the reforms of 1966–7 which aimed at
bringing them closer to the German model of universal banks. This chapter will discuss this issue by studying the role of the Banque de Paris et des
Pays-Bas (Paribas) in the electricity industry, an industry which experienced important changes during the 1920s, and in which Paribas had large
interests in both France and Belgium. It will try to draw some conclusions
about the role of banks in the economy, particularly about their relation-

ship with industrial firms in France and Belgium during the first half of the twentieth century.

1. PARIBAS AND INDUSTRY: A GENERAL PERSPECTIVE

From the time of its foundation in 1872 Paribas may be considered the model of the French *banque d'affaires*, very different from the commercial banks such as Crédit lyonnais. One of its major functions was the financing of firms. Of all French banks Paribas was perhaps in the best position to promote change in the structure of industry. However, its relationship with business enterprises was not constant but displayed important changes in the course of the twentieth century.[1] These changes are remarkable if one looks at the position of industrial securities in the total investment portfolio of the bank. The proportion represented by such securities increased markedly in the 1890s, the early 1920s, and during the 1950s, but these increases were separated by periods of stability and even by falls, as, for example, after 1900.[2]

These developments were clearly linked to the general economic climate. Around 1900 and just after the First World War, Paribas participated in many firms, under the stimulus of boom conditions. In both cases, however, those initiatives were challenged by the downswing which followed; the bank had to take part in rescue operations for several firms in which it had interests and to make extensive write-offs on its portfolio of securities. Thus, after 1900, following difficulties in Russia and in the chemical industry (Société norvégienne de l'azote), Paribas decided to give up, for some time, its investment in industry. Likewise, the ventures which had been launched after the First World War ran into so many difficulties that the bank was forced, once more, to cut down its commitments. However, the 1920s were not simply a replay of the difficulties of the pre-war period. After 1918, Paribas went back to industrial investment within the broad framework of a global strategy and—for the first time—of an analysis of the role of the *banques d'affaires* in the economy.

During the war Paribas participated in the formulation of 'offensive strategies', influenced by an economic nationalism directed against Germany, and it implemented them in co-operation with industrial partners. In the steel industry Paribas helped the Forges et aciéries du nord et de l'est to establish a European-sized group by contributing to the financing of an important programme of acquisitions in Lorraine and the Saar. In the same way, the bank participated in the creation of Chantiers navals français and of the Compagnie nationale des matières colorantes,

---

[1] Eric Bussière, *Paribas, Europe and the World: 1872–1992* (Antwerp, 1993).
[2] See ibid. 307, table 3A.

and it co-operated in the preparation of a scheme to establish a national nitrogen industry; in 1919 it also began to invest heavily in the oil industry. Finally, as we shall see, it sought to create an integrated group in the electrical industry.

The bank was not alone in defining and undertaking such a policy. Several of its initiatives were made in co-operation with 'government engineers' (*ingénieurs de l'État*) who helped government in the wartime industrial mobilization. The development of this new strategy was also linked with important changes in the top management of Paribas. Horace Finaly, who became managing director in 1919, was not an engineer; however, before the war he was in charge of the interests of Paribas in the Norvégienne de l'azote (Norskhydro) and at the end of the war he tried to make it the axis of the French nitrogen industry. During the 1920s he also personally supervised some of the bank's important industrial interests, for example oil. The war was also the cause of the entry into the bank of two engineers who played the main role in the definition of its industrial strategy: Louis Wibratte and Henri Urban.

Urban was a member of a leading family of businessmen who in the 1880s promoted several holding companies in the field of public utilities (tramways and electricity) in association with the Banque de Bruxelles and the Belgian branch of Paribas. As a refugee in France during the war, he was commissioned by the Belgian Government in exile to undertake a study of the Belgian economy; in 1917, in his book *L'Effort de demain*, he developed the idea of an economic war against Germany after victory. In 1916 he had accepted the post of managing director of Paribas's Bruxelles branch after the war, with the task of creating a multinational group in electricity including engineering, production, transport (tramways), and distribution. Louis Wibratte, a graduate of the École polytechnique, was first a railway engineer; his relations with Paribas started when he helped in the reorganization of the Brazilian Railway Co., of which he became chairman in 1916, before joining the bank as director in 1920. He then took charge of the main businesses of the bank which were managed from Paris.

If Urban played a major role in the definition of the 'offensive' industrial strategy of Paribas, Wibratte became from 1922 onwards its 'theoretician' of industrial rationalization. As already mentioned, the depression of 1921 revealed the weakness of several ventures in which Paribas was engaged. Wibratte extended the necessary reorganization of those firms into a plan for rationalizing industrial structures at the national level, in order to prepare for the negotiation of international agreements. The originality of Wibratte's schemes lay in the role he attributed to the banks: a role of initiative and arbitration between industrial interests, if necessary by using the pressure of granting credits. In 1922 he wrote about the steel industry: 'an arrangement between banks ought to exist to stop credit and to create a central company in charge of financing the metallurgical industries which accept mergers and their conditions of financial and technical rationalization.' In studies of 1924 and 1926, he forecast that the deflationist effects of the French franc's stabilization would allow banks to control the rationalization of industry: 'the banks, and in particular the *banques d'affaires*, will play an important role in the rationalization of companies and in the distribution of available savings.'[3]

These great ambitions were not fulfilled. The rationalization of corporate structures was less important than Wibratte anticipated, and, above all, it was achieved by the industrialists themselves and not by bankers. The analysis of the strategy of Paribas in the sector of electricity and of its contribution to the creation of Alsthom will help to specify the role played by the *banques d'affaires* in the French economy during the first half of the twentieth century.

2. PARIBAS AND THE ELECTRICAL INDUSTRY: GREAT AMBITIONS AND THEIR LIMITS

The birth of an industrial project

Before the First World War, Paribas regarded its activity in the electricity industry as one in a public utility, along the lines of its earlier investment in railways; the development of a specific industrial strategy was not its objective. Through a policy of multiple participation in companies concerned with the production, sale, and transport of electricity, the bank's aim was to profit from the large number of financial operations resulting from the rapid development of such firms. In France, Paribas had interests, together with Schneider, in the Franco-Suisse pour l'industrie électrique, created in 1898; it participated in the foundation of the Compagnie parisienne de distribution d'électricité in 1907 and of the Omnium lyonnais de chemins de fer et de tramways; it played a part in the financial operations of the Empain group in 1912–13. It was also associated, with other French banks and German interests, in the creation of an important holding company: the Société centrale pour l'industrie électrique.[4]

The Brussels branch of Paribas, which enjoyed a large degree of autonomy from the headquarters of the bank in Paris, developed a more systematic policy. In 1880 it founded, with the Banque de Bruxelles, the Société générale des chemins de fer économiques (Les Économiques) a specialized holding company that became very prosperous and invested in a large scale in tramway companies, especially in Italy. The creation in

---

[3] Paribas archives: 508/1.   [4] Bussière, *Paribas*, ch. 3.

1895 of the Société générale belge d'entreprises électriques (La Générale belge) was stimulated by the wider application of electricity to public utilities. Its purpose was larger than that of the Économiques: the creation of subsidiaries concerned with the supply of electricity and tramways, as well as with the technical and financial management of those enterprises. The investors in the Générale belge were the Économiques and some of its main shareholders, such as the Banque de Bruxelles and the German holding company Gesfürel, itself a subsidiary of the UEG, which held the patents of American Thomson-Houston for Germany. With the merger of UEG and AEG in 1903, the Générale belge became potentially a subsidiary of this dominant German firm, which was also represented in Belgium by the holding company Sofina. Paribas seems to have been present for the first time as a shareholder of the Générale belge in 1898; its interest became greater in 1907 and 1914, through large subscriptions to new capital issues. So, on the eve of the war, the Franco-Belgian shareholding had supplanted the German one as the dominant presence in the Générale belge.[5] Strongly represented in Belgium and Italy, the Économiques–Générale belge group also had branches in France, where it created, in 1911, Les Exploitations électriques, a holding company with the same object and a capital of 10 million francs.[6] Thus, if Paribas acted in France mainly with a financial perspective, its aim being to play the role of an intermediary between the main national and international groups, it was associated in Belgium, where the tradition of universal banking was dominant, with the definition of a global strategy for utilities, in an international perspective. It is from this Belgian springboard that Paribas tried, after the war, to develop a more integrated strategy. Urban's intention was, as has already been said, to build, on the basis of the Économiques–Générale belge group, a completely integrated entity in the electrical industry of France and Belgium. His programme was: first to develop the Exploitations électriques in France, if necessary through mergers and acquisitions (some had already been under discussion just before the war, for example with the Société des applications industrielles of Louis Loucheur); secondly, to create additional industrial capacity. This second part of the plan was put into effect at the end of 1917. Urban reached an agreement with an English electrical engineering firm, the English Electric Company, which wanted to expand its activities on the Continent. The industrial programme, elaborated at the end of 1918, involved the creation of two industrial companies, the Constructions électriques de Belgique (CEB) and the Constructions électriques de France (CEF), which were to benefit from the processes and patents of their British partner. The two companies were constituted in 1920 with a capital of 40 million francs

[5] M. Dumoulin, *Les relations économiques italo-belges (1861–1914)* (Brussels, 1990), 193–8.
[6] Paribas archives: 576/35 and 578/6.

each. Their main shareholders were, for the CEF, Paribas (Paris and Brussels), the Exploitations électriques and their Belgian shareholders, and the English Electric Co.; for the CEB the CEF, Paribas, and the Générale belge. The industrial establishments in France were located at Vénissieux, near Lyons, and at Tarbes. The Vénissieux factory was set up in 1919 to build and repair the tramway equipment intended for the French subsidiaries of Exploitations électriques. The Tarbes factory, inaugurated in 1922, was designed to build electric locomotives for the Compagnie des chemins de fer du Midi and equipment for power stations. As for the CEB, two old factories at Ghent and Liège were complemented by building a modern one at Herstal. The agreements with the English Electric Co. provided for technical assistance from its side, combined with a commercial partnership based on the geographical sharing of markets.[7]

The new group took a new direction and a larger dimension by its participation in the hydroelectric equipment of the Massif Central and the creation of the Énergie électrique du Rouergue in June 1923, with a capital of 30 million francs. The object of this undertaking was to establish, in the South of the Massif Central, an electrical network capable of supplying the Toulouse area and to create a link between the Pyrenean producers and those of the Rhône valley. For that purpose the Énergie électrique du Rouergue acquired the power stations of the Énergie électrique de la Sorgue et du Tarn and started building the Pinet barrage on the Tarn. From its creation, it also signed commercial agreements with the Compagnie du Midi, the producers of electricity in the eastern Pyrenees, and later with industrialists such as ONIA (Office national industriel de l'azote, which had been established in Toulouse during the war) and Vieille Montagne. The Sorgue et Tarn and the Exploitations électriques were the main shareholders of the Rouergue.[8]

Difficulties

This industrial group soon experienced difficulties, which were serious enough to oblige the bank to make a general revision of its strategy. These problems had two origins: the weakness of the industrial scheme itself and an unfavourable economic climate. The Urban scheme aimed to supersede the German electrical industry by means of a Franco-Belgo-English alliance. But it failed to take into account the position of the American companies, which had taken advantage of the war to develop their technical superiority and, at the end of the conflict, had renewed

---

[7] Ibid. 101/18; CEB 590/1 and 2; CEF.   [8] Ibid. 573/10 and 11, 574/18: Rouergue.

their agreements with their former partners. In France, Thomson-Houston was the axis of a new technical and industrial alliance and could rely for its development on the technological and financial assistance of the American firm. British technological and financial assistance was ultimately less effective than American.

Moreover, the model of integration defined by Urban became gradually obsolete during the 1920s. Traction equipment, in which the CEF specialized, did not offer the same prospects as before the war. Cities were beginning to neglect their tramway networks and orders for locomotives from railway companies were not large enough and often were not profitable for the builders. The Tarbes factory had been built to execute large orders from the Compagnie du Midi, which were expected to represent the largest share of its activities for several years and to permit large amortizations on the plant. The results were disappointing. The locomotives had many failures due to constructional defects, resulting in financial penalties and delays in payment; at the end of 1924 a technical reorganization of the CEF was successfully undertaken with the assistance of the English Electric Co., but the financial consequences of these difficulties were serious: payments by the CEF were more and more financed by banks and financial charges became too heavy. In 1927 Paribas, which had made advances to the firm of over 28 million francs, decided on a complete reorganization. The capital was reduced from 50 million to 20 million francs and then raised to 67.5 million by the conversion of debts into shares.

The CEB also met with difficulties. They did not obtain the orders they expected from their French and English partners and the Herstal plant was only completed thanks to credit from the banks. So in 1925 the capital of the CEB was reduced to 30 million francs and the bank debts were converted into shares. As for the Énergie électrique du Rouergue, it experienced increasing financial problems in 1925, because of cost overruns on the building of the Pinet barrage; in the autumn of 1927 the contract with the construction company was broken and new financial resources were found through a 3.5 million florin 7 per cent loan raised in Holland and help from new shareholders, in particular the Compagnie vieille montagne, which took up part of the new 40 million franc capital issue. During the spring of 1928, new advances amounting to 54 million francs were obtained from the Exploitations électriques (12 million) and the Union financière d'électricité (Petsche group: 42 million). All these were later converted into shares.

Thus, these failures of the bank's industrial policy in electricity were caused by inexperience in the field as well as by its inability, in a time of inflation, to finance that kind of long-term project until the first return on investment. The stabilization of economic conditions in Europe in 1927 gave Paribas the opportunity to reduce its risks in this sector.

3. THE 1928–30 PERIOD AND THE STRUCTURAL REORGANIZATION OF THE ELECTRICAL SECTOR IN FRANCE AND IN BELGIUM

Paribas did not take the initiative in rationalizing the French electrical industry, where the main development was the foundation of Alsthom in 1928: the decision came from the top management of the latter's two founders, Thomson-Houston and the Alsacienne de construction mécanique. They wanted to give the new firm the critical size necessary to control the French market and to compete efficiently with the Germans. These events offered Paribas an opportunity to extricate itself from its industrial ventures. On the contrary, in Belgium Paribas tried to establish itself as the hub of a general rationalization of electrical networks, by the creation of Électrobel. This attempt was not entirely successful.

The bank was approached at the end of 1927 when the idea of merging CEF and the embryonic Alsthom was first raised. The offer was rejected because of the poor state of CEF. In the spring of 1929 a new opportunity occurred and Paribas did not miss it. The CEF had, by that time, recovered, from the technical, commercial, and financial points of view. With a productive capacity of fifty-five locomotives per year and an activity in repairs and turbine-building, it could achieve a turnover of 100 million francs per year. The CEF was therefore a recognized specialist in France for large electrical traction units, but was still a middle-sized enterprise, in quite a vulnerable position owing to its strong specialization (locomotives represented 85 per cent of its turnover). At the end of 1929, with orders for over 200 million francs and potential profits of 10 million for 1930, the firm was in good health, but vulnerable over the medium term. Its agreements with the Compagnie du Midi were due to end in 1935 and their renewal, in a context of acute competition, was likely to be on less favourable terms. Consequently there was a good opportunity for Paribas to return to a less exposed position in this sector.

The agreements, concluded on 26 June 1929 between the French giant Le Creusot and Westinghouse, and which resulted in the creation of Le Matériel Électrique Schneider-Westinghouse, provided Paribas with an opportunity for negotiations. Le Creusot offered to extend its talks with Westinghouse to the CEF, while the American firm began negotiations with the English Electric Co., which succeeded in 1930. Consequently, Paribas had the opportunity to close the circle according to the agreements which still existed between English Electric and CEF. This offer was in fact used by Paribas to resume its conversations with Alsthom. The latter was a much more interesting partner for the bank, because of its size and the potentialities of its shares on the market. On the other hand, we have to remember that the Petsche group had helped Paribas to solve the financial difficulties of the Rouergue some months earlier and that Paribas was the leading manager for the bond issues of Union d'électricité, which was part of the Petsche group.

Auguste Detœuf, managing director of Alsthom, took the initiative and met a representative of Paribas on 6 July 1929. Alsthom renounced competition with the CEF on the market, and the CEF broke off their negotiations with Schneider. A scheme of integration of the CEF and Alsthom was devised in October 1929 and came into effect in April 1930: it consisted of an exchange of shares between Alsthom and the CEF; the Tarbes factory was integrated in the 'Alsthom system'. The Chemins de fer du Midi agreed with this programme, in which they saw a guarantee of development for the Tarbes establishment. All this actually amounted to a merger, which was formally achieved in 1932.[9] So, at the beginning of 1930, Paribas had left industrial and commercial leadership in France to the Petsche group. It also had to renounce its great ambitions in the field of electricity distribution in Belgium.

In May 1927 a general rationalization of electricity supply was recommended by an official commission. The main private sector groups, such as Sofina and Société générale de Belgique, prepared plans with that perspective. It was to avoid being isolated by these major Belgian groups that Urban took the offensive with a merger between the Économiques, the Générale belge d'entreprises électriques, and some other companies (e.g. the Compagnie pour l'éclairage et le chauffage par le gaz, the Union financière d'électricité et de transport). The name of this new holding company, constituted at the end of 1928, was Électrobel. Its total assets were over 2.5 billion Belgian francs, and it had interests in several countries of Europe.

However, this new strategy of Urban's did not prove successful, due to mistakes made during the first year of Électrobel's existence.[10] Paribas was not in a dominant position in the holding company: with 30 per cent of the controlling shares it had to take into account a major shareholder, the Banque de Bruxelles (50 per cent), and a minor but influential one, the Société générale de Belgique (13 per cent). Urban's aim was to force the latter to join more firmly in the new holding company by bringing its major assets in electricity to Électrobel. As president of the board of Électrobel, he competed with Sofina in Spain, by creating Hispanobel, and with the Générale, by acquiring large stakes in its Belgian subsidiaries. This aggression resulted in an agreement between Sofina and the Société générale to block the expansion of Électrobel by completely reorganizing it. The Banque de Bruxelles, whose main shareholder and depositor was Sofina, was not in a position to support Urban. In February 1930

[9] P. Lanthier, 'Les Constructions électriques en France: financement et stratégies de six groupes industriels internationaux, 1880–1940' (thèse de doctorat, Université de Paris X, 1988), 672–4. Paribas archives: 549/7.

[10] E. Bussière, *La France, la Belgique et l'organisation économique de l'Europe 1918–35* (Paris, 1992), 307–16.

Électrobel's capital was divided equally between Sofina, the Banque de Bruxelles, the Générale, Paribas, and a newcomer: Solvay. So, as in France, Paribas returned in 1930 to a less ambitious and more prudent policy.

This general attitude was confirmed by the creation of a specialized holding company, the Compagnie financière d'électricité, with a capital of 25 million francs in March 1928, increased to 50 million in 1929. The initial contribution of the bank was made up of most of the stocks in its head office portfolio which concerned electricity. The new holding company participated in credits to and issues by the Rouergue and developed its relations with new partners. Paribas kept for itself the controlling shares of the new company, but it benefited from the help of the American bank Kuhn-Loeb and of the Union financière pour l'industrie électrique, the holding company of the Petsche group and of Rothschild, who were bankers to this group. Albert Petsche became vice-president of the Compagnie financière d'électricité. This *rapprochement* with the Petsche group was in line with the policy which led Paribas to call for its help to finance the Rouergue, to realize the merger with the CEF, and to give up the fight with Sofina, partner of the Petsche group in several ventures in France.

So Paribas reverted, at the beginning of the 1930s, to its pre-war approach to electricity. It abandoned its global industrial ambitions and decided to concentrate on its financial and banking activities. Paribas adopted the same policy in other industries, such as iron and steel, motor car, and shipbuilding. In the same way, the bank favoured cartelization in the late 1920s, but did not lead it. However, Paribas showed its ability to reduce significantly some risky positions in industry before the crisis of the 1930s and, thanks to this prudent attitude, escaped the serious difficulties which other banks experienced.

This analysis is, in my view, a confirmation of that presented by Jean Bouvier, in the *Journal of European Economic History* in 1984, concerning the weakened position of the banks during the inflation of the 1920s. If Wibratte was correct in his pessimism about industry at the end of the inflation period, the banks were equally correct in doubting their ability to sustain the numerous enterprises launched at the end of the war. The capital and reserves of Paribas grew less quickly than inflation, in spite of the increase in capital made by Paribas in 1929. So numerous firms supported by Paribas were under-capitalized and suffered from the high cost of short-term advances which the bank only granted reluctantly. Beyond specific difficulties resulting from wrong investment decisions, the weakening of the *banques d'affaires* prevented them from playing a decisive role in the rationalization of industrial structures in France during the inter-war period.

13

Big Business in Britain and France, 1890–1990

YOUSSEF CASSIS

In the last few decades, the role of the large enterprise has been one of the central issues in business history.[1] Perhaps surprisingly, the debate has taken a similar turn in Britain and France. In both countries it has often been assumed that the emergence and development of large enterprises took place later than in other industrialized countries, in particular the United States and Germany. This may seem surprising since for a long time the French suffered from a 'British complex', their concern about a lack of large enterprises deriving from comparisons made with Britain rather than with Germany. And the British did not think they had much in common with the French in terms of business development, preferring comparisons with the Americans and the Germans.[2]

As a corollary the persistence of the family firm has been strongly underlined in both countries, with, however, diverging conclusions concerning its long-term economic effects. In France, the 'revisionist' school has rejected the thesis of the country's 'economic backwardness' put forward by American scholars in the 1950s: economic growth has been judged satisfactory in the long term and firms are considered to have responded adequately to such constraints as technological development, available resources, or internal demand.[3] In Britain, on the other hand, the responsibility of the family firm for the country's relative economic decline has recently been brought back to the forefront by Alfred Chandler, although some reservations have been expressed by British scholars.[4]

[1] See in particular A. D. Chandler, Jr., *Scale and Scope: The Dynamics of Industrial Capitalism* (Cambridge, Mass., 1990), and the essays in A. D. Chandler and H. Daems (eds.), *Managerial Hierarchies: Comparative Perspectives on the Rise of the Modern Industrial Enterprises* (Cambridge, Mass., 1980).

[2] Interesting remarks on this question can be found in C. P. Kindleberger, *Economic Growth in France and Britain 1851–1950* (Cambridge, Mass., 1964).

[3] See e.g. M. Lévy-Leboyer, 'Le Patronat français a-t-il été malthusien?', *Le Mouvement social*, 3 (1974) and 'La Grande Entreprise française: un modèle français?', in M. Lévy-Leboyer and J. C. Casanova (eds.), *Entre l'État et le marché: l'économie française des années 1880 à nos jours* (Paris, 1991).

[4] Chandler, *Scale and Scope*; L. Hannah, 'Scale and Scope: Towards a European Visible Hand?', *Business History*, 33/2 (1991). See also Robert Fitzgerald's chapter in this volume.

These two historiographical debates are more amply discussed in the first chapter.

The question of big business in Britain and France in the twentieth century goes far beyond the scope of this chapter, which cannot seriously pretend to be much more than a few comparative remarks on a selection of themes. The three following points will be discussed. First, the concern about the lack of large enterprises existing in the two countries. Secondly, the nature of big business in Britain and France and its evolution in the twentieth century. Thirdly, the major characteristics of business leadership in the two countries. A comparison between two countries, however fruitful, can only take its full meaning when set against a third party. Occasional comparisons will therefore be made with Germany.

1. THE LARGE CORPORATION

Comparative discussions of business development are usually based on the analysis of the largest industrial companies of the relevant countries. Well-known lists have been established for most industrialized countries, although the situation remains unsatisfactory in the case of France.[5] A different approach has been chosen here. In the first place, the notion of big business will not be limited to manufacturing industry, but will include trade and finance, which have formed an integral part of big business during the period under review.[6] Secondly, comparisons between the two countries will not be made on the basis of the 50, 100, or 200 largest companies of each country. This could be misleading as there is no guarantee that all these companies were large firms and that one is comparing like with like. In 1930, for example, a company with £5.5 million in paid-up capital would rank in 65th position in Britain, in 20th position in Germany, and in 1st position in France—taking together the industrial and financial sectors. Instead, it is preferable to compare all companies above a certain size which may arbitrarily be considered as the minimum to qualify for 'big business' status.

[5] The only published lists were established some forty years ago by J. Houssiaux, *Le Pouvoir de monopole* (Paris, 1958). For Britain, see in particular L. Hannah, *The Rise of the Corporate Economy* (2nd edn. London, 1983) and Chandler, *Scale and Scope*. For Germany see J. Kocka and H. Siegrist, 'Die hundert grössten deutschen Industrieunternehmen im späten 19. und frühen 20. Jahrhundert', in N. Horn and J. Kocka (eds.), *Recht und Entwicklung der Grossunternehmen im 19. und frühen 20. Jahrhundert* (Göttingen, 1979); H. Siegrist, 'Deutsche Grossunternehmen vom späten 19. Jahrhundert bis zur Weimarer Republik', *Geschichte und Gesellschaft*, 6 (1980); Chandler, *Scale and Scope*; W. Feldenkirchen, 'Concentration in German Industry 1870–1939', in H. Pohl (ed.), *The Concentration Process in the Entrepreneurial Economy since the Late 19th Century* (Stuttgart, 1988).

[6] The recent lists established by D. J. Jeremy, 'The Hundred Largest Employers in the U.K.: 1907, 1935 and 1955', *Business History*, 33/1 (1991) and P. Wardley, 'The Anatomy of Big Business: Aspects of Corporate Development in the Twentieth Century', *Business History*, 33/2 (1991) include companies from the service industries.

Table 13.1. *Large companies in Britain, France, and Germany, measured by paid-up capital*

	Britain	France	Germany
1907 (£2m. or more)	93	21	45
1929 (£3m. or more)	186	2	55
1953 (£5m. or more)	150	12	67

From this perspective, the concern about a lack of large enterprises which exists in both the French and English historiographies does not appear to rest on very solid ground.[7] During most of the twentieth century, Britain was in fact the European country where big business reached its highest development, well ahead of France and Germany. This has not only been the case, as is often assumed, since the Second World War, but since the very beginning of the century and even before. In that respect, Britain can be considered as having been a rather exceptional case. French companies were smaller than their British, and also German, counterparts. However, on the whole, France was closer to the European norm than is usually assumed.

Several criteria can be used to measure and compare the size of firms: turnover, paid-up capital, market value of capital, total assets, work-force. None of them is perfect. Turnover is usually considered as best suited for international comparisons but is not readily available before the 1960s. Two criteria have been used for this study, which correct to a certain extent each other's bias: paid-up capital and work-force. The figures given in Tables 13.1 and 13.2 are only intended to give broad general comparative indications.[8]

As can be seen from Table 13.1, Britain had a much higher number of large firms measured in terms of paid-up capital than both France and Germany. Table 13.2 also shows that Britain had a larger number of companies employing 10,000 people or more than its two main European competitors, apart from the pre-1914 years, when it was surpassed by Germany. However, if Britain had the highest *number* of large companies,

[7] Peter Wardley has expressed doubts about this concern in 'The Anatomy of Big Business', in conclusion to his analysis of the largest British companies in the 20th cent. measured by market value. Similar doubts arise from the lists of the largest American, British, and German firms in 1912, and of the leading world industrial corporations in 1937 in Christopher Schmitz, *The Growth of Big Business in the United States and Western Europe, 1850–1939* (Basingstoke, 1993), 30 and 32.

[8] Tables 13.1 and 13.2 have been compiled from a variety of sources, in particular the *Stock Exchange Yearbook*; *Annuaire Chaix des sociétés anonymes*; *Handbuch der deutschen Aktiengesellschaften*; Jeremy, 'The Hundred Largest Employers in the U.K.'; Kocka and Siegrist, 'Die hundert grössten deutschen Industrieunternehmen'; Siegrist, 'Deutsche Grossunternehmen'; as well as several company histories.

Table 13.2. *Large companies in Britain, France, and Germany, measured by work-force* (10,000 employees or more)

	Britain	France	Germany
1907	17	10	23
1929	39	22	27
1953	65	(15–20)	26

the *largest* companies, measured in terms of work-force, were to be found in Germany until the end of the Second World War. In 1907, for example, Krupp was the largest employer in Europe, with 64,000 workers, whereas the largest British employer—excluding the railways companies, which had been nationalized in Germany—was the Fine Cotton Spinners and Doublers' Association with 30,000 workers. In 1929 three German firms employed more than 100,000 people—IG Farben, Vereinigte Stahlwerke, and Siemens—while there were none in Britain. The situation was different in France. In terms of capital, its companies were during the first half of the twentieth century significantly smaller than those of Britain and Germany. In the 1920s in particular, this gap was widened by the devaluation of the franc, while most firms' capital remained in pre-war gold francs. In terms of work-force employed, however, France, apart again from the pre-1914 years, was much closer to Germany than to Britain, even though giant firms never appeared in France in the inter-war years.

This trend continued until the 1970s. In 1973 there were fifty companies in Britain employing 20,000 people or more as against twenty-nine in Germany and twenty-four in France.[9] There were, however, fewer differences in terms of turnover, and they had almost disappeared by the late 1980s. In 1973 Britain had twenty-three companies with a turnover of $1 billion or more as against fifteen in France and eighteen in Germany, and in 1989 twenty-one companies with a turnover of $5 billion as against sixteen in France and twenty-two in Germany.[10] In the early 1970s France was therefore still closer to Germany than to Britain in terms of both work-force and turnover.

Size is of course a very imperfect measure of business activity, which can be independent, although not in the long term, of other variables such as productivity, market share, exports, or profits. A comparative analysis of the performance of the largest European companies would go far

[9] Chandler, *Scale and Scope*, 19.   [10] *Fortune*, Sept. 1973, 30 July 1990.

beyond the scope of this chapter. However, in connection with the theme discussed in this section, an attempt has been made to measure one aspect of business performance: survival as an *independent* and *large* company.[11] The criterion is not perfect, as the survival of a large company is not solely affected by economic factors; but business life is a complex matter, involving socio-political as well as economical factors. Its value, however, cannot be doubted from a business leader's point of view: the maintenance of his company's independence is a mark of success, the surrender of its independence a mark of failure. Moreover, hostile take-over bids have been justified as a sanction against bad management.

The French large firms of the pre-1914 years survived longer than their English and German counterparts: all of them were still in existence twenty-five years later, as against 90 per cent of British firms and 80 per cent of German firms. These same French firms also had a higher rate of survival in the longer term: 42 per cent of them were still companies of a significant size eighty years later as against 39 per cent in Britain and 23 per cent only in Germany.[12] However, the larger British firms of the late 1920s were more successful than their French and, even more, than their German counterparts: 89 per cent of them were still large companies in the early 1950s, as against 79 per cent in France and 60 per cent in Germany; and 56 per cent in the late 1980s, as against 51 per cent in France and 35 per cent in Germany. On this particular count, the performance of the large British and French companies was quite similar and superior to what was achieved by their German competitors. However, this is a domain where business history cannot be entirely separated from political history, as Germany's defeats in two World Wars, in particular the Second World War, resulted in greater changes in its business organization than had occurred in Britain and France, even though Germany did not have large-scale nationalizations like Britain, and still more France.[13] Since the Second World War the rate of survival of large companies has been very close in the three countries.

[11] Estimates based on a sample of 59 British, 29 French, and 40 German companies in 1907 and 63 British, 47 French, and 46 German companies in 1929, from the industrial, financial, and commercial sectors. Although all companies above a certain size have been included, a few large companies which would not rank among the thirty, fifty, or sixty largest have been included in order to have a sample representative of various industrial branches. In case of mergers on equal terms between major companies, I have considered that the two, or more, firms involved had survived.

[12] On the longevity of the French large corporations, see Houssiaux, *Pouvoir de monopole*, 494–5.

[13] Nationalized companies which have maintained their identity have been considered to have survived. This mainly applies to the large French deposit banks (Crédit lyonnais, Société générale), the management of which remained at first unchanged and did not differ in later years from that of the privately owned large corporations. The fact that they have been, or are about to be, privatized is a sign of continuity in the companies' history. The same applies to the motor car company Renault, but not to the coal-mines, which constituted the bulk of French big business before the Second World War.

2. SECTORAL DISTRIBUTION

In the first half of the twentieth century, big business was much more diversified in Britain than in the other European countries. Several large firms were to be found in all branches of manufacturing industry as well as in banking and finance, the distributive trades, shipping, and overseas companies. Big business was much less diversified in France and in Germany. Before 1914, in both France and Germany, big business was almost synonymous with banking and heavy industry. In France in 1911 there were thirteen banks among the twenty-one companies with a paid-up capital of £2 million or more and eight coal, iron, and steel companies among the eleven employing 10,000 people or more. In Germany in 1907 there were twenty banks and twelve firms from the heavy industries among the forty-five companies with a paid-up capital of £2 million or more, i.e. 71 per cent. In Britain, by contrast, only eighteen financial companies and ten from the heavy industries were to be found among the ninety-three working with the same amount of capital, i.e. 30 per cent, which left room for a number of other activities.

There were of course large French and German firms outside banking and heavy industry. In 1907 the two largest industrial firms in France, measured by their paid-up capital, were Saint-Gobain, in the glass and chemical industries, and Thomson-Houston, in electrical engineering. In Germany there were the giant electrical firms Siemens and AEG and, to a lesser extent, BASF, Bayer, and Hoechst in the chemical industries. Both countries also had large companies in electricity supply as well as in shipping. However, in France, as in Germany, big business was much more restricted than in Britain, where the range of business opportunities existing at that time in the economy was much wider. These differences remained for another fifty years or so despite the development of the 'new' industries in the inter-war years in both Britain and France and the emergence of large firms in the electrical, chemical, and motor car industries.

In some industrial sectors, however, there were more similarities between big business in Britain and France: in the first place in the heavy industries, coal, iron, and steel, which during most of the twentieth century epitomized the idea of big business. The largest French and British firms were of a similar size; and, although by no means small, they did not reach the gigantic scale of their German competitors.[14] This was partly due to the fact that the French and British iron and steel producers did not integrate backwards, into coal-mining, to the same extent as their German competitors. In 1907 eighteen German coal, iron, and steel companies

---

[14] For details on the size of the French iron and steel companies see J. M. Moine, *Les Barons du fer: les maîtres de forges en Lorraine du milieu du 19e siècle aux années trente: histoire sociale d'un patronat sidérurgique* (Nancy, 1989).

employed 10,000 workers or more, as against eight in France and seven in Britain. In 1929, while the Vereinigte Stahlwerke employed more than 180,000 workers, no British or French firm had a work-force exceeding 50,000 people. This changed, however, with the dismantling of the Vereinigte Stahlwerke and other large concerns by the Allies after the Second World War, and the mergers and rationalization of the European steel industry in the 1970s, which were often imposed by government. In 1990 the largest European steel producer was the state-owned French firm Usinor-Sacilor, followed by British Steel, which had been privatized in 1988.

The impact of big business in the new industries also followed a similar pattern in Britain and France. Electrical engineering started slowly in the two countries. Before 1914 the market leader was a foreign subsidiary— Thomson-Houston in France, British Westinghouse in England—while the identically named General Electric Company and Compagnie générale d'électricité were of a similar size and not yet truly large companies. Coincidentally, the driving force in each of them was a man of foreign origins: Hugo Hirst (1863–1943), born in Bavaria, at the GEC, and Pierre Azaria (1865–1953), born in Cairo of Armenian descent, at the CGE. In the chemical industries the French and British firms lagged behind their German competitors not so much in terms of size—Saint-Gobain, Brunner Mond, even United Alkali in its early days were large companies—as in terms of technological advance in organic chemistry and its various applications, in particular to dyestuffs.

British firms grew faster than their French conterparts from the 1920s to the 1950s. In electrical engineering, General Electric Company and the Associated Electrical Industries were substantially larger than the Compagnie générale d'électricité and Thomson-Houston. In chemicals, the foundation of ICI in 1926 provided Great Britain with a powerful international group, whereas a merger of such magnitude did not take place in France before the 1960s.[15] Since then, there has again been a convergence between the two countries, France being ahead in the electrical industries, Britain in chemicals and pharmaceuticals. In the motor car industry, France's early lead did not induce significant differences between the sizes of the largest firms in the two countries until the decline of the British motor car industry in the 1970s.[16]

Another similarity between the two countries lay in the role played by their respective capitals, London and Paris. Both countries were very

[15] For the reasons for the absence of such a merger in the 1920s see Jean-Pierre Daviet's chapter in this volume.

[16] See S. M. Bowden, 'Demand and Supply Constraints in the Inter-war UK Car Industry: Did the Manufacturers Get it Right?', *Business History*, 33/2 (1991), for interesting European comparisons. On the decline of the British motor industry see R. Church's recent book *The Rise and Decline of the British Motor Industry* (Basingstoke, 1994), and N. Tiratsoo's chapter in this volume.

centralized, with the logical consequence that a large share of big business was concentrated in the capital. This concentration, however, took place earlier in France than in Britain, especially as far as manufacturing industry was concerned. As early as 1910, 75 per cent of the largest French companies had their head office in Paris, as against 37 per cent of the largest British companies in London: before 1914, the majority of the large British industrial companies did not have their head office in London. In Britain, separation between capital and region meant, at least for the early part of the century, a separation between finance and industry, the consequences of which have remained a controversial issue up to the present day.[17] The situation started to change in the inter-war years, and in the early 1950s 59 per cent of British companies had their head office in London, as against 85 per cent of French companies in Paris.[18]

For over a century, London and Paris have been the two leading European financial centres, well ahead of Berlin between 1871 and 1939. This opened various opportunities for big business, in particular, before 1914, in the field of foreign investment, and undoubtedly contributed to the role played in both capitals by a financial aristocracy of private bankers. But there also were differences between London and Paris, the main one being that, despite its international importance, Paris was never a financial centre of the same calibre as London. Before 1914 London was the undisputed financial centre of the world. Paris could probably claim.second place, ahead of New York and Berlin, but way behind London. To give only a few examples: London was the leading centre for the issue of foreign loans and equity. The London Stock Exchange was larger than the Paris and Berlin Stock Exchanges combined. British banks had 1,387 foreign branches in 1913, as against an estimated 500 branches for French and German banks.[19] London was also home to a greater number of large financial institutions: in 1910 ten British insurance companies, but not a single French one, had premium incomes in excess of £2 million. The largest banks, however, were of a similar size, with total assets amounting to about £100 million; but three of them were based in London (Lloyds Bank, London City and Midland Bank, London County and Westminster Bank), and one in Paris (Crédit lyonnais).

The First World War put an end to London's unrivalled financial supremacy. However, the challenge came from New York rather than Paris (which also suffered from the war), and this challenge was only gradual, for, if capital was henceforth in New York, experience and expertise

---

[17] For recent overviews of these controversies see Y. Cassis, 'British Finance: Success and Controversy', in J. J. Van Helten and Y. Cassis (eds.), *Capitalism in a Mature Economy: Financial Institutions, Capital Exports and British Industry 1870–1939* (Aldershot, 1990) and M. Collins, *Banks and Industrial Finance in Britain 1800–1939* (Basingstoke, 1991).

[18] Estimates based on a sample of companies. See n. 9.

[19] G. Jones, *British Multinational Banking 1830–1990* (Oxford, 1993), 414; R. Z. Aliber, 'International Banking: A Survey', *Journal of Money, Credit and Banking*, 16/4 (1984).

remained in London. Although Paris never developed the range of financial expertise which would have enabled it to challenge London seriously, the gold reserves and the sterling assets held by the Banque de France as a result of the over-valuation of the pound and the under-valuation of the franc put Paris in a strong position *vis-à-vis* London and enhanced its international status, particularly in the immediate aftermath of Britain's departure from gold in 1931. Otherwise, London actually widened the gap which separated it from Paris. This is reflected, for example, in the size of the largest banks in each country: the total assets of the Midland Bank and the Crédit lyonnais were respectively £408 million and £78 million in 1929 and £1,492 million and £381 million in 1952. Here again there has been greater convergence since the 1960s. London has remained, alongside New York and Tokyo, one of the three main financial centres in the world, but the size of the largest British, French—and German—financial institutions is again very similar.[20]

3. BUSINESS ÉLITES

Business élites will be considered here in connection with the development of big business in the last hundred years. It has now been widely acknowledged that in all European countries family ownership persisted in large enterprises well into the twentieth century.[21] In that respect European countries had more in common with each other than any of them, including Germany, had with the United States of America. Family ownership or, as was more common in the larger firms, strong family interests did not mean, however, that salaried managers were not called on to run such companies. An important question, therefore, concerns the degree to which salaried managers were integrated in the business élite.

In both Britain and France the responsibility of running a company rested with the board of directors. In the earlier part of the period under review, directors were usually responsible for strategic decisions, leaving day-to-day routine to salaried managers. Some boards, in Britain more often than in France, could however be more actively involved in the management of the company.

A first measure of the integration of salaried managers into the business élite can be provided by the frequency of their accession to the board of directors. Before 1914, although France had fewer large companies than Britain, these companies were more often run, at their highest level, by salaried managers. In 1907 44 per cent of the chairmen and managing directors of the French largest companies were salaried managers, as

---

[20] See Y. Cassis, 'Financial Elites in Three European Centres: London, Paris, Berlin, 1880s–1930s', *Business History*, 33/3 (1991).

[21] See the recent special issue of *Business History*, 35/4 (1993) on 'Family Capitalism', ed. G. Jones and M. B. Rose.

against 25 per cent in Britain—and 47 per cent in Germany. Things changed, however, after the First World War. Since then there has broadly been the same proportion of salaried managers among the chairmen and managing directors of the largest companies in the three countries, that is, around 50–5 per cent in 1929, 60–5 per cent in 1953, 70–5 per cent in 1972, and 85–90 per cent in 1990.[22] The proportion, however, might well be lower, particularly up to the 1950s, if the entire board of directors were considered, as the founding families could be willing to delegate the responsibility of running the company to an outside managing director, or even chairman, while exerting a certain amount of control through a number of seats on the board.

A second, more qualitative measure of the integration of salaried managers is given by the status enjoyed by directors and managers. In Britain there was a strong separation, both socially and professionally, between the two functions.[23] Managers usually came from a lower social background, entered the firm at the age of 16, and rose step by step to a managerial position. Whatever the importance of their role, senior managers ultimately remained in a subordinate professional position and during the first half of the twentieth century promotions to the board before retirement age remained exceptional. The situation was in some respects similar in France. One important difference is that French managers were usually better educated than their English counterparts. Many of them in the large companies were graduates of a *grande école*, very often the École polytechnique, which increased the prestige of their position and brought them closer to the directors, who had sometimes attended the same schools.[24]

These differences between directors and managers have lost much of their significance with the increased professionalization of the boards of directors since the 1960s. The two countries have therefore converged in that respect. But the combinations of the functions of chairman and general manager into that of *président directeur général*, introduced by the law on companies of 1940, created an extremely powerful executive in the French companies, whose equivalent in Britain has been rarer and has aroused stronger opposition, as witnessed by the Cadbury Report of 1992, which recommended the separation of the functions of chairman and chief executive.

French top businessmen have been the best educated in Europe in the twentieth century. If higher education is used as a criterion, they have been well ahead of their British—and German—counterparts. As can be

[22] Author's estimates based on the chairmen and managing directors of a sample of major British, French, and German companies.

[23] See e.g. D. C. Coleman, 'Gentlemen and Players', *Economic History Review*, 2nd ser. 26 (1973).

[24] See e.g. P. Lanthier, 'Les Dirigeants des grandes entreprises électriques en France 1911–1973', in M. Lévy-Leboyer (ed.), *Le Patronat de la seconde industrialisation* (Paris, 1979); Moine, *Barons du fer*.

Table 13.3. *Top businessmen with university education (%)*

	Britain	France	Germany
1907	35	75	57
1929	47	88	62
1953	45	96	75
1972	59	90	87
1990	64	95	88

Source: Author's estimates based on the chairmen and managing directors of a sample of major British, French, and German companies. Percentages have been calculated on the basis of the cases with available information.

seen in Table 13.3, French businessmen were once again closer to their German than to their British counterparts. However, recent studies on the theme of business and education have emphasized the differences between the German system on the one hand and the French and British ones on the other hand, arguing that the former was better suited to the needs of business.[25]

France and Britain have had in common a system of élite education that has never existed in Germany: the *grandes écoles* in France, the public schools and Oxbridge in Britain. On the whole, about two-thirds of university-educated top businessmen (Table 13.3) went to a *grande école* in France—Polytechnique alone taking some 35 to 40 per cent—and to Oxford or Cambridge in Britain. A third of the top British businessmen were educated at a public school, with a peak of 46 per cent for the generation active in 1929, and a low of 9 per cent for the generation active in 1990, when a new meritocracy formed after the Second World War attained top positions.[26] This educational system combined with other factors such as political centralization and the role of the capital cities provided Britain and France with a national business élite.

Did these systems provide a similar type of education for businessmen? Apparently not. The French *grandes écoles* mostly turned out a scientifically trained élite of engineers, and for that reason were highly thought of in England.[27] The public schools and Oxbridge, on the other hand, have been criticized for favouring a classical education which, according to

---

[25] See in particular R. Locke, *The End of the Practical Man: Entrepreneurship and Higher Education in Germany, France and Great Britain 1880–1940* (Greenwich, Conn., 1984).

[26] See L. Hannah, 'Human Capital Flows and Business Efficiency', in K. Bradley (ed.), *Human Resource Management: People and Performance* (Aldershot, 1992) for a discussion of this change in the social composition of British top management.

[27] See Michael Sanderson's chapter in this volume.

some authors, had the most detrimental effect on British industry.[28] Behind these apparent differences there was, however, much similarity between the French and British systems. The practical knowledge acquired at a *grande école*, in particular the most famous of them, Polytechnique, seems to have been of little use in top businessmen's actual careers. But they did give to their pupils the sense of belonging to an élite, ensured that they were perceived as such by the outside world, and laid the foundations of their vast network of relationships.[29] In other words they prepared them to play a leadership role, whether in business, in politics, or in the state service to which their graduates were primarily destined. The public school and Oxbridge basically played the same role, the formation of an élite, and for that reason they were highly praised and even imitated in France.[30]

At the highest level of the business hierarchy, leadership qualities are more important than technical expertise. The German educational system had the same function but fulfilled it through different channels. It is significant that about 40 per cent of German top businessmen studied law and that a majority of those who studied science went to a university, rather than to a Technische Hochschule, until the latter became properly established in the late nineteenth century. In the end, France was perhaps closer to Germany in the sense that, in both countries, belonging to the élite required a university education, whereas in Britain a secondary education at a public school was for a long time sufficient.[31]

4. CONCLUDING REMARKS

Three points emerge in conclusion to this brief comparative overview of big business in Britain and France. First, contrary to some assumptions, the main common feature between the two countries was not the lack of large companies and the persistence of medium-sized family firms. Britain had by far the highest number of large companies in Europe and France was in the European norm. And although France did not have as

---

[28] The best-known exponent of this thesis is M. J. Wiener, *English Culture and the Decline of the Industrial Spirit, 1850–1980* (Cambridge, 1981). For a recent and valuable clarification of the role of the public schools see H. Berghoff, 'Public Schools and the Decline of the British Economy 1870–1914', *Past and Present*, 129 (1990). For a powerful rejection of Wiener's thesis see W. D. Rubinstein, *Capitalism, Culture and Decline in Britain, 1750–1990* (London, 1993).

[29] The testimony of Roger Martin, chairman and managing director of Saint-Gobain from 1970 to 1980, is particularly revealing in that respect. See his autobiography, *Patron de droit divin* (Paris, 1984).

[30] The École des Roches, one of the most exclusive French private schools, was founded in 1899 by Edmond Demolins, a great admirer of the English educational methods, but it remained exceptional and its impact small.

[31] Interesting comparisons between the French and German educational systems can be found in F. Ringer, *Fields of Knowledge: French Academic Culture in Comparative Perspective* (Cambridge, 1992).

many large companies as Britain, these companies were earlier headed by professional salaried managers, who enjoyed the highest level of university education in Europe. Secondly, the main similarities between France and Britain were the role played by their respective capitals as the major centre of big business; and the rhythm of development of the new industries. In balance, however, France appears to have been closer to the German model. This is particularly apparent in the number of large companies to be found in each country, in the relatively narrow field of big business activities where large companies developed, and in the professionalization and level of education of top businessmen. And thirdly, convergence in all aspects related to big business has greatly increased between Britain and France in the last thirty years.

Index